T0340375

The Economic Thought of William Petty

William Petty (1623–1687), long recognised as a founding father of English political economy, was actively involved in the military-colonial administration of Ireland following its invasion by Oliver Cromwell, and to the end of his days continued to devise schemes for securing England's continued domination of that country. It was in that context that he elaborated his economic ideas, which consequently reflect the world of military-bureaucratic officialdom, neo-feudalism and colonialism he served.

This book shows that much of the theory and methodology in use within the economics discipline of today has its roots in the writings of Petty and his contemporaries, rather than in the supposedly universalistic and enlightened ideals of Adam Smith a century later. Many of the fundamental ideas of today's development economics, for example, are shown to have been deployed by Petty explicitly for the purpose of furthering England's colonialist objectives, while his pioneering writings on fiscal issues and national accounting theory were equally explicitly directed towards the raising of funds for England's predatory colonial and commercial wars.

This book argues that exploring the historical roots of economic ideas and methods in this way is an essential aspect of assessing their appropriateness and analytical power today, and that this is more relevant than ever. It will be of interest to advanced students and researchers in the history of economic thought, early modern economic history, development economics and economic geography.

Hugh Goodacre is currently a Senior Lecturer in Economics at the University of Westminster, and a Teaching Fellow at University College London. He was formerly a Senior Curator for Asia, Africa, Pacific Collections at the British Library, where he worked from 1972 to 1996, specialising in Arabic. His research project is to explore the influence of colonialist ideology on the economics discipline.

Routledge Studies in the History of Economics

For a full list of titles in this series, please visit www.routledge.com/series/SE0341.

The Economic Thought of William Petty

Exploring the Colonialist Roots of Economics

Hugh Goodacre

LONDON AND NEW YORK

First published 2018
by Routledge
2 Park Square, Milton Park, Abingdon, Oxon OX14 4RN

and by Routledge
52 Vanderbilt Avenue, New York, NY 10017

First issued in paperback 2020

Routledge is an imprint of the Taylor & Francis Group, an informa business

British Library Cataloguing-in-Publication Data
A catalogue record for this book is available from the British Library

Library of Congress Cataloging-in-Publication Data
A catalog record has been requested for this book

ISBN 13: 978-0-367-66665-1 (pbk)
ISBN 13: 978-0-8153-4815-3 (hbk)

Typeset in Bembo
by Out of House Publishing

Contents

Figures

Tables

Preface
Economic thought and the intellectual legacy of colonialism

The economics discipline as it now exists in much of the academic world – internationally as well as in the countries where it initially took its now familiar form – has an intellectual ancestry which is inextricably interlinked with colonialist currents of thought in the West. This book aims to cast light on this interconnection in the case of a formative chapter in the emergence of modern colonialist ideology – that which concerned England's colonialism in Ireland, "the colony *par excellence*" of early modern times[1] – and specifically in the case of the writings of one of its foremost ideologists, who has also long been recognised to be a founding father of English political economy, William Petty (1623–1687).

The book argues that the role of the history of economic thought is essential if we are to assess the ideas and methods used by economists today; if we lose a perspective on where those ideas and methods came from, and on their performance in different historical periods and circumstances, then we lose an essential aspect of assessing their appropriateness and analytical power in application to economic issues in the world today. It is with that aim that this book brings to the fore Petty's close engagement – practical as well as ideological – in the history of English colonialism in early modern Ireland, a chapter of history which has been described as having "presaged the future form of capitalist imperialism", and as having been consciously adopted by England as a "model of empire".[2] Petty, who first "began to define colonial populations by looking at Ireland",[3] directed all his considerable intellectual energy towards providing ideological legitimation for this colonial relationship. His was a not inconsiderable contribution to the construction of modern colonialist ideology at this formative stage when England's colonial rule in Ireland was the context in which the very idea of the colonial system, in its modern form, was beginning to be defined. Ireland was indeed providing the archetype of the colonial relationship which was subsequently to be globalised – a relationship whose legacy lives on in the situation of international inequality that exists today. Such was the soil in which the roots of much modern economic thought were first planted, and it is the aim of the present study to explore the continuing effects on today's economics discipline of this intellectual ancestry.

Interlinked with this motivation is the book's call for the economics discipline to broaden its research remit – and, indeed, its teaching curriculum – into one of open-ended interdisciplinarity if it is to break out of the intellectual isolation in which it has landed itself, not only in the academic sphere but among the public at large. This isolation has meant that generations of intellectual episodes and currents of thought within other fields of enquiry, including its neighbouring social sciences, have quite simply passed over the heads of the economics discipline, with dissenters herded into the galaxy of different schools of thought marginalised as 'heterodox'.

The book pursues these objectives by placing Petty's economic writings in apposition to some central issues in three fields of economic enquiry: development economics; the economics of taxation; and spatial economics.

Part 1 of the book illustrates the extent to which the ideas and methods familiar in much of today's development economics were originally forged within the context of early modern colonialism. This enquiry also serves to counter the impression given in many mainstream economics textbooks of recent decades that the analytical starting point in the development of the concepts dominating in today's economics is to be sought in the 'closed economy'. It is here illustrated how, on the contrary, the origin of today's concepts is more often found in an international context, and not least in the context of the relation between colonising power and colonised peoples.

Part 2, on Petty's fiscal writings, takes forward lines of enquiry, which have long been current within the field of economic history, on what is now termed the 'fiscal-military' aspect of early modern economic thought. It is an example of the disciplinary isolation of economic thought that, when economists discuss the origin of the concepts and methods they deploy, they rarely mention the fact that they were largely forged in connection with the raising of war funds. Indeed, in the conflict-free fantasy world of many mainstream economics textbooks, it is often hard to find any mention at all of either international or social conflict.

Finally, in Part 3, the book explores those aspects of Petty's writings which illustrate the interrelation between economic and geographical issues, and takes this as a starting point for a critique of today's neoclassical spatial economics, as formulated in particular by Paul Krugman. While a technical exposition of Krugman's theory is provided, this may be skimmed over by the non-technical reader, for whom it is enough to note, first, that the hyper-technical language of today's mathematical economics in fact expresses perfectly simple ideas that have been discussed in informal terms for centuries and, secondly, that exploring the historical roots of these ideas and methods is an essential aspect of assessing their validity and performance with respect to the world today.

The time for publication of this book is more suitable than ever, since the issues it explores are all coming increasingly to the fore. The issues discussed in the first part, for example, are now widely debated in such fields of study as postcolonial studies and critical development economics. The second part addresses topics that continue to preoccupy fiscal historians and researchers in war studies. The third part is particularly relevant at this time, when the framework of analysis used in Krugman's 'new economic geography' – the 'market failure' approach – has assumed a new significance in academic economics. Krugman has established himself as a prominent US radical, courageously going against the tide with an oppositional stance on many economic and political issues of current concern, while at the same time remaining, in his own words, "quite fanatical about defending the relevance of standard economic models".[4] The framework of analysis exemplified by his work has thus been seized upon as an opportunity to reboot the teaching of the economics curriculum in such a way as to keep it strictly along neoclassical lines but in a more attractive guise than heretofore.[5]

In any event, the present study aims to illustrate how the writings of William Petty, as well as the voluminous and steadily expanding secondary literature on those writings, offer abundant material which can serve to enrich all such current discussion and debate, and to substantiate the imperative for the history of economic thought as an essential aspect of the assessment of ideas and methods still in use by economists today.

Notes

1 Hull cites, for example, PAI 193, 219, 222.
2 Wood 2002: 156.
3 Chaplin 2001: 318–320. Similar comments are made by Goblet 1930: I, 23f.
4 Krugman 1996, where he describes himself as "basically a maximization-and-equilibrium kind of guy". See also chap. 5.4, note 29, for an example of his dismissive standpoint towards other schools of thought.
5 Not least in the widely publicised CORE course pioneered at University College London. There are, of course, other schools of thought that function within the 'mainstream' that currently dominates much of the economics profession, but these are confined to schools of thought that, like game theory and behavioural economics, effectively acknowledge the hegemony within that mainstream of the neoclassical school.

Acknowledgements

Many people have given me generous advice, encouragement and assistance in my work on the present study, which has proceeded in two stages. The first stage was my work on my PhD at the School of Oriental and African Studies, London, during which time my supervisor, Ben Fine, contributed invaluable guidance. Others closely followed my work during those years, including my former colleague at the British Library, Peter Hogg, and my brother, the local historian John Goodacre, both of whom kindly read and discussed much of the text in draft. Others from whom I received assistance at that time include other former colleagues at the British Library, Frances Harris and Peter Barber, as well as John Andrews, former professor of geography at Trinity College Dublin. I am also grateful to Kwame Sundaram Jomo, then United Nations assistant secretary-general for economic development, who, along with Ben Fine, brought about the publication of some of my research during the final months of my work on the thesis. The thesis as a whole, however, was not deemed suitable for publication as an academic work at that time, evidently due in no small part to the perceived radicalism of its anti-colonialist standpoint, which, despite my best efforts, I found it impossible to soften without losing the work's intended message.

In the following years, during which I have published a number of articles on related subjects, I have been fortunate to benefit from the encouragement and interchange of ideas with many of the acknowledged authorities on the writings of William Petty, including (in alphabetical order): Tony Aspromourgos, Toby Barnard, Anthony Brewer, Paul Dockès, Rhodri Lewis, Ted McCormick and Holger Wendt along with historians of relevant subjects including John Cunningham. I have also benefited from the encouragement of many colleagues of the European Society for the History of Economic Thought (ESHET) and the Annual UK Conference on the History of Economic Thought, which has now been reconstituted as The History of Economics Society (THETS). Of these, I am particularly indebted to Andy Denis of City University London, who launched me on my lecturing career, as well as to Richard van den Berg, Harald Hagemann, Bertram Schefold, Heinz Kurz, Geoffrey Harcourt, Cristina Marcuzzo, Antoine Murphy, Annie Cot and the late Alain Clément, to name just a few.

I am also grateful to the University of Westminster for granting me a generous research allowance, and for hosting the inaugural conference of THETS in 2013. Colleagues at Westminster who have kindly taken an interest in my work, as well as in my career as a lecturer, include my successive heads of department there, Nicos Zafiris and Vincent Rich, as well as Karen Kufuor, with whom I am currently developing a course entitled, topically, 'Crises and controversies in economics', and my late colleagues Ron Skinner and Ray Bayldon. I am also grateful to the Department of Economics at University College London (UCL) for giving me the opportunity of reintroducing the history of economic thought into their teaching curriculum there, and I have also benefited from the friendship and encouragement in that department of Victoria Chick, as well as of other colleagues in other UCL departments, including Julian Hoppit of the History Department.

Fashions change, and an anti-colonialist standpoint has become increasingly widely voiced within the academic world, not only among students but also in published work, as illustrated in my survey of recent literature on William Petty in Chapter 5. This welcome change in atmosphere, as well as persistent prodding over the years from the external examiner of my thesis, Roger Backhouse, encouraged me to return to this book project, and a second stage of work on it has resulted. In this stage I have updated the text in the light of recent research, as well as adding the above-mentioned fresh chapter, though admittedly the reference work remains thicker for items published before the conclusion of the first stage. The editors of the book at Routledge, Natalie Tomlinson and Lisa Lavelle, the production manager Daniel Fowler, along with the Out of House project managers, Zeba Talkhani, Eleri Pipien and Jamie Hood, and copyeditor, Mike Richardson, have patiently guided me through the publication process, while throughout this second stage Sue Dale, author of an outstanding PhD thesis on Petty, has provided discussion and suggestions which have been invaluable in helping me to bring the project through to completion.

I am also grateful to my daughter Su Goodacre and all other family and friends for their forbearance at times when I have shelved other commitments to focus on this work.

Much of the text of Chapter 2 is substantially the same as my chapter entitled "William Petty and early colonial roots of development economics", in Jomo, Kwame Sundaram, editor, *The pioneers of development economics*, 2005, and is included by kind permission of the publishers, Zed Books. Figure 4.1 is reproduced by kind permission of Oxford University Press from Willan, Thomas S., *River navigation in England, 1600–1750*, 1936. Figure 4.4, taken from the 1875 edition edited by H. Schumacher of von Thünen, Johann H., *Die isolierte Staat*, is reproduced from a 1966 reprint of that work by Wissenschaftliche Buchgesellschaft of Darmstadt, who have kindly waived any claim to copyright over their reproduction. Figure 4.7 is reprinted by permission of Pearson Education from Dicken, Peter, and Lloyd, Peter E.,

Location in space: theoretical perspectives in economic geography, third edition, 1990. Figures 4.8 to 4.12 are adapted from Fujita, Masahisa, Krugman, Paul, and Venables, Anthony J., *The spatial economy: cities, regions, and international trade*, 1999 (figures 5.4, page 68; 5.5, page 71; 9.4, page 142; and 7.6, page 109, respectively), by permission of the MIT Press. Figures 4.1, 4.3, 4.4, 4.5 and 4.6 are reproduced, with kind permission, from items in the British Library.

1 William Petty

Biographical and historical background

1.0 Introduction

The English writer William Petty (1623–1687) has attracted such widespread acclaim from historians of economic thought that, as Joseph Schumpeter comments, it seems that "economists whom no other topic could unite… have…joined forces in extolling him".[1] Petty is described, for instance, as "the initiator of English classical economics",[2] "an economic thinker of the first order, the best or equal to the best that existed before 1730",[3] "the outstanding economist of the seventeenth century",[4] "the most important economic figure of the seventeenth century",[5] "the most prominent of the first generation of political economists",[6] "the most important of the forerunners of Smith and Ricardo",[7] "the initiator of classical English economics [who] laid the foundations on which his successors – Smith and Ricardo – could erect their structures",[8] "widely acknowledged to be a founder of classical political economy",[9] "the true founder of modern economics",[10] whose "great analytical quality and clarity of theoretical purpose place [him] above all other economic writers of the seventeenth century",[11] and so on.[12]

This unusual level of unity among economists is readily explained, for no economist – of whatever school, current or tendency – could fail to be impressed by the "cornucopia of words and concepts"[13] in Petty's writings, which "in time became the stock-in-trade of economic thought".[14] One writer even goes so far as to claim that "the ideas that inhabit the pages of later writers are basically his inventions", and, in support of this claim, supplies a list of thirteen such ideas: "[T]he labour theory of value; surplus value; differential rent; the theory of interest; the distinction between price and value; the role of monopolies; velocity of circulation; the multiplier; natural law; national accounting; division of labour and economies of scale; public works as a remedy for unemployment."[15] This is only one example of a number of such lists, selected by various authors, in which yet more items appear: cycles, 'contingencies', 'ceteris paribus', substitutes, full employment, the preference of averages over single data and even the popularisation of the term 'economics' itself.[16] Other economists who read Petty's work would undoubtedly find all such existing conceptual catalogues to be deficient, and would add another half-dozen or so equally eligible items in accordance with their own specialist interests.[17]

A number of these concepts had, of course, been formulated previously, in some cases even in ancient times; others were topical ideas which were in common currency in the political, commercial and legislative discussions of the day; others, again, appear to be original to Petty, or at any rate to the circles he frequented. But, while the originality, as well as the significance, of his contribution in particular instances varies widely, the fact that his writings include an extraordinarily high concentration of 'anticipations' of subsequent economic theory, whether original or otherwise, appears to be uncontested.[18]

There is, in contrast, less emphasis, let alone agreement, on the more difficult matter of how to explain this phenomenon. Clearly, the first task in this connection is to explore the context in which Petty's ideas were forged and the requirements to which they responded. This task benefits from a substantial body of research on the biographical and historical background, not least McCormick 2009, which usefully summarises and enriches this literature.[19] The aim of the following brief and very selective survey of this background is not to add anything new to the known facts of Petty's life and activities; it is solely to bring to the fore the colonialist roots of his economic thought. It accordingly takes as its starting point an account of Petty's activities when, reaching the peak of his official career quite early in life, he held a series of senior positions in Cromwell's army of occupation in Ireland during the 1650s. In the course of that notoriously brutal episode of early modern colonial history, Petty seized extensive lands which had been expropriated from the Irish, as a result of which he has been described, by the Irish nationalist John Mitchel, as "the most successful land-pirate…and voracious land-shark who ever appeared in Western Europe".[20]

Subsequently, following the overthrow of the Cromwellian regime and the ensuing restoration of the monarchy in 1660, Petty never ceased, throughout the remaining 27 years of his life, to retain the ambition of relaunching his military-administrative career on the high-flying course it had taken under the Cromwellian regime. To this end, he concocted an unending series of schemes, which he vainly hoped would be adopted by the monarch and entrusted to him for implementation, comprising all kinds of fiscal, cadastral, administrative, naval and military projects, including proposals for the depopulation of Ireland and the wholesale transfer of much of the population of Ireland to England. It is in the text of these proposals, whose form varies all the way from extensive treatises to brief jottings, that Petty set out his pioneering mode of economic analysis, and it is in this context, by the same token, that much of the conceptual apparatus which, even now, remains in use by economists first saw the light of day.

1.1 Petty and the Cromwellian settlement in Ireland

Mitchel's allusion to piracy in connection with Petty's seizure of Irish lands cannot be dismissed as a mere flight of rhetoric; on the contrary, it is fully consistent with the verdict of today's historians on the nature of the colonial administration under whose aegis those lands were seized. This was the military-colonial administration imposed on Ireland, following the invasion of that country led by Oliver Cromwell in 1649, an invasion which restored the colonial rule which the Irish had successfully thrown off during the preceding period of civil wars in England. Far from making any attempt to gloss over the piratical basis on which they launched this invasion, the English parliamentary authorities had themselves set up a fund to finance it, which was to be raised by public subscription, on the security of prospective shares in land to be expropriated from the Irish! As a result, historians readily compare this invasion to the maritime privateering enterprises of the period, describing it as "a land-based equivalent to a privateering expedition",[21] or likewise as "predatory speculation"[22] conducted by "polite buccaneers".[23] Significantly, the arrangements also "resembled those of a joint stock company",[24] and, in some ways, even set an institutional precedent for the Bank of England, which was to be founded half a century later.[25]

Although the invasion fund had been established in the months following Ireland's successful rebellion against English rule in 1641, a long delay ensued, due to the civil wars in England, and it was not until 1649 that the victorious English parliamentary forces, having executed the monarch Charles I, on the one hand, and suppressed the egalitarian elements within their own army, on the other, were eventually in a position to dispatch Cromwell's invasion force.[26]

After a bloody campaign lasting three years, whose infamous massacres have "continued to reverberate to the present day",[27] colonial rule was re-established. By this time the cost of the invasion had risen far above the relatively small amount advanced by the speculators, or 'adventurers', who had subscribed to the original fund, and the bankrupt parliamentary regime, unable to meet the army's arrears of pay, accordingly resorted, in this case also, to the same expedient of granting land in lieu of cash.[28] Meanwhile, Cromwell and the parliamentary authorities, who "had no intention of sinning through excessive mercy",[29] had begun to issue a series of legislative instruments, which embraced blood-curdling punitive measures including, initially, plans for mass executions of Irish 'rebels' – defined sufficiently broadly to include the great majority of all adult males in the country – as well as deportations and enslavements, and the complete removal of the remaining Irish population from three of the country's four provinces to a kind of reservation in the west.[30] The borders of this reservation were largely to coincide with those of Connaught, the westernmost of the country's four provinces, and the intentions of this, the notorious 'transplantation' policy, were accordingly expressed in the expression 'To Hell or Connaught!'.[31] Subsequently it has been described as a scheme for the creation of an "immense concentration camp".[32]

The aim of the English parliamentary authorities was that the army of occupation, after receiving its arrears of pay in the form of entitlements to expropriated Irish land, would form the core of a massive colonial immigration. Such an immigration would, it was hoped, replace the executed or 'transplanted' population and transform the Irish countryside into a replication of that of

England – a landscape dominated by smallholdings cultivated by a peasant 'yeo-manry', interspersed with larger manorial estates.[33] Although, as it transpired, neither the planned executions nor the 'transplantation' to Connaught were carried out on the massive scale originally envisaged, the expropriation and distribution of land went ahead, and, in this process, Petty's role was of pivotal importance, for it was to him that the army assigned the crucial task of surveying the expropriated land for distribution.

Petty arrived in Ireland, with the position of physician general to the army of occupation, in 1652, just as the military campaign was drawing to a close.[34] By this time he had already had a varied career, having spent some years in the Royal Navy, as well as attending university, first on the Continent and then at Oxford, where, following a purge of royalists by the victorious parliamentary forces, he had been appointed professor of anatomy.[35] He soon exchanged his academic career, however, for the more profitable occupation of providing medical services to the wealthy elite of the parliamentary regime.[36] His reputation as a physician was evidently due as much to "a talent for self-promotion"[37] as to his newly acquired medical qualifications themselves; in particular, he had famously resuscitated a woman who had been hanged, an incident which he publicised in a pamphlet entitled *Newes from the dead*, which consisted of his own narrative account, accompanied by a collection of poetic tributes to his skills, including one by Christopher Wren, then an Oxford student in his late teens.[38] Petty was clearly successful in securing contacts in high places, and, besides his medical activities, also operated as a 'solicitor', a term which at the time was not necessarily confined to the legal field, and may best be rendered in modern terms as a 'fixer'.[39] His supreme achievement in this capacity was to 'fix' for himself the most senior position that was open to any physician in the English army at the time, thus laying the basis for his meteoric rise through the world of military-bureaucratic officialdom in the following years – a rise that was to bring him not only high office but riches, for "profits upon pills in London suburbs were nothing in comparison with the victorious sharing of these wide vales of Munster".[40]

On his arrival in Ireland, Petty was, thus, already well connected and ambitious, and, within barely two years of his arrival, he had come to assume a central role in the complex factional politics relating to the interlinked issues of military disbandment and land distribution.[41] A situation had emerged in which the great majority of the rank-and-file soldiery of the army of occupation lacked not only the competence and capital[42] but also the desire to make a success of farming in Ireland, and wished only to sell their allotments of land and hurry home to England as soon as possible. The senior army officers, as well as the established English settlers (the 'Old Protestants'[43]), were eager to seize this opportunity and buy up the soldiery's entitlements to land ('debentures'), which were thus bound to come up for sale at knock-down prices.[44] But these transactions could not be concluded until the lands in question had been surveyed. As a result, the one thing which all the different factions in the military-colonial establishment had in common was their urgent desire for such a survey to be completed, and, in consequence, "that the soldiery should, with what expedition is possible, be put into possession of their lands".[45]

Even two years after the conclusion of the military campaign, however, the vast majority of the soldiery, bivouacked around the country and living off the land as best they could,[46] had still not received their allotments, and, with land prices plummeting and showing no sign of bottoming out, were increasingly impatient with the slow pace of the surveying process, which was eating away at the value of their only prospective asset.[47] As a result, the atmosphere was becoming increasingly tense, and the military-colonial administration in Dublin was facing the real prospect of losing control of the situation. Eventually, in the closing months of 1654, the various factions – army officers, rank-and-file soldiery and Old Protestants alike – all swung into a consensus for a drastic overhaul of the surveying procedure, and, since the only effective administrative structure was the army itself, they effectively decided that the survey should be carried out as a military operation. In this situation, Petty, who was evidently well served both by his naval-military background and his skill as a 'fixer', managed to negotiate the rowdy meetings which debated this issue,[48] and so to secure, against intense factional competition, a contract from the army to conduct a new survey of the lands allotted to it,[49] to be known as the 'Down Survey'.[50]

It has been the verdict of historians, friend and foe alike, that Petty was "one of the ablest brains ever exercised over the area of a conquered country",[51] and, certainly, his survey of Ireland, which he conducted with energy and enthusiasm, was a very substantial operation,[52] the total distance measured being, as he subsequently pointed out, equal to several times the circumference of the Earth.[53] That such a massive operation should be supervised by a "cartographic trouble-shooter" such as Petty, rather than a specialist surveyor as such, was only to be expected, and was, in fact, the rule rather than the exception for surveys in early modern Ireland.[54] He referred to his staff as his "ministry of about one thousand hands",[55] but in fact it would be more apt to compare it to a regiment than a ministry, since the vast majority of the claimed 'one thousand' consisted of military guards, along with local auxiliary assistants and informers ('meresmen' and 'bounders') pressed or bribed into service for the purpose in particular areas. Actual surveyors, as such, numbered considerably fewer than a hundred, and many of these were little more than hastily trained soldiers.[56] For the survey had to be carried out in still hostile territory, and, accordingly, each field team had to be accompanied by "seven soldiers and a corporal".[57] They faced armed opposition not only from remnants of the defeated Irish army but also from the more determined guerrilla forces known as 'Tories',[58] by whom, on one occasion, an entire field team was captured, tried and executed.[59]

All in all, Petty's role in the survey has aptly been described as that of "director of field operations".[60] Indeed, a careful reading of Petty's account demonstrates that his survey comprehensively fulfils the criteria listed in a work of military history for defining a military operation:[61] for it was military factors which dominated the situation to which it responded; its aims and objectives were military, as were the terms in which it was debated, and the forums within which those debates took place;[62] equally military were its personnel, planning, preparation, execution and evaluation; its relationship to friendly and hostile forces in the country at large; its mode of gathering intelligence; its arrangements for travel, billeting and provisioning;[63] its security, discipline, requisitioning of equipment, its command, control and communication, its leadership, strategy and tactics. Thus, while former assessments have tended to attribute the principles of organisation adopted for the survey to Petty's "creative imagination",[64] an impression which his own egocentric account readily confirms,[65] the reality is that it was, in general, performed in accordance with military procedures and regulations which were already in force in any case. As he himself, on one occasion, acknowledged: "'Tis by this army that I am what I am."[66]

Having thus come to prominence in the conduct of the survey, Petty went on to become centrally involved in the actual land distribution itself, a process whose details remain "shrouded in obscurity",[67] but whose overall character has aptly been described as "a sordid confusion of non-applied theories, plans abandoned, hesitations followed by purposeless acts of cruelty, and procedural quarrels stirred up by mean-minded jealousies".[68] Petty took to all this like a duck to water, eagerly exploiting the opportunities his position gave him for benefiting from bribery and corruption. As surveyor, he was responsible not only for the measurement of expropriated Irish lands[69] but also for the assessment of their profitability, and was, in addition, uniquely well informed on which lands were 'encumbered' with legal complications which might subsequently threaten the tenure of those to whom they were allotted.[70] He was thus in possession of "so many advantages over his brethren of the carpet bag"[71] that he was able to outmanoeuvre them at every stage of the distribution process, and before long he had become one of the foremost landowners in the country, in the same league as the wealthiest of the 'Old Protestants' and the Cromwellian *nouveaux riches* who had now joined them – senior army officers, wealthy adventurers and profiteers of all kinds. Once these elements had bought out the bulk of the land entitlements of the rank-and-file soldiery, Ireland fell into their hands. The outcome was a kind of neo-feudal situation, in which this coalition of large landowners were left lording it over the Irish population, who remained effectively enserfed on the land they had formerly owned.[72]

Petty claims that his role in the military-colonial administration became so central that he "was forced to manage the executive part of that vast and intricate work, as it were alone".[73] Although allowance must be made for his evident desire to create the greatest possible impression of his own importance, it certainly seems that he eventually became a linchpin of the ruling establishment, being appointed to the position of joint clerk to the military-colonial administration and, concurrently, secretary to Oliver Cromwell's son, Henry Cromwell, who headed it.[74] It was apparently in this latter capacity that he was sent to London in the summer of 1658 to conduct negotiations between the colonial administration and the 'adventurers',[75] in the course of which he effectively became the chief link between the Cromwellian administrations in Dublin and London.[76]

In September 1658, while Petty was still in London conducting these negotiations, Oliver Cromwell died, and his son Richard Cromwell succeeded to his father's position as head of state, or 'Lord Protector', while Richard's "abler brother"[77] Henry remained as head of the administration in Ireland. By the spring of the following year, however, elements within the army in England were posing a threat to the continuation of the Protectorate regime. In this situation, opponents of the Protectorate who hesitated to make direct attacks on Henry Cromwell's rule in Ireland saw Petty as a convenient proxy for their polemics; this resulted in a vigorous debate in the short-lived parliament called by Richard Cromwell at this time, to which both Petty and one of his leading critics had been elected.[78] During these tense months the army in Ireland commanded by the Protector's brother was widely perceived as the last card in the regime's hand, and the only hope for a revival in its fortunes.[79] It consequently spelt the end of the Protectorate's rule when, in June 1659, Henry Cromwell sent a 'letter of acquiescence' to the group of army officers who were, by then, in the process of deposing his brother Richard in England. The bearer of this momentous document was none other than Petty, who was thus the 'fat lady' who sang the curtain down on the very last moments of the Cromwellian regime.[80]

In this way, having just entered his 36th year, Petty's career as a military-bureaucratic high-flyer came to an abrupt end, and never again was he to regain the position at the heart of affairs of state to which he had risen.

1.2 Aftermath

Following the collapse of the Cromwellian regime during 1659 and the restoration of the monarchy in England the following year, the dominant coalition of neo-feudal landowners in Ireland, to which Petty belonged, effortlessly transferred its political allegiance to the new monarch, Charles II.[81] That Petty should escape retribution from the restored monarchy was not a foregone conclusion, however. He had been an intimate of the Cromwell family circle, and had even been accused of having entertained hopes of marrying one of Oliver Cromwell's daughters.[82] He had, in addition, been a close associate of Hardress Waller, a 'regicide', or signatory of the death warrant of Charles I.[83]

As it turned out, Petty was readily forgiven his Cromwellian past, and was willingly accepted back into Restoration 'society'. Not only was he allowed to retain most of the land he had seized in Ireland but, before long, he even received a knighthood for services to science. His official career, was another matter, however, and, from that point of view, he had entered the 'doldrums'.[84] For, despite his evident experience, talents and skills, the authorities were evidently unwilling to risk placing heavy responsibility on him, presumably due to his unusual temperament, a peculiar mixture of 'genius', eccentricity and querulousness which was doubtless perceived as unmanageable,[85] and which, on one occasion, even landed him in prison, in the course of a disagreement with the colonial authorities.[86] One leading official told him frankly that he was held "by some to be a conjurer, by others to be notional and fanciful near up to madness, and also a fanatic",[87] while another expressed the fear that, if placed in high office, "he will make so many objections and propose so many notions that much of our time will be lost in them".[88] Petty did not get the message, however, merely commenting, in his correspondence, that "my hearers are as deaf as haddocks",[89] and continuing, to the end of his days, to deluge the authorities with precisely such 'notional and fanciful' proposals. "Schemes, projects, prospectuses, sketches and outlines flowed from his pen by the ream",[90] and his efforts to promote these continued to bring him "into collision with nearly all the different parties successively which governed the country under the Commonwealth and during the reign of Charles II".[91]

Thus handicapped in his quest for high office by his inflexible adherence to his own "peculiar method of reasoning",[92] Petty had to make do with a role in public life which, though not insubstantial, was evidently far below his ambitions. He was appointed judge and president of the High Court of Admiralty of Ireland, a position which offered him ample opportunity for venal activities, which he exploited to the full.[93] The chain of command under which he served in this capacity was a curious anomaly. For, in the 1670s, the future James II (then Duke of York) had been 'excluded' from his position as Lord of the Admiralty, following his conversion to Catholicism; it appears, however, that it was not specified that this 'exclusion' should apply to Ireland as well as England, and Petty, in his capacity as an Admiralty official there, continued to report to him. This resulted in a personal connection which Petty subsequently attempted to exploit when the duke succeeded to the monarchy. Besides his Admiralty duties, Petty also sat on the Navy Commission, a newly established and prestigious body, as well as on the Council of Trade of Ireland,[94] and was a member of the colonial parliament which was established in Ireland after the Restoration.[95]

These positions were evidently not, as has sometimes been suggested, sinecures.[96] Nor does it appear, as was assumed by some commentators in the past, that his status at court was insubstantial – that his role was comparable with that of a court jester, or, less charitably still, that he was perceived as a "kind of freak, whose considerable material success was regarded as completely abnormal".[97] Indeed, new evidence has been brought to light by Dale 2011 that in his final years he had access to the monarch and was by no means excluded from discussions of state policy on a variety of issues, not least, of course, those concerning Ireland. Indeed, she finds that, following Petty's death, James II conferred the title of baron on his son "in consideration of his [father's] services", and, most remarkably, found the time to do this on 6 December 1688, less than a week before he fled London for France at the outbreak of the 1688 revolution.[98]

Petty's enterprises on the lands he had seized in Ireland included trading in timber (or, rather, ruthless deforestation[99]), fishery and the establishment of an iron foundry.[100] His tenure of these lands was precarious, however, and he, like all his fellow beneficiaries of the Cromwellian settlement, lived in the fear that "a new settlement, unsettlement, resettlement, a new 'resumption', confiscation, revolution, or general bedevilment of all things, might come upon them any day".[101] He was, as a consequence, involved in an interminable process of litigation to ward off the attempts of the expropriated owners to regain their lands, as well as to defend himself against the lawsuits of rival beneficiaries who had been worsted by him in the Cromwellian period; he also engaged in fierce disputes with the colonial authorities regarding tax liabilities due in respect of his estates.[102] This litigation continued not only throughout his own life but into the lives of his descendants as well. The outcome was largely successful, however, and, though he unwillingly "disgorged some of his acquisitions",[103] most of them remained in his hands. As a result, he secured for his descendants a position in the landed aristocracy; shortly after his death, his son was ennobled with the title of Baron Shelburne, while subsequent titles which came into the family were that of Lord Kerry (with the rank of count),[104] and, ultimately, Marquis of Lansdowne, a title which they have retained to the present day.

Petty was, furthermore, involved in large-scale financial dealings in connection with the lease ('farm') of tax collection in Ireland, and also unsuccessfully tried to engage in the lucrative task of searching out the 'concealment' of defective titles to land which made their holders liable to expropriation.[105] Both these activities had been strongly denounced by Petty when carried out by others, and even a sympathetic biographer expresses shock that he should be so ready to enter this "tribe of drones and parasites" and "professional blood-suckers".[106]

Intermittently, when his official duties, his activities as a landlord and his speculative enterprises permitted, Petty also participated in the movement for the promotion of scientific and technological advance that was fashionable in his time.[107] His scientific interests dated back to his days as a student in Holland and France in the mid-1640s, following which he had, while in London, participated in the activities of circles established for the advancement of useful science along Baconian lines.[108] During his subsequent period of medical studies at Oxford he had for a time hosted, in his own rooms, the regular meetings of the 'Oxford Experimental Club', another such circle of scientific enthusiasts.[109] In the early Restoration period, when these London and Oxford scientific circles merged to form the Royal Society, Petty was a founder member, and he remained active in that institution for the rest of his life, at any rate during his periods of residence in London.[110] He was also the leading figure in the establishment of its sister organisation in Ireland, the Dublin Philosophical Society,[111] and participated in the activities of the Dublin College of Physicians.[112]

Petty's scientific and technological interests ranged widely, from medicine to ship design, and from chemistry to astronomy. Despite the customary assumption that he was in the vanguard of scientific and technical progress,[113] however, his supposed achievements in this regard have, in fact, received specialist assessment in only one field, that of surveying and cartography, where it has been shown that he lagged significantly behind the advanced practice of his time.[114]

Petty liked to represent himself as a seaman, uneasy with life on shore. This was a fashionable pose in that era, when 'headline economics' was largely a matter of international maritime trade, combined with predatory naval warfare and overseas colonial adventures. In Petty's case, however, there was more than mere fashion in the adoption of such a pose, as is reflected in the fact that his supreme technological achievement, or at any rate his most notable technological enterprise, lay in the field of ship design, wherein he aimed to persuade the naval authorities that their vessels should be built with twin hulls. He even arranged for the construction of prototypes of such a vessel, a kind of giant catamaran, which he termed the 'double bottom'. This project has received less thorough assessment than it deserves, despite the fact that substantial documentation has been made available, and certainly does not deserve to be dismissed, as it frequently is, as no more than a quaint example of Petty's eccentricity.[115] Although his most ambitious prototype was lost in a storm, much of the experimentation was surprisingly successful. Besides, the very fact that he was able to undertake such substantial ventures, which were spread out over a period of 20 years, is, in itself, an indication that, for all the efforts of his detractors, he must nevertheless have been able to muster a certain amount of influence in naval and naval-administrative circles, and, certainly, his project was the object of intense debate among the various factions at court.[116]

To the end of his days Petty's lifestyle remained set in a neo-feudal mode. His London residence was described by a contemporary diarist as a "splendid palace",[117] while his fiefdom in county Kerry in south-west Ireland was run along the lines of a small principality, as is graphically illustrated in his correspondence with his family and agents.[118] It was in Ireland that he spent much of his time from 1666 onwards, punctuated by extended periods of residence in London, where he eventually settled in the last two years of his life.[119]

On one occasion, while wintering in London in 1679–80, Petty related his life story to the writer and purveyor of gossip John Aubrey, whom he evidently held spell-bound with his intriguing rags-to-riches yarn of how he had risen from comparatively humble origins in a family of clothiers and dyers in Hampshire, who sent him to sea to seek out markets in the cross-Channel trade. Following an accident on board a ship, he had been left on the coast of Normandy, where he managed to talk himself into being accepted as a student at the Jesuit college of the University of Caen. He went on to relate how he studied medicine and other subjects in Holland and France, during which time, while in Paris, he associated with the philosopher Thomas Hobbes.[120] He also provided a selective account of his subsequent career in the Cromwellian and Restoration periods. Fortunately for posterity, Aubrey was so impressed with this tale that he wrote it all down, whereupon it became the prototype for his project to compile 'brief lives' of the 'eminent men' of his time.[121]

For some time after Petty's death the only written source of information on his life story remained Aubrey's 'brief life', and even that in very abbreviated form.[122] Then, in 1769, came the publication of his extraordinary 'Will', in which he strains the definition of that genre to the limit, taking the opportunity not only to list his wealth but also to provide a narrative account of how he had amassed it.[123] A number of subsequent biographical compilations included entries for Petty, relying largely on these two sources,[124] though in 1851 this material was augmented by the publication of his own account of his survey of Ireland. Eventually, in the 1890s, the first biographical monographs were published,[125] and though over half a century passed between the time of the next such biography in 1955 and the most recent in 2009,[126] the present study benefits from the fact that, quite apart from the brief accounts of his life that are routinely included in studies of his economic thought,[127] many aspects of his eventful life story have continued to be explored within a variety of specialist historical fields.[128]

Such, then, is the biographical and historical background to the economic thought of this intellectually enterprising 'land-pirate', a background which must be fully taken into account if his status in the history of economic thought is to be assessed in a balanced way. It is reasonable to state, for example, that he was "conspicuous for his connection with science",[129] and that this influenced the presentation, character, and even the mode of analysis, of his economic writings. To place a one-sided emphasis on this aspect of his work risks underestimating the paramount influence of its underlying motivation, however, and here it is essential to take due account of the frustration of his ambitions and his efforts to relaunch his career that have here been outlined. For it is, above all, to his policy proposals that he owes his singular position in the history of economic thought, since it was in that form that he elaborated those distinctive 'notional and fanciful' conceptions which were to receive so much more enthusiastic a reception from subsequent historians of economic thought than they did from the 'deaf haddocks' of the Restoration court.

1.3 Petty's status in the history of economic thought

Many historians of economic thought provide little more by way of explanation of the phenomenon of Petty's 'anticipations' than the assertion that he was endowed with exceptional intellectual gifts. Such an assertion falls into a long tradition, since he has been "regularly described as a genius, by discerning contemporaries, as well as admiring biographers".[130] He was, in his own lifetime, praised for his "genius",[131] or "admirable inventive head",[132] and was subsequently credited with "a prodigious working wit",[133] "the most refined invention"[134] and, in more florid terms, "his understanding genius, which like a meteor moved above the sphere of other mortals";[135] the term "genius" has stuck,[136] in particular the idea that his was a "pregnant geny [genius]",[137] an epithet which has been endlessly repeated in modernised form as his "fertile genius",[138] "fertile brain",[139] "fertile mind",[140] "tumultuously fecund" intellect[141] and "teeming brain",[142] along with more general references to his "great power of imagination",[143] "highly ingenious inquiring mind",[144] "perceptive mind",[145] "creative brilliance",[146] "general intellectual brilliance",[147] "immense natural energy",[148] "intensely inquiring mind",[149] and so on.

None of this amounts to any more than representing Petty's brain as a kind of grandly labelled black box, and plainly does not even begin to address the question of why such a large proportion of the conceptual apparatus of subsequent economic analysis should have passed through this particular individual's mind at this particular time. Clearly, a more substantial line of enquiry is called for, and the present study aims to cast new light on the matter by bringing to the fore elements of his writings to which historians of economic thought have customarily accorded only secondary attention, when indeed they have paid them any attention at all. A prime example of this reordering of priorities is that the relative amount of attention devoted to each of Petty's four full-length works on economic subjects will differ from that which has been usual. Hitherto, the focus of attention has normally been directed towards the first three of these works – namely *A Treatise of Taxes and Contributions*, *The Political Anatomy of Ireland* and *Political Arithmetic* – while the fourth and last of his major economic works, *A Treatise of Ireland*, has attracted relatively little attention. In the present study, in contrast, this final *Treatise* will be the focus of much of the discussion, representing, as it does, the culmination of Petty's efforts to apply his new-fangled quantitative methodology to the practical issues of his day, and, in the first instance, to the formulation of colonial policy.

This work, the *Treatise of Ireland*, was completed in September 1687, barely three months before Petty's death in December of that year. It represents an unusual feat of authorship: densely packed with quantitative propositions, tabular presentations of data and a labyrinthine maze of arithmetical calculations, it was composed after Petty's eyesight had very largely failed him, and he was almost entirely reliant upon dictation to commit the text to paper, very occasionally inserting amendments, in his own faltering hand, to the otherwise neatly written manuscript copied down by an 'amanuensis'.[150] Its contents are no less remarkable than the manner of its composition, for it sets out the final, and by far the most elaborate, version of his scheme for the demographic restructuring of England and Ireland through massive transfers of population and intermarriage arrangements, which, at any rate in some of his earlier versions of the scheme, would have involved the systematic depopulation of the latter country.[151]

The immediate stimulus for the composition of this *Treatise* was provided by the accession to the monarchy of James II in 1685, when Petty, with characteristically unfounded optimism and equally unerring misjudgement, thought that, at last, his time had come, and that he would now be able to assume the role, to which he had so long aspired, of elder statesman and policy adviser to the monarchy. The new monarch did indeed appear disposed to reward him for the personal loyalty he had displayed as an Admiralty official, and accorded a courteous response to the policy proposals which now began to arrive from this old retainer.[152] Although this courtesy amounted, in reality, to no more than an assurance that the proposals would be passed to the relevant officials for assessment,[153] Petty chose to interpret this response as an indication that the monarch was prepared actually to take them seriously. Thus encouraged by what he perceived as a more favourable policy environment, he began to dust off and refurbish various past proposals "on lines which he hoped would secure the Royal approval",[154] and, of these, it was his scheme for Ireland which focused his most concentrated attentions.

This scheme, which he had been putting forward in increasingly elaborate forms for many years,[155] had, in all its successive versions, two principal aims. First, it would increase the advantages of compactness of population in England, such compactness being, in his view, the key to the advantages enjoyed by Holland, which was, in his time, not only Europe's most densely populated country but also its most economically advanced.[156] The second main aim of the scheme was to put an end to Ireland's independent national life and its associated anti-colonial traditions, and thus to bring about a "perpetual settlement" (or, in the term used prophetically by his editor in 1899, a "final solution") that could, at last, "cut up the roots of those evils" which "have made Ireland, for the most part, a diminution and a burthen, not an advantage, to England".[157] A further central element of the scheme, in the fully elaborated form which it took in his final *Treatise*, was the transformation of the whole of Ireland into a "kind of factory"[158] for rearing livestock for England, or, in today's terms, "one large cattle ranch".[159]

The 'evils' Petty sought to rectify had, then, in his eyes, "made Ireland, for the most part, a diminution and a burthen, not an advantage, to England", and his final *Treatise* aimed precisely to quantify the supposed balance of this 'burthen' and 'advantage', and to suggest that it could be reversed by the implementation of his scheme; in today's terms, his aim was to carry out a cost–benefit analysis. His conclusion was that England would benefit to the tune of many tens of millions of pounds,[160] and, more particularly, that there would be a 10 per cent increase in its national income[161] and a 20 per cent increase in tax revenue.[162] Assuming that there would continue to be, as in the previous period, one year of war to every three of peace,[163] the fiscal surplus resulting from the scheme would enable the state to accumulate, and permanently sustain, a war chest which would, he calculated, always stand £6 million in credit in the event of all prospective wars, or, in his words, would "make a Bank of 6 millions pounds for the one year of war";[164] the result would be to tip the balance decisively in England's favour in the ongoing naval and military struggles among the European powers for international maritime and commercial hegemony.

Historians of economic thought, when they have alluded to Petty's final scheme at all, have, in general, limited themselves to a perfunctory mention, occasionally tinged with disapprobation or embarrassment, and the overall impression that emerges from the existing literature is that the subject can safely be passed over as an unfortunate and eccentric aberration of his later years, and, by the same token, that his final *Treatise* lacks resonance with subsequent economic theory.[165] Much of the present study will, in contrast, be concerned to show that there is, on the contrary, plenty of scope for correlating the contents of this *Treatise* with Petty's economic thought as a whole, and that it does indeed cast much light on the roots of economics in general.

In addressing this task, it will constantly be necessary to emphasise the specific characteristics of the historical context, since the *Treatise* is presented in a format which is so familiar today that it is easy to forget that it was, at the time, Petty's own singular innovation. For it is he who pioneered the very concept of an 'economic policy proposal', in the sense in which the term has since come to be understood. It is true that there had been precedents, in a general sense, from Xenophon's *Phoroi* (*Ways and Means*) in the fourth century BC to the innumerable proposals of the 'projectors' who preceded Petty; what he did that was new, however, was to back his recommendations with a combination of statistical and cost–benefit analysis within an explicit theoretical framework. In this sense, the entire tradition of 'applied economics', as it is now understood, follows in the footsteps of Petty's pioneering documents, of which his final *Treatise* is by far the most elaborate.[166]

1.4 Conclusions: Petty, Smith and the roots of economics

Much of the existing literature on the history of economic thought adopts a retrospective, or 'Whig', approach,[167] resulting in the assessment of the contribution of pioneering writers such as Petty in terms of the extent to which they anticipated the theories of Smithian and post-Smithian economic thought. An associated effect is that it tends to compartmentalise the enquiries undertaken by particular specialist authors; thus, as will be seen, writers on the emergence of classical political economy commonly focus on Petty's value and distribution theory, writers on quantitative techniques on his 'political arithmetic' methodology, and so on for writers on the history of finance, fiscal theory, development economics and other economic subdisciplines. Such partial studies, while in many cases invaluable within their own respective fields, are, almost inevitably, short on cross-reference to each other, a shortcoming which has drastically impeded the development of a consolidated and cumulative discussion of Petty's economic thought as a whole.

The approach of today's economic mainstream to its own intellectual ancestry may be seen as an extreme case of such compartmentalism, amounting, in fact, to a situation of self-imposed isolation among the social sciences. As a result, a recurring theme in what follows will be that a broader and more constructive assessment of Petty's economic thought could, long since, have been developed, had historians of economic thought been more disposed to respond to advances in neighbouring social science disciplines. For, as will be shown, there exists, within these neighbouring disciplines, a long backlog of insights which have, as yet, made no impact on the history of economic thought, despite the fact that, in a number of cases, those insights have involved detailed discussions of highly relevant aspects of the historical background to Petty's writings, and even, in some cases, of those writings themselves.

This self-imposed intellectual isolation has had, in turn, a further, and yet more profoundly distorting, effect, which is that it has allowed the orthodoxy's own complacent view of its intellectual roots to escape serious challenge, at any rate within the bounds of the economics discipline itself. The core element of that self-image is the assumption that those roots are, for all intents and purposes, located in Adam Smith's *Wealth of Nations*, or, at any rate, within the current of thought broadly termed the 'eighteenth-century Enlightenment'. On the basis of such an assumption, any concern with pre-Smithian authors such as Petty becomes a largely antiquarian enterprise, useful only to the extent that it provides Smith with 'predecessors'. From this point of view, Smith's work is customarily represented as the definitive systematisation of all the progress that had hitherto been made in the development of economic analysis, and the function of such 'predecessors' is merely to serve as a source of material which can be quoted in corroboration of this view.

The comfortable consequence of relying on such a fundamentally truncated theoretical history is that the roots of the discipline of economics can be assumed to lie in the world of eighteenth-century Enlightenment philosophy and the early modern 'scientific revolution' (or, as some would have it, the 'seventeenth-century Enlightenment') which had preceded it,[168] reflected respectively in Smith's concept of 'natural liberty', along with the suggestion that his theoretical system is a kind of economic application of Isaac Newton's concept of a self-regulating universe.[169] From here, it is only a short step to the acceptance of a whole set of further such rosy assumptions. The origins of economics may, from this point of view, be assumed to be inseparable from the emergence of capitalism, often identified simplistically with free competition. The roots of economics, accordingly, are portrayed as lying in the triumph of free enterprise over feudal restrictions, of the productive individual over the 'rent-seeking' society[170] and of enlightened self-interest over the destructive ethos of the previous century, when wars between competing despotisms had torn much of Europe apart.[171] Likewise, economics represents the triumph of science over superstition, and of an associated advance of political secularism over survivals of medieval theocracy, which may be represented, according to taste or prejudice, in terms of the advantages of the 'Protestant ethic' over Catholicism,[172] of Christianity over other religions, and so forth. Smith thus emerges as the Newton of the economy,[173] the figurehead not only of a science but of an entire ideology of individual liberty, religious toleration and even pacifism, in which a self-regulating economy enables the free competition of individual agents, each seeking their own advantage, to contribute, unknowingly, to a universal and peaceful progress, so that to maximise the benefit of each is, at the same time, to maximise the benefit of all.

Such a depiction of the self-image of economics is, admittedly, something of a caricature, but it is nevertheless still possible to read many accounts of the rise of modern economic thought without encountering any serious challenge to such a reassuring set of assumptions. The present study, in contrast, will subject each and every one of these assumptions to explicit reappraisal, and will argue that such a reappraisal is far from being of antiquarian interest alone. For, if, as will be suggested, the roots of the analytical apparatus still in use within economics can be traced back to the military-bureaucratic and colonial context which is so ingenuously revealed in Petty's pioneering writings, then questions inevitably arise as to the capacity of that apparatus to provide an adequate conceptual basis – let alone an acceptable ethical foundation – for the analysis of the economic issues facing the world today.

These questions arise in particularly acute form in connection with that economic subdiscipline which is most directly concerned with the colonial context and its legacy, namely development economics, and this will, accordingly, be the first branch of economic enquiry to be considered in the present study.

Notes

1 Schumpeter 1955: 210.
2 Beer 1938: 168.
3 Letwin 1963: 114 (1730 being the approximate date of compilation of Cantillon's *Essai*).
4 Hutchison 1997 [1988]]: 24.
5 Pressman 1999: 7.
6 Jones 1994: 77.
7 Roll 1973: 111f.
8 Beer 1938.
9 McNally 1988: 35.
10 Routh 1975: 35.
11 Aspromourgos 1996: 148.
12 For further such laudatory comments, see Cossa 1880 [1876]: 130; Kuhn 1963: 25f.; Spiegel 1983: 124; Robbins 1998: 56; and Landreth and Colander 2001: 50.
13 Spiegel 1983: 134.
14 Routh 1975: 36. See also Whittaker 1960: 59.
15 Routh 1975: 36, who also, however, points to the significant absence from Petty's writings of the concept of "the demand–supply paradigm" (p. 47), as discussed further in Chapter 3.3.
16 For example, Johnson 1937: 98; Spiegel 1983: 134; and Finkelstein 2000: 107.
17 For a discussion of the changing character of these positive assessments of Petty's thought over the centuries since his death, see Goodacre 2014.
18 The term 'anticipations' is used by Robbins 1998: 55.
19 No attempt will be made to cross-reference that work comprehensively, much of the following material having been compiled before it was published; it is well indexed, however, and can readily be consulted for supplementary detail.
20 Mitchel 1873: 53.
21 Braddick 2000: 213.
22 McKenny 1995: 199.
23 Letwin 1963: 119.

24 Bottigheimer 1971: 44.

25 *Ibid.*: 45. See also, on the founding of the Bank of England, Dickson 1993: chap. 3.

26 For accounts of the campaign, see Gentles 1992: 350–384; Wheeler 1999; and Ó Siochrú 2008.

27 Gentles 1992: 362 – though, for a revisionist account, see Reilly 1999.

28 For a succinct summary of the resulting profile of the debt, along with its equivalent in promises of Irish land, see Butler 1917: 161f. See also Bottigheimer 1971: 119f.; Corish 1976: 360; and Wheeler 1999: 227–230.

29 Strauss 1954: 53.

30 Gardiner 1899: 703f estimates that the provisions of the initial legislation effectively prescribed upwards of 100,000 executions, and his grizzly calculations have continued to receive endorsement from later historians (see, for example, Corish 1976: 359; McKenny 1995: 193; Wheeler 1999: 228; and Coward 2002: 145, 147).

31 The 'transplantation' itself "has never been comprehensively studied" (Canny 1987: 232); the most authoritative studies remain Gardiner 1899; Simington 1970: introduction; and Corish 1976. More progress is being made in elucidating the more limited issue of the transfer of landownership: see, for example, McKenny 1995.

32 Goblet 1930: I, 74, the term at that time still referring primarily to British policy in the Boer War of 1899–1902. The term has also been used subsequently, for example by Olson 1993: 61.

33 The case of Ireland thus breaches the neat distinction, which is current in some of the literature on the geography of development, between the 'neo-Britains', or 'neo-Europes', of early modern colonial policy in the temperate zones, and the more oppressive 'extractive states' established in the tropics; see Chapter 5.1.4.

34 DS: 1f. See also Firth 1962 [1902]: 253; and Barnard 2000 [1975]: 216–219, 241f. On the role of army physicians in early modern times, see Cantlie 1974: I, 27 (on Petty), 8, 11, 23–25, 32; and Tallett 1992: 112.

35 For narrative accounts of this earlier part of his life, see Fitzmaurice 1895: 1–22; and Strauss 1954: 13–42.

36 Hughes 1999: 15, in a study of Petty's medical career at Oxford, on which see also PSC: 213f.; and Aspromourgos 2001: 11–14. On his political standpoint in this period, see Sharp 1975: 120–126.

37 Barnard 1981b: 204.

38 Petty's narrative account of the revival of Anne Green is reprinted in PP2: 157–167. Mandelbrote 2017 explores the extensive commentary that immediately surrounded this affair in the context of the political situation in Oxford at the time. Sivado 2017 argues that the incident influenced Petty's subsequent schemes for Ireland, as discussed in Chapter 5.2. For previous commentary, see DNB ("Ann Green, criminal, fl. 1650"); Strauss 1954: 36f.; Aspromourgos 2001: 13, 22 (note 7); and, for an account which includes some technical assessment, Hughes 1982. Anne Green's entire life, both before and after her near-death on the gallows, is narrated – in fictional form – in Hooper 2008, a historical novel entitled, unoriginally, *Newes from the Dead*.

39 Aubrey [1971]: 90, who comments that "no doubt he was an admirable good solicitor". On early modern usage of this term, see OED. For wider discussion of the recruiting of such 'virtuosi' into the Cromwellian military and administrative apparatus, see Fitzmaurice 1895: 17; Goblet 1930: I, 203; Webster 1975: 84f.; and Barnard 2000 [1975]: 225f., 243.

40   Mitchel 1873: 60, Munster being the province in which Petty's principal acquisitions of expropriated Irish land were to be located.

41   Start-up and disbandment costs occasioned the 'fiscal peaks' of military campaigning in this period, rather than the costs of campaigning in progress. See Tallett 1992: 171.

42   These 'micro-financial' aspects of settlement were long ago alluded to by Prendergast 1870: 82, but have not hitherto been adequately addressed. See also the note on Gookin 1655 in Chapter 4.1.5.

43   On this term, see Barnard 1973b: 33.

44   Prendergast 1870 for long remained, for all its shortcomings, a fundamental source; for an assessment of this work, see Barnard 1993: 192–196. Coward 2002: 139–158 is a later account of the overall context, which Cunningham 2011 has at last begun to cover in detail.

45   DS: 4.

46   Prendergast 1870: 205, etc.

47   For Petty's estimates of the decline in land prices, see PAI: 178, 152 ("freely and openly sold for 4s and 5s per pound"); and TI: 606f. See also Bottigheimer 1971: 85, 111, 113, 119.

48   DS: 208 refers to the "clashings" which characterised the "clamorous" gatherings involved. The course of the meetings is discussed in detail, with the text of the resulting documentation, in DS: 3–42.

49   Two surveying operations preceded Petty's Down Survey. The achievements of the first, the Gross Survey, are obscure. The second, the Civil Survey, laid the basis for that performed by Petty. On the relation between the three surveys, see Simington 1931–61: introduction; and Andrews 1985: 61–63, 79.

50   This term, which Andrews 1985: 64 aptly describes as 'Cromwellian newspeak', was evidently adopted with reference to the fact that the survey was to be laid 'down' on maps, the previous surveys having been without a cartographic element. The first recorded usage is by Hardress Waller (DS: 41). See also Larcom 1851: vii–viii; and Goblet 1930: II, 237–239.

51   Mitchel 1873: 54.

52   The main source is Petty's own account, DS, on which Larcom 1851 provides extensive editorial comment. Goblet 1930 expounds the same material, with discussion. Andrews 1985 and 1997 advance the understanding and assessment of the technical aspects, and furthermore open out new perspectives on the wider social and economic significance of the survey. Strauss 1954: 43–90 provides a generally excellent narrative account, while Webster 1975: 435–444 also remains useful as a brief summary of the tasks performed. Historians of economic thought commonly omit any detailed consideration of the subject, though, for exceptions in the past, see McNally 1988: 36, 46–48; and Poovey 1994: 20–32. Smyth 2006 provides an admirably succinct and authoritative narrative account of the Survey, and Andrews and Rankin 2012 provide an authoritative account of the surveying technology, with some case studies of its application, placed in the broader context of the history of topography and cartography.

53   As for the actual number of such circumferences, that was a story which grew in the telling, as discussed further in Chapter 4.1.1.

54   Andrews 1985: 56f.

55   DS: 295, though he elsewhere uses expressions such as "some hundreds" (107) and "many" (103).

56 See *ibid.*: 45 ("one hundred instruments") and 108 (a meeting in Dublin of "about fifty surveyors").

57 *Ibid.*: 45.

58 This term, derived from the Irish *toiridhe*, a 'pursued person' (Ellis 1988: 32), was subsequently adopted by Whig politicians to denote their opponents; hence the current usage. On the armed resistance, see Gentles 1992: 380. Petty's own account is pervaded with reference to security issues, as at BA: xv; and DS: 16, 29, 45, 50, 125. See also Bottigheimer 1971: 129f.

59 The leader of the group which carried out this operation was Donogh (Donagh, Donnogh) O'Derrick (O'Derrig, Doyle), known as 'Blind Donogh'. See Prendergast 1870: 206, 336f., who aptly comments that he "could see well enough for this purpose". See also Webb 1878: 436; Fitzmaurice 1895: 52; Dunlop 1913: 2, 542 (document 731 and editorial note); Goblet 1930: I, 246; Strauss 1954: 69; and Ellis 1988: 156, 161f. For other instances of attacks on surveyors in early modern Ireland, see Andrews 1970: 181; and 1985: 61, 78 (note 42).

60 Andrews 1985: 72.

61 Van Creveld 1991: 1. Kitson 1994: 273 provides criteria for the evaluation of a military commander, by which Petty would probably be estimated quite highly at the operational level.

62 See, in particular, DS: 3–16.

63 See, for example, the observation by Larcom 1851: 320, discussing DS: 35, etc., that the arrangements for local provisioning, transport, requisitioning and billeting were made according to the current legislation (to which he refers, anachronistically, as 'Mutiny Acts'). For examples of relevant legislation then in force, see Firth and Rait 1911: I, 1048; II, 110f.

64 Strauss 1954: 62–65. See also Fitzmaurice 1895: 51 ("clever and judicious"); Masson and Youngson 1960: 83 ("master of practical organisation"); and Roncaglia 1985 [1977]: 7 ("highly developed organisational ability").

65 As Barnard 2000 [1975]: 226 cautions, this is the only detailed account available on which to assess his achievements. It is, nevertheless, an almost uniquely valuable document in itself, since at that time "it never occurred to any contemporary writer to draw up a description of the system of military administration". Firth 1962 [1902]: 182. See also Thomson 1938: 474 ("administrative history was largely ignored until the present century"); and Andrews 1985: 64.

66 *Reflections*: 156f.

67 Andrews 1985: 95, though light is beginning to be shed on the subject, notably in Cunningham 2011 and other items by that author. Bottigheimer 1971 does not attempt to elucidate how distribution was carried out on the ground. A complicated series of sequential lotteries was involved; see Prendergast 1870: 187–238 (the army), 239–244 (the adventurers); Fitzmaurice 1895: 57–60 (whose account is nevertheless criticised by the reviewer in *Edinburgh Review* 1895: 47, 57, for not having adequately "dwelt on this subject"); Firth 1962 [1902]: 202f.; Dunlop 1913: 522f (document 386); Goblet 1930: I, 80–91; and, for Petty's own account, DS: 184–211.

68 Goblet 1930: I, 56. (This and all other translations from this work are mine.)

69 Petty's survey in general under-measured lands by around 15 per cent. Since under-measurement is identically equal to over-granting (Andrews 1985: 40), it has been suggested that this is evidence of corruption on a colossal scale. This issue is not as

simple as it might appear, however; his estimate in fact represented a considerable increase on previous estimates. For discussion, see Goblet 1930: I, 332–337; and II, 160–163 (with maps); and Lynam 1932: 417. Andrews 1985: 72f., 81f., 300f. (with table), is not convinced that sharp practice provides a fully satisfactory explanation for this under-measurement, and considers that hitherto unexplained technical factors are more likely to have been the main influence at work.

70 The evidence for this is largely contained in Petty's own account, due to his predilection for narrating the wiles and manoeuvres by means of which he outwitted his accusers. For summary accounts, see Prendergast 1870: 235–238; Fitzmaurice 1895: 90–93; and Strauss 1954: 78–83.

71 Mitchel 1873: 55.

72 Firth 1909: II, 144, calls them a "new aristocracy". On the concept of neo-feudalism, or the 'new feudalism', see further in Chapter 2.2.

73 *Reflections*: 116. This self-assessment is accepted by Strauss 1954: 78; Masson and Youngson 1960: 83; and Thomson 1987: 232.

74 Fitzmaurice 1895: 73; and Strauss 1954: 84, who both evidently rely on Petty's own reference to his tenure of these offices, in DS: 209 and *Reflections*: 10, 37f., 119f.

75 The aim of his mission was to persuade the adventurers to accept the same principles of land division as had been used for the soldiers' lands, which he referred to as his 'perfect rule'. His own account of the mission is at DS: 227–257. Alternative versions of some of the relevant documentation are in Mahaffy 1903: 357–365. See also *Reflections*: 134, 259; Prendergast 1870: 243f.; Fitzmaurice 1895: 62–64; Strauss 1954: 84f.; and further discussion in Chapters 3.2.2 and 4.1.1.

76 Ramsey 1933: 230–233 (withdrawal of the previous linkman), 340f (Petty commended as a trustworthy representative), 238, 259. See also the letter from Henry Cromwell to Lord Broghill, May 1658, in Thurloe Papers (1742): VII, 115. See also McCormick 2009: 110–111.

77 Firth 1909: II, 306.

78 DS: 258f , 289–307. *Reflections* as a whole is largely a reply to this debate, on which see Fitzmaurice 1895: 78–86; Ramsey 1933: 301f., 309; and Strauss 1954: 84–88. On the position of MPs for Ireland in this and the two preceding Protectorate parliaments, see Little 2000. Petty in fact sat for an English constituency, to which he had been hurriedly transferred at the last moment, to ensure his successful 'election', following disagreements within Ireland over the selection of MPs; see Barnard 1973a: 356–359.

79 Ramsey 1933: 272–287; Strauss 1954: 84–86.

80 DS: 301, which records the date of his dispatch to deliver the letter as 16 June 1659. See Hull 1899: xvi; Ramsey 1933: 338f.; and Strauss 1954: 88. Petty's own account displays such a narrow focus on his own immediate affairs that he gives the impression of having barely noticed the wider historical significance of the events in which he had become caught up.

81 Bottigheimer 1972.

82 DS: 261.

83 He was later to marry Waller's daughter, Elizabeth. This was in 1667, shortly after Waller died in prison in Jersey; see DNB (Waller); and Strauss 1954: 102. On Petty's business relations with Waller, see DS: 32–34. Waller played a prominent role in Ireland in the months following the fall of the Protectorate regime, as narrated at length in Clarke 1999.

84 Barnard 1981b: 204, 214. See also Strauss 1954: 90, 173 ("involuntary retirement"); and Goblet 1930: II, 180f. An alternative, more positive, spin is occasionally placed on this, by suggesting that he was thereby relieved from "arduous administrative duties", and so freed for the service of science; see Johnson 1937: 95; and Strauss 1954: 180. On Petty's acceptance by the monarchy in the years immediately following its restoration, see McCormick 2009: 120–125.

85 See Fitzmaurice 1895: 104f.; Strauss 1954: 105, 120–134; and Evelyn [1971]: 94. For a comment on Petty by Charles II, see PSC: 281.

86 On Petty's imprisonment, which occurred in 1679, see PSC: 14–19.

87 *Ibid.*: 103f.

88 See Strauss 1954: 129 for this and other similar quotations from correspondence among the officials concerned.

89 PSC: 91. In DS: 102 he had similarly complained of "spiteful and ignorant persons, deaf adders, that will not hear, though they be charmed never so wisely". See also his scathing characterisation of 'politics' in DPA: 121f.

90 Letwin 1963: 121.

91 Fitzmaurice 1899: 100. Lynch 2001: 229 adds that his habit of accompanying his proposals with petitions relating to his personal grievances "did not help".

92 Furniss 1920: 35.

93 His activities in this position are narrated with gusto by Costello 2005 and 2011. See also PSC: xix, 37–39, 62–67, etc.; Fitzmaurice 1895: 246–251; PP1: 253 (editorial comment); and Strauss 1954: 127f.

94 Strauss 1954: 123. The text of a 1676 report by this Council, which largely takes the form of a summary of PAI, is printed in EW: 211–223.

95 Fitzmaurice 1895: 130 ("as member for Inistiogue in Kilkenny"); see also Fitzmaurice 1899: 100b; Fitzmaurice 1896: 115a ("as member for Enniscorthy"); and Strauss 1954: 96. His advocacy of legislative union between England and Ireland, involving a joint parliament along the lines of the Protectorate parliaments (of the third and last of which he had been a member, as noted in Chapter 1.1), have been described as "the most incisive and ambitious schemes" advanced on that subject in the Restoration period; see Kelly 1987: 238–240.

96 Letwin 1963: 120. Similarly, Strauss 1954: 127f describes his Admiralty post as a "mock appointment".

97 Strauss 1954: 145, 154.

98 Dale 2011: 78–9. See further below on the particular connection between Petty and this monarch.

99 As Mitchel 1873: 58 points out, uncertainty about the long-term tenure of lands provides a powerful incentive for such short-termism. See also Strauss 1954: 103.

100 Macaulay 1848–62: chap. 12 provides a whimsical account of these "benevolent and enlightened" projects. See also Lansdowne 1937: 12–46; and Wood 1934 (a transcription of some relevant documentation). Subsequently, Barnard published four authoritative studies of this aspect of Petty's life: Barnard 1979 (on connections between his estate management and his writings on population), 1981a (on his fishery enterprise), 1981b (on his landownership in relation to his career as a whole) and 1982 (on his iron foundry). For a later study of the general background, see Barnard 2003. Even in his notes on his estate affairs, Petty persisted in his relentless theorising; see Aspromourgos 2000: 58–60, as discussed in Chapter 4.1.5.

101 Mitchel 1873: 58.

102 Fitzmaurice 1895: 125–153; Strauss 1954: 85–108.

103 Mitchel 1873: 57.

104 As part of the arrangement under which they acquired this title, his family changed their name to Petty-Fitzmaurice, or, as Mitchel 1873: 57 puts it, "bribed one of the high-born but beggared Geraldine Fitzmaurices to marry his daughter, and also to take his paltry name of Petty". Naturally, a more favourable spin is placed on this arrangement by Petty's descendants Fitzmaurice 1895: 311f. and 1896: 118a, and Lansdowne (editorial comment at PP2: 245), both of whom retained the family name to whose origins Mitchel alludes (though Lansdowne does note that the daughter in question was "a very ugly woman"). See also Strauss 1954: 137.

105 Fitzmaurice 1895: 251f.; Strauss 1954: 125–127.

106 Strauss 1954: 126.

107 For general accounts, see Strauss 1954: 109–119; and Masson and Youngson 1960.

108 The principal outcome of this was his 1648 treatise, *Advice*.

109 See Ward 1740: 218; Purver 1967: 117–120 (with picture facing page 110), Webster 1975: 153; and Lynch 2001: 15f.

110 Hoppen 1965: 129–134 and Masson and Youngson 1960: 85–88 are undocumented but useful summary accounts. See also Hunter 1989: 159f., etc.; and Finkelstein 2000: 109f., 300.

111 This society is the subject of a monograph study, Hoppen 1970, which is criticised by Barnard 1974 for its neglect of the work of the efforts of precursor groups and individuals, on whom see also Barnard 2000 [1975]: 244–248. See also Fitzmaurice 1895: 253–255; PP2: 87–92; and Webster 1975: 428–444.

112 Hoppen 1970: 18–20, 233. See PP2: 171–179 for an important lecture which he delivered to the College in 1676. See also editorial comment at PP2: 156; and Strauss 1954: 113.

113 See, for example, Sharp 1977: ix; and Feingold 2001: 94.

114 See Andrews 1985: 65–66 and other studies by the same author. For a brief selective survey of the steadily expanding literature on possible influences on Petty's economic and social thought from his interest in the natural philosophy of his time, see Chapter 5.2. For earlier discussions, see Kargon 1965, who places Petty's views on chemistry in the context of the transmission of continental European science to England. Sharp 1977 provides valuable documentation and general discussion on many relevant subjects, though this remains largely non-technical (with the exception of a meticulous study of Petty's 'double writing machine': 238–241), as does earlier commentary on his medical career and views, with the exception of Hughes 1982. Aspromourgos 2001: 13f. provides an account of the source material on Petty's medical activities. See also Chapter 4.1.1.

115 For further discussion, see Chapter 4.1.4.

116 See Strauss 1954: 117–119; PSC: 283; and further discussion in Chapter 4.1.4.

117 Evelyn [1971]: 94.

118 See, in particular, Wood 1934.

119 He resided in London in 1673–76 (for nearly three years), 1679–80 (an overwinter visit of under three months) and 1682–83 (for about a year). See Hull 1899: xxiv–xxxii; and Strauss 1954: 103.

120 There is an extensive literature on the intellectual influences to which Petty may have been exposed in this early period of his life, which is authoritatively summarised and updated in McCormick 2009: 19–28 (on Jesuits and their

eductional system), 28–36 (on universities in Holland), and 36–39 (on Petty's ssociation with Hobbes in Paris).

121 See Hunter 1975: 80, 46 (note 9). Aubrey [1971] is a valuable verbatim transcript of the original manuscript.

122 Aubrey's full manuscript was not published till 1813 (the life of Petty being at Aubrey [1813]: II, ii, 481–491), but he lent it to his contemporary Anthony À Wood, who drew on it extensively for his own biographical compilation (the entry for Petty being at Wood 1691–92: IV, 214f.).

123 Extracts from the Will had already been included in Ward 1740: 217f., but it was first published in full in a 1769 volume containing the texts of TTC, PA and PAI (i.e. *Tracts, chiefly relating to Ireland…*, the Will being on pp. ii–xiii). The Will is also included in Fitzmaurice 1895: 318–324, after the original in the Irish Probate Court.

124 For example, Ward 1740: 217f.; Ware 1745: 353–356; *Biographia Britannica* 1747–66: V, 3342–3349; Munk 1861: I, 252–254; and Webb 1878: 435–437.

125 Bevan 1893, 1894; and Fitzmaurice 1895 (usefully summarised in Fitzmaurice 1896). The last of these remains essential, not least for its inclusion of a large amount of valuable documentary material, more of which is contained in Hull 1899: xiii–xxiii, and in Lansdowne's editorial commentary in PP1/PP2 and PSC.

126 Strauss 1954. Dale 1987 is an undocumented but readable pamphlet by a local historian in Petty's home town of Romsey in Hampshire.

127 For example, McCulloch 1845: 211f.; Marx 1970 [1859]: 52–54; Pasquier 1903: 27–41; Gooch 1914: 242–250; Goblet 1930: I, 181–206; II, 179–193; Letwin 1963: 114–122; Kuhn 1963: 25–27; Deane 1968; Keynes 1971: vii–ix; Sharp 1977: 1–195; Roncaglia 1985 [1977]: 3–18; and 1987; Olson 1993: 59–62; Aspromourgos 1996: 9–19; and 1998; Pressman 1999: 4f.; Finkelstein 2000: 108–110; and Harris 2000: ix–xii.

128 For example, the studies by Barnard on Petty's activities as a landowner in Ireland, as listed above, and items by various authors on his scientific activities, which will be cited as appropriate.

129 Robbins 1998: 56. Similarly, Mirowski 1989: 151 describes him as "located at the core of the fledgling British scientific community".

130 Letwin 1963: 114.

131 Evelyn [1971]: 94

132 Aubrey [1971]: 89.

133 Ware 1745: 354.

134 Gadbury 1691.

135 Wood 1691–92: IV, 215.

136 Strauss 1954: subtitle ("portrait of a genius") and *passim*.

137 Wood 1691–92: IV, 214. Wood commonly used the term 'genie' in the sense of a natural bent or disposition. See OED: genie 2a.

138 Bonney 1995b: 179.

139 Strauss 1954: 201, 225.

140 Routh 1975: 36. See also Christensen 1989: 706; and Spiegel 1983: 134.

141 Sharp 1977: 365.

142 Strauss 1954: 150.

143 Macaulay 1848–62: chapters 12, 28.

144 Mitchell 1967: I, 148.

145 Studenski 1958: 27.

146 Riley 1985: 35.
147 Robbins 1998: 56.
148 Deane 1968: 666.
149 Walsh and Gram 1980: 16.
150 The *Treatise* was completed by the first week of September 1687; Petty died on 16 December of that year. Hull's editorial introduction (TI: 546–548) provides an indispensable guide to its contents. The sole manuscript is British Library Add. 21,128, ff. 52–129.
151 On Petty's various discussions of Ireland's population in connection with his population transfer schemes, see Chapter 5.1.
152 For an account of Petty's meetings with the monarch, see Dale 2011: 69–77. See also McCormick 2009: 261–262.
153 TI itself, for example, was passed for assessment to Samuel Pepys: see TI: 547 (editorial comment).
154 PP1: 46 (editorial note). These included other measures to increase the population of England and promote the union of Ireland and England, as well as schemes to regulate coins and exchange rates, to reduce the incidence of the plague by half, to "get Hispaniola and Cuba", to choose suitable spouses for the monarch's natural children, to forge an alliance with Denmark, to reform the postage system, and so on. For these and a great many other examples, see PP1: 251–276; and, for much detailed assessment, see Dale 2011: *passim*.
155 See, for the first two versions, PAI: 157f.; and PA: 285–290.
156 See Chapter 4.1.2; and Goodacre 2009, 2010c.
157 TI: 551, 546 (editorial comment), 558 §5.
158 *Ibid.*: 560 §19.
159 PP1: 48 (editorial note); and, similarly, Lynam 1932: 418. For further discussion, see Chapter 4.1.6.
160 By capitalising the flow of the prospective increase in England's national income, he suggests a direct benefit of £100 million (TI: 563 §3); set against this, the "expense or damage" is only £4 million (TI: 555). Much of his argumentation centres on the concept of the 'value of people'; on this concept, see Chapter 3.1.4. For a recent detailed analysis of the costs and benefits, see Dockès 2013.
161 The figures he provides suggest an increase of 10.6 per cent.
162 The figures he provides suggest an increase of 21.6 per cent.
163 TI: 549 §9, 567.
164 *Ibid.*: 549 §9; 567, 572 §5.
165 A notable exception is provided by Poovey 1994: 20–32, and 1998, though the focus of these studies is on general issues of theory and methodology, rather than on colonial policy. See also McNally 1988: 46–48.
166 Though his *Verbum Sapienti* of 1665 is his most succinct and, arguably, the most persuasive, as further discussed in Chapter 3.1.2.
167 For further discussion of the 'Whig interpretation of history' in relation to Petty's writings, see Chapter 5.4.
168 The concept of such a scientific revolution pervades the discussions of Petty's work in Webster 1975 and Sharp 1977, though it is contested by other writers, such as Shapin 1996.
169 Not that the eighteenth-century Enlightenment movement in European philosophy was by any means without its limitations when it came to those termed by Smith "barbarous and uncivilized nations", as discussed in Goodacre 2010b.

170 See, for example, Ekelund and Tollison 1981; and 1997.
171 "Smith anticipates the neoclassical theory of peaceful market economies..." (Coulomb 1998: 315).
172 For a critique of this 'Weberian' thesis as applied in the history of science by Merton, see Jacob 1992; and, for an endorsement, see Kaldor 1954: 67.
173 On the concept of Smith's theoretical system as 'moral Newtonianism,' see Thomson 1984 [1965]: 332–335; Skinner and Wilson 1975: 3f.; and, for a later critical assessment of the concept, Montes 2003. For further discussion of the influence on Smith of Newtonian physics, see Chapter 3.3.

2 Petty and the colonialist roots of development economics[1]

2.0 Introduction

The first of the three branches of economic enquiry to be considered in the present study, development economics, became established as an academic subdiscipline at a time when the history of the British and other old colonial empires was entering its final phase. The first university in England to provide a course in the subject was Oxford, where it was introduced, in the late 1930s, as an element in the 'colonial studies' curriculum for students being trained for the British colonial service,[2] some two and three-quarter centuries after Petty had abandoned his promising career at that same university for more lucrative pursuits in Ireland.

Barely had this new subdiscipline been established, however, when the requirement for training colonial officials was overtaken by the policy of training replacements for them from among the nationals of the countries emerging into independence from the 1950s and 1960s onwards. In the course of reorienting towards this new task, development economists found themselves increasingly confronted with yet another requirement of the times, which was the modification of the attitudes prevailing within the home countries of the colonial rulers towards those whom they had long been accustomed to regard as subject peoples. In contributing to this task, development economists were participating in a wider process of reappraisal of the intellectual legacy of colonialism, as a result of which "areas that had been considered in the eighteenth century as 'rude and barbarous', in the nineteenth century as 'backward', and in the pre-war period as 'underdeveloped', now became the 'less developed countries' or 'the poor countries' – and also the 'emergent countries' and 'developing economies'".[3]

If the contribution of development economics to such a reappraisal of colonialist attitudes was to be truly heart-searching and thorough, then it might surely be expected to entail a search for the historical and conceptual roots of the categories of analysis hitherto prevailing within its parent discipline of economics. In particular, Petty's pioneering works would appear to be of unmistakable relevance, especially in the case of his writings on Ireland, in which he discusses so many of the issues which remain central for the development economists of today: for example, the relation between the subsistence and commercial sectors of the economy; the relation of town to country, and of manufacture to agriculture; the obstacles to the consolidation of a wage-earning labour force in an agrarian context; and the influence on economic life of traditional society and culture. Even apart from this range of direct analogies in specific fields of concern, the mere fact that his economic thought was forged very largely in a colonial context is surely enough, even on its own, to justify according him a prominent status in the intellectual ancestry of development economics in his own right, rather than being relegated, as he customarily is, to the status of a mere 'precursor of Adam Smith'. Indeed, Amartya Sen appears to endorse such an assessment, describing Petty as, quite simply, "a founder of development economics".[4]

Unfortunately, however, it turns out that Sen's allusion to Petty in these terms is a mere passing remark, and that, though not unique, it does not reflect any sustained or substantial discussion of Petty's writings in the development literature. In what follows, it will be shown that this failure of development economists to address the seemingly inescapable task of thoroughly exploring Petty's writings can readily be explained by the uncomfortable nature of the questions which any such exploration inevitably raises regarding the intellectual roots of the subdiscipline as it exists today. To this end, the literature, such as it is, on the relevance of Petty's writings to developmental issues will first be critically reviewed. His approach to some central issues in the intellectual ancestry of development economics will then be analysed – the emergence of a wage-earning labour force in an agrarian context, the ideology of a 'civilising mission', the role of institutions in economic transformation and the political-economic status of the state in the colony. In each case, it will be shown that his writings provide a valuable historical vantage point from which to assess the extent to which development economics has, or has not, surmounted the intellectual legacy of colonialist thought and moved forward to the construction of a truly post-colonial perspective on economic development in the world today.

2.1 Petty, Smith and development economics: a literature review

Such few passing references to Petty as may be gleaned from the literature on the history of development economics are predominantly found in writers of the pioneering period, including Colin Clark, Arthur Lewis and Amartya Sen, as well as the work of subsequent authors who continue to adhere to the same general approach.[5] Their comments commonly amount to little more than an antiquarian flourish on more substantial discussion of Adam Smith, however, whose *Wealth of Nations* is widely regarded as the true starting point in tracing the subdiscipline's intellectual ancestry, this work being perceived by Sen as "also an inquiry into the basic issues of development economics".[6] Seen from such a point of view, the fate of the developmental approach to economic issues encapsulated in Smith's concept of the 'natural progress of opulence' was that, "in the neoclassical epoch, it was just put to bed",[7] or was to "almost die out",[8] only to be reawakened, or "resurrected",[9] by the pioneers of today's development economics almost two centuries later.[10]

Those elements of Smith's theoretical system adduced in support of this view are conventionally grouped together in what is categorised, collectively, as his theory of economic growth, which is, in turn, sometimes cited as evidence of his orientation towards an ideal of social and economic progress. These elements are his celebrated concept of the increase in the division of labour in response to the extension of the market, his discussions of the effects of increase of population and of capital ('stock'), his remarks on technological progress and his concept of a 'progressive state' of society.[11]

The assumption that reference to Petty can, somehow, deepen the historical perspective on this theoretical heritage leads, inevitably, to a tendency among development economists to overestimate the extent to which his discussions of analogous subjects anticipate the Smithian theoretical system. In this, they are by no means alone; for example, historians of economic thought have, in general, been inclined to exaggerate the extent to which Petty's discussions of division of labour – significant though these are – anticipate Smith's highly distinctive and far more elaborate theory.[12] With even less justification, Petty has been credited with the origination of the theory of economic growth, on the dubious basis of his contention, described as "part of one of the earliest discussions of development economics", that "the French grow too fast".[13] A further assertion to be found in the development literature – which anyone who is at all acquainted with Petty's writings will find astonishingly wide of the mark – is that, in his time, "economists are no longer occupied with military power".[14]

Colin Clark stands alone among development economists in showing that he has actually studied Petty's writings, and, in his seminal textbook first published in 1940, he not only makes use of Petty's statistical estimates of world trade but also attributes to him a "brilliant and entirely correct generalisation" – or "what must be called, in all fairness, Petty's Law": the idea that there is a long-term tendency for the working population to move "from agriculture to manufacture, and from manufacture to commerce and services", or "from primary production to secondary and tertiary".[15] One commentator, who prefers the term 'Petty–Clark Law', also suggests that wider affinities exist between the methodologies of the two authors.[16] Clark also notes Petty's advocacy of the advantages of compactness of population, commenting that it contrasts with the subsequent prevalence of "Malthusian propaganda".[17] Clark is, moreover, apparently unique among development economists who have commented on Petty in at least alluding to the need for "deploring his mercantile morality"; as an example of this morality, he cites Petty's inclusion, "without a blush", of the proceeds of piracy and slavery in his estimate of England's import-export statistics.[18]

With the exception of Clark, then, references to Petty by development economists have largely been restricted to cursory, and not always fully informed, assertions by those who evidently presume that counting him in as a 'precursor' will, in some way, add historical depth to the thesis of the Smithian intellectual ancestry of their subdiscipline. This situation clearly indicates the need for a dedicated literature to clarify the issues involved, yet there is, unfortunately, only one study addressed specifically to the subject of Petty's relevance to development economics, a 1988 article by Alessandro Roncaglia, entitled "William Petty and the conceptual framework for the analysis of economic development". This study does indeed provide a salutary corrective to a number of 'retrospective' distortions of the kind that currently prevail, taking as a case study the concept of a distinction (or 'dichotomy') between manufacture and agriculture.

Roncaglia argues, in particular, that Petty did not represent the 'dichotomy' between manufacture and agriculture in terms of an inter-sectoral input–output system of the kind subsequently formulated by the Physiocrats and further elaborated by Adam Smith;[19] rather, he argues, Petty perceived the relationship as one of 'vertical integration', a perception which would, moreover, have accorded with his own first-hand experience in establishing mining and other industrial ventures on his estate in rural Ireland.[20] Unfortunately, however, this study, while highly sensitive to the emergence of the fundamental categories of early modern political economy, includes only minimal engagement with the development literature it purports to address: all that is offered in this regard is a passing reference to a well-known 1954 article by Lewis, which, he states, discusses "the contrast between 'natural' and market-oriented activities",[21] and a rather pedantic criticism of Clark's use of the term 'Petty's Law'. It is not until the conclusion to his study that Roncaglia eventually raises the question of whether Petty's writings are relevant to the validity of the concepts used within development literature today, but this is a question he raises only to leave unanswered.

Despite its useful critique of some retrospective distortions, Roncaglia's study nevertheless takes subsequent classical political economy as its reference point, and moreover totally ignores the colonial context of Petty's writings. The result is that the study ultimately has the effect of reducing his status to that of a precursor of Smith, which, of course, in turn has the effect of implicitly endorsing the idea of the Smithian ancestry of development economics, so that, to find a challenge to this central tenet of the subdiscipline's doctrine on its intellectual origins, it is necessary to turn elsewhere.

One line of enquiry which runs counter to the 'Smithian ancestry' thesis lies in the literature on Smith's concept of the 'states of society'[22]. It has long been pointed out that these 'states' – progressive, stationary, declining – can by no means be assumed to embody unidirectional economic 'progress'. On the contrary, such an optimistic idea is uneasily grafted by Smith onto what remains, essentially, a pessimistic cyclical theory inherited from ancient times – a point conspicuously absent from the arguments of those adhering to the 'Smithian origins' standpoint,[23] though familiar to other writers on the history of economic thought.[24]

A further critique, which is also of more direct relevance in the present context, has been advanced by Michael Cowen and Robert Shenton. They argue that to identify Smith as the intellectual forebear of development economics is to misconstrue the motivation of the nineteenth-century writers whose standpoint – whether under the banner of positivism, utilitarianism, or imperial 'trusteeship' – began to prefigure the idea of economic development as it is now understood. They suggest that these nineteenth-century authors, far from being advocates of progress, were, on the contrary, searching for means to "ameliorate the perceived chaos caused by progress" – the "social disorder of rapid urbanisation, poverty and unemployment". They consequently criticise those who, in their attempts to 'legitimise' development economics, ignore this formative period and, instead, "rummage through the writings of the Scottish Enlightenment, especially those of Adam Smith", to say nothing of even less historically minded writers who "truncate development's historical domain" yet more drastically by confining their attention to the period since 1945.[25] But, while there is much of value in this critique, it is itself founded on another historical truncation, which, as will now be argued, has the consequence of eliding a previous, and even more profoundly relevant, field in which to seek an alternative to the idea of the Smithian roots of development theory.

For to bring Petty's writings on Ireland into currency in these debates is to cast a new light on the points at issue, and inevitably leads to a break with a number of other approaches to the question of the intellectual roots of development economics. First of all, it leads to a break with the tradition, represented by Roncaglia, of centralising the fundamental categories of political economy without reference to the colonial context in which they were first forged and set to work. Secondly, and by the same token, it breaks with the centralisation of Smithian 'growth theory'; for, though Smith frequently makes reference to colonies in this connection (almost exclusively the settler colonies of North America), his purpose is to explore general economic issues such as the effects of labour shortage and the plentiful supply of land,[26] rather than to single out issues which are specifically colonial as such, in the sense of relating to the conquest and administration of subordinate territories. Thirdly, turning to Petty also breaks with, or, at any rate, requires a reverse extension of, the critical theory advanced by Cowen and Shenton, whose analysis effectively discounts the relevance of the period prior to the more mature industrial and colonial theory of the nineteenth century.

One further study, though it makes no attempt to address the literature on development economics, nevertheless deserves mention in the present context. This is the 1997 article by Patrick Welch entitled "Cromwell's occupation of Ireland as judged from Petty's observations and Marx's theory of colonialism". This study consists, primarily, of a correlation of aspects of Petty's writings on Ireland with Karl Marx's theory of the role of colonialism in the primitive accumulation of capital. To this end, a selection of citations of relevant texts is discussed under three headings: "Brutality and religious factionalism", "The supply of labour and the creation of markets" and "Public debt and taxation".

The outcome is that the study directs its focus unequivocally onto the realities of the colonial context in which Petty formulated his economic thought, something which none of the development literature reviewed above has done.[27] It is to the task of continuing down the path thus opened up that much of what follows will be directed, widening the narrow base of the existing literature on the subject by incorporating insights developed within neighbouring fields of historical, social and literary research. It will be shown, on the basis of such a broader perspective, that Petty's approach to what are now identified as development issues was influenced, to an extent not hitherto appreciated, by the colonialist thought of his time; this, in turn, gives an ironic twist to the suggestion by Sen that he should be accorded the status of "a founder of development economics".

2.2 Petty on labour in early modern Ireland

Mainstream economics is singularly unsuited to the task of analysing the process of transition from one kind of socio-economic formation to another. Development economics, however, is inevitably concerned in the first instance with precisely such a process, and, for this reason, its pioneering practitioners, for all the profound differences between their respective approaches, have commonly been perceived as falling into the one broad category – very different from that of the mainstream – of theorists of structural change.[28] Petty's writings on Ireland provide an opportunity to assess their efforts in this respect against his first-hand experience and direct observations of socio-economic life in an era of momentous significance for world history – the era when the world stood on the brink of the emergence of the capitalist system and the 'great divergence' in fortunes between the rich and poor countries to which that system gave rise.

It is hard to see where to begin this task if not from the phenomena which Marx associates with the primitive accumulation of capital, since it was these phenomena which constituted the day-to-day reality reflected in Petty's life and thought: violence, social upheaval, expropriation of the cultivators from their land, the centrality of the state as the prime economic agent, and "passions the most infamous, the most sordid, the pettiest, the most meanly odious".[29] But what is more difficult to identify in Petty's writings – and what at the same time constitutes their unique value – are his observations and comments regarding the various stages and processes through which labour was beginning to be brought into subjection to capital. For his writings embrace three successive, though overlapping, phases in his perspective on labour, each of which illustrates an aspect of the preliminary stages through which early modern political economy had to pass on its path towards a formulation of the concept of capitalist accumulation.

The first phase in Petty's perspective on labour in Ireland can readily be associated with the orientation he adopted with respect to the factional struggles within the colonial establishment in the Cromwellian period. These struggles centred around the fact that, by the time he had risen to high office in the mid-1650s, the faction of large landowners into which he was eventually to be integrated had become increasingly opposed to the implementation of the 'transplantation' of the Irish en masse. They were naturally more than happy to see 'rebel' landlords out of the way, but wanted the actual cultivators of the land to be left where they were. For these cultivators constituted the population they aimed to enserf under their neo-feudal domination, and they had no wish to see them swept away from under their feet; least of all did they want them replaced by the soldiery of the Cromwellian army of occupation, who were, from their point of view, factious and uncontrollable 'fanatics' who had performed the task of restoring colonial rule, and were now best sent back to England as soon as possible.[30]

The neo-feudalism of Petty and his fellow land magnates was far from being a mere reversion to 'true' feudalism as it had existed in the Middle Ages. On the contrary, as the enterprises which Petty subsequently established in his own fiefdom illustrate, a more commercial orientation differentiated such new seigniors as him from the feudal lords of the former epoch, just as the trade in grain surplus underlay the equivalent 'new feudalism' arising in areas of central and eastern Europe in the same period.[31] Nevertheless, from a conceptual point of view at least, Petty's standpoint towards labour at this stage shared more in common with feudalism than capitalism, in the sense that he advocated a situation in which labour was to be retained in situ, as, effectively, an adjunct to the land.

It has been claimed that Petty "elaborated the theory of value...in response to the very concrete practical requirements of his position as Cromwell's Surveyor General".[32] While this statement undoubtedly represents a welcome attempt to situate the formative period of early modern political economy in a colonial context, it needs qualification if it is taken to imply that Petty's celebrated propositions on the labour theory of value were formulated in the course of his actual conduct of his survey.[33] For such theoretical preoccupations clearly responded to issues arising in the development of the wage system and emergent capitalism, whereas the manner in which he conducted his survey was, on the contrary, designed precisely to counter, rather than to promote, such forces as then existed in Ireland for the emergence of agrarian capitalism and the wage system, these being, in that particular context, represented primarily by the rank-and-file Cromwellian soldiery to whose interests he was opposed. Indeed, ironically, the map which resulted from his survey was, "though nobody said so, ...essentially an atlas of Catholic Ireland"[34] – or, in other words, an atlas of the feudal, and even pre-feudal, pattern of land use, whose preservation was demanded by the landowning magnates as the basis of the neo-feudal domination they sought to impose. It was only subsequently that Petty's attention shifted to the issue of wage labour and value, a shift which represented a second and distinct phase in his perspective on labour.

This new phase in Petty's approach may be discerned following the restoration of the English monarchy in 1660. He now remained in England for a number of years, during which time his attention naturally focused more on English than on Irish affairs. In this phase a contradiction opened out between his own continuing neo-feudal status and his increasing interest in the advance of the wage system. The idea that labour is, or should be, an adjunct to the land, in feudal style, now gave way in his writings to ideas and concepts that pointed forward to the world of emergent capitalism. Indeed, at the 'macro' level, he even ran ahead of the times in his celebrated formulation of a system of national accounts, in that he categorised the income of the entire labouring population purely and simply – and as yet surely unrealistically – as 'wages'.[35] At the 'micro' level, his discussions of the motivation of labour anticipated the concept which has subsequently been termed the 'backward-bending labour supply curve': the idea that an excessive wage level, or, in real terms, "over-feeding of the people", results in "indisposing them to their usual labour".[36]

Such simplifying assumptions and schematic concepts exemplify the manner in which Petty's writings prefigure what was eventually to become economics; they also, however, misrepresent the actual situation in England at the time. For, while dispossession of the peasantry was indeed far advanced, it by no means follows that the resulting dispossessed population had as yet become a wage-earning labour force, let alone a homogeneous one. The reality was that the social dislocation, vagrancy and high mortality suffered by the dispossessed in the sixteenth century had to a large extent been replaced only by the political and national upheaval, civil wars and high mortality of the seventeenth. If such was the case in England, then it was incomparably more so in Ireland, and, when Petty returned to that country in 1666, his writings began to express increasing frustration over the problems involved in establishing a wage-earning labour force at all in the conditions prevailing there. For the Irish socio-economic system, which retained features of communal, as well as individual, patterns of land use, remained, even at this time, "highly flexible and uniquely suited, in environmental terms", to its material circumstances,[37] and was fully capable of reabsorbing into itself those who might otherwise have constituted the demographic base for a wage-earning class.[38]

Petty rooted his comments on this situation in observation. The Irish, he states,

> are able to perform their husbandry with such harness and tackling as each man can make with his own hands, and living in such houses as almost every man can build; and every housewife being a spinner and dyer of wool and yarn, they can live and subsist after their present fashion, without the use of gold or silver money.[39]

Such being the case, the cash economy constitutes, by his estimate, only a fifth of all their "expense", the rest of their consumption being "what their own family produceth";[40] the principal exception is tobacco, which was evidently spearheading the introduction of cash transactions for consumption goods into the agrarian economy – the Coca-Cola of its day.

Petty furthermore asserts that the Irish are able to supply themselves with "the necessities above-named without labouring two hours per diem".[41] He consequently asks:

> What need they to work, who can content themselves with potatoes, whereof the labour of one man can feed forty, and with milk, whereof one cow will in summertime give meat and drink enough for three men, when they can everywhere gather cockles, oysters, muscles, crabs, etc., with boats, nets, angles or the art of fishing, [and] can build an house in three days?[42]

Petty's discussions of how the Irish are to be "kept to their labour"[43] thus illustrate the obstacles to the subjection of labour to capital in conditions where they have the alternative choice of an independent livelihood on the land – conditions which were to remain characteristic of much of the colonial world in the following centuries.[44]

From frustration and oversimplification it is only a short step to fantasy, and it was to this mode of speculation that Petty turned in what signalised a third and final phase in his changing perspective on labour – his scheme for the wholesale transfer of the Irish population to England – which he initially put forward "rather as a dream or reverie than a rational proposition".[45] The scheme nevertheless took on an increasingly realistic character, until it finally assumed the elaborate form in which it appears in his final *Treatise of Ireland* in 1987. In this final form, moreover, his proposal further developed his perspective on labour, whose role in his scheme is that of what would, in today's spatial-economic analysis, be termed a 'mobile factor of production'.[46] As such, it falls into the same category as mobile physical capital, and is distinguished from the immobile factors of land and real estate ('housing').[47]

To indulge in such retrospective analogies, however, only highlights the limited extent to which Petty actually anticipated the 'factors of production' approach of subsequent economic theory, despite his pioneering adoption of a threefold division of the sources of economic output into labour, land and "money and other personal estates", a category occupying the conceptual space that was subsequently to be filled by the various successive and differing concepts of capital.[48] For the subsequent concept of factors of production is predicated upon the endorsement of capitalist competition in the market, an institution which Petty regarded with suspicion.[49] Rather, he turned spontaneously to the state as the sole force capable of imposing a solution to the problems of consolidating a wage-earning labour force in general, let alone implementing his own scheme.

Such was the long and complex process through which Petty's perspective on labour evolved, from the neo-feudal standpoint of his Cromwellian years to the empirical and observational approach of the subsequent period and, finally, to a more abstract approach which began to foreshadow – though only dimly and partially – that of the mature classical political economy of the following century, and, beyond it, the economics that was to follow.

2.3 Petty, the Cromwellian invasion of Ireland and the 'civilising mission'

The tone of Petty's writings on Ireland, however harsh it sounds to modern ears, is restrained and dispassionate by comparison with the fulminations against all things Irish or Catholic which characterised much of the English political literature of the Civil War period of the 1640s.[50] This contrast might appear to accord with the complacent assumption still commonly found in the writings of English historians that Cromwell's invasion of Ireland coincided with a passing moment when fanatical forces temporally seized control of affairs of state in England; the ferocity of the accompanying anti-Irish hysteria was thus, according to this view, an aberration of English history, and was, moreover, soon rectified by more moderate counsels emanating from within the mainstream of the ruling establishment in England, in coordination with the supposedly paternalist land magnates in Ireland.

This interpretation has been challenged by the historian Norah Carlin, however, on the basis of her analysis of a body of propaganda material commissioned by the parliamentary authorities in support of the invasion. She points out that this propaganda explicitly de-links the invasion issue from matters of religion, and, to a certain extent, also from the crudest forms of anti-Irish hysteria; rather, what marks it out as distinctive is its centralisation and systematisation of the argument that English colonial rule in Ireland could be justified by reference to "Irish barbarism and the idea of an English civilising mission".[51] In other words, the ideology used to justify the invasion was not a manifestation of a passing wave of fanaticism but a systematic exposition of England's long-term colonial objectives, and was not formulated from within a political fringe but from within the mainstream of the ruling establishment of the time.

Petty shares with much of this literature a relatively dispassionate tone, and surpasses it all in his relentless efforts at theoretical systematisation; his writings on Ireland can, thus, be seen as a continuation and further elaboration of the new wave of propaganda which originated in attempts to justify the Cromwellian invasion. Although he does not display direct acquaintance with the particular texts analysed by Carlin, he would undoubtedly have been aware of the substance of their argumentation, with which, as will now be shown, there is frequently resonance in his writings of the following decades.

For example, Petty castigates the Catholic priesthood for propagating rebellious aspirations among the Irish people, and for effectively constituting an "internal and mystical government" which allows Ireland to be "governed indirectly by foreign power".[52] His comments are thus directed overwhelmingly towards political issues, and, while he comments disparagingly on certain aspects of Catholic religious practice which he considers "peculiar to those Irish",[53] he makes it clear that he is not concerned to extend such comment into wider discussion of issues relating to Catholic doctrine as such.

Besides de-linking Irish political issues from the religious sphere in this way, Petty also attempts to provide materialistic explanations for a range of other economic and social issues relating to Ireland and the Irish. For example, as has already been seen, he associates the supposed laziness of the Irish with their ready access to means of subsistence requiring only "two hours per diem" for their production, rather than attributing it to anything in their physical make-up: "For their shape, stature, colour, and complexion, I see nothing in them inferior to any other people, nor any enormous predominance of any humour."[54] He concludes that "their lazing seems to me to proceed rather from want of employment and encouragement to work than from the natural abundance of phlegm in their bowels and blood".[55]

But, while the intractability of Irish labour to subjection to capital could thus not be attributed to their physical characteristics, it was, he suggests, nonetheless deeply rooted, in consequence of "their ancient customs, which affect as well their consciences as their nature"; for, he asks,

> Why should they desire to fare better, though with more labour, when they are taught that this way of living is more like the patriarchs of old and the saints of later times, by whose prayers and merits they are to be relieved, and whose examples they are therefore to follow?[56]

Petty's secular explanatory framework accords broadly with much of the propaganda justifying the 1649 invasion. A further range of correlations can also be identified with a body of argumentation commonly used during that period to justify rule by conquest.[57] Such arguments corresponded with Petty's view that it was only by conquest that the Irish could be made to realise that "'tis their interest to join with them and follow their example who have brought arts, civility and freedom into their country".[58]

In connection with the 'arts', a category which then included technology, Petty claims that there were "not ten iron furnaces" in the whole of Ireland.[59] That which he established on his own estate was manned primarily, if not exclusively, by colonists from England,[60] and his experience in this and his other enterprises doubtless strengthened his prejudice that only colonialism could introduce technological progress into Ireland. An associated argument was that, left to themselves, the Irish would fail to develop the natural resources of their country. This argument was used to justify colonial rule in Ireland in a 1652 work by Gerard Boate, a writer who had frequented the same intellectual circles as Petty during the 1640s, and of whose work he must surely have been aware.[61] The same argument remained a familiar feature of colonialist writings throughout the subsequent era, and was, indeed, one of the principal contexts in which the term 'economic development' first came into currency two centuries later.[62]

A further characteristic feature of this ideology of conquest is the belittlement of the history of the colonised people prior to the arrival of the invader. Petty took up this standpoint and elaborated on it with enthusiasm:

> There is at this day no monument or real argument that, when the Irish were first invaded, they had any stone housing at all, any money, any foreign

trade, nor any learning but the legends of the Saints, Psalters, Missals, Rituals, etc., viz. nor geometry, astronomy, anatomy, architecture, enginery, painting, carving, nor any kind of manufacture, nor the least use of navigation or the art military.[63]

The ultimate insult in this connection was the assertion that the Irish were intruders in their own country, a common suggestion being that they were of 'Scythian' origin, an idea which supposedly explained the apparently 'nomadic' (in fact, transhumant) aspect of Irish pastoral society.[64] Petty's own 'conjecture' was in fact less exotic, though perhaps intended to be no less wounding, suggesting as he did that Ireland's first inhabitants were likely to have come from Scotland, rather than being "Phoenicians, Scythians, Biscayers, etc.".[65]

The generally positive estimation that Petty receives from development economists for his contribution to their theoretical heritage is thus in contradiction with the assumption, which presumably most of them would share, that much of the impulse to the formative work of their pioneering representatives came from the perceived need to supersede the colonialist ideology of the 'civilising mission' and provide a post-colonial alternative to it.[66] Once it is taken into account, therefore, that Petty was in fact deeply engaged in an early, but crucial, stage of the formulation of this very ideology, questions inevitably arise as to the level of self-awareness prevailing in the subdiscipline regarding the intellectual roots of the conceptual apparatus on which its practitioners continue to rely.

2.4 Petty on institutions and their transformation

There is some remarkably close resonance with aspects of the development economics literature in Petty's comments on what would now be termed 'institutions', or, more specifically, the commercial and financial infrastructure, the legal institutions relating to the security of property rights, and the conditions for a culture of enterprise.

Regarding commercial institutions, Petty poses the question: "Why should they [i.e. the Irish] raise more commodities, since there are not merchants sufficiently stocked to take them of them, nor provided with other more pleasing foreign commodities to give in exchange for them?"[67] Moreover, commercial transactions are impeded by corresponding deficiencies in the financial institutions, in the form of "difference, confusion and badness of coins, [and] exorbitant exchange and interest of money".[68]

As for what are now termed property rights, Petty asks the question: "Why should men endeavour to get estates, where the legislative power is not agreed upon, and where tricks and words destroy natural right and property?"[69] This issue of secure land tenure was, of course, one with which he was deeply concerned throughout his career, first as both surveyor of Ireland and beneficiary of the Cromwellian confiscations, and subsequently in ongoing legal battles to retain possession of the lands he had seized. It is, consequently, no surprise to find that he repeatedly returns to this theme, calling for "clear conditions" upon leases,[70] and, in the political sphere, "certainty" over where ultimate legislative authority lies.[71] At the same time, he cautions that laws might not be readily transferable between countries, since, if "first made and first fitted to thick-peopled countries", they might overload the more summary legal apparatus available in "thin-peopled countries such as Ireland".[72]

Against the background of such weak commercial, financial and legal institutions, it is no surprise that a culture of enterprise was failing to take root, and, reflecting on the "indisposition" of the Irish to take to maritime trade, Petty complains that "the Irish had rather eat potatoes and milk on dry land than contest with the wind and waves with better food".[73]

This entire range of discussion, based as it is on his own lifelong practical preoccupations and frustrations, gives Petty's writings on institutional matters a more concrete and immediate aspect than the rather unspecific and general observations on equivalent subjects that had been propagated by the English parliamentary authorities at the time of the 1649 invasion. He also, for that matter, strikes a more modern note than is subsequently to be found in Smith's discussions of colonialism, which, based as they are on second-hand information, are Olympian, academic and unrealistic by comparison.

This realism endows Petty's population transfer proposals with a grimly practical character, designed as they were, perfectly explicitly, to wipe out Ireland's national traditions — economic, social and cultural — which had proved so resilient to transformation in accordance with the requirements of colonialism and emergent capitalism. The English had never been able to muster sufficient colonists to swamp these traditions in situ; his scheme was, he argued, a more realistic means to achieving the same aim. It would, for example, facilitate the eradication of the Irish language, along with the replacement of "those uncertain and unintelligible" Irish place names.[74] It would prescribe cross-marriages on a massive scale, in particular between Irish men and English women, so that the offspring would be reared in the language and culture of their mothers.[75] In short, "the manners, habits, language and customs of the Irish…would all be transmuted into English".[76]

History is full of ironies, and, by dismissing market institutions in favour of continued reliance on the blunter instrument of action by the absolutist state, Petty was, in fact, turning his back on precisely those forces that, in the centuries to come, were to achieve what, for him, had been only a "dream or reverie": the catastrophic decline of the Irish population,[77] the devastation of their traditional way of life, the decline of their language to the verge of extinction and the reduction of their economy to export dependence, centring particularly — at any rate in the southern, 26-county, state till quite recent decades — on cattle ranching.[78]

2.5 Petty and the state: metropolitan and colonial

As has now been shown, what the tone of Petty's discussions lacks in fanatical invective is amply compensated by a clinical note which is, arguably, even more chilling. This reaches its extreme in his use of anatomical imagery to justify his methodological approach to socio-economic analysis, and, in particular, his argument that Ireland presents an ideal opportunity for such 'political anatomy', just as "students in medicine practice their inquiry upon cheap and common animals".[79] The English state's experiments in this 'laboratory' of Ireland encompassed "governmental modernisation, colonial expansion, religious reformation and identity formation all in process simultaneously".[80] In the case of each of these processes, everything that constituted an advance from the English point of view necessarily entailed measures to suppress Ireland's cultural, political and religious life and annihilate its national identity: "[T]he development of 'Englishness' depended on the negation of 'Irishness'."[81] Petty's writings disingenuously reveal both sides of this equation with a frankness and clarity which contrasts with the distorted perspective which results from the all-too common tendency to focus in a one-sided manner on those aspects of his writings which are susceptible to representation in a positive light, or even as socially progressive.

The history of England's colonial policy in Ireland provides ample illustration of the paradoxical fact that the fundamental institutions of what is now perceived as capitalist private enterprise, such as the joint-stock company and even corporate enterprise in general, first emerged in inseparable combination with state – usually military – activity.[82] It was through his engagement in such activity, for which, in another context, he coined the term 'privato-public',[83] that Petty made his fortune; in this, he exemplified the rise of neo-feudal upstarts of all kinds in the Europe of his time, a rise which, for all its local variation, had in common the fact that it was predicated on the strength of the state rather than, as in the 'true' feudalism of the medieval period, its weakness. It is therefore no surprise that Petty's economic thought is concerned, above all, with the problem of how to maximise England's taxation revenue, and his writings on colonial Ireland are no exception. Although, in this connection, he at times criticised the English authorities for imposing restraints on aspects of the Irish economy – particularly by restricting its cattle exports[84] – this was clearly motivated by defence of the profits reaped by colonial landowners such as himself rather than being an expression of sympathy with the idea of an independent economic life for Ireland, let alone an independent Irish nation state.

The idea of economic planning by the state was, in Petty's time, closely linked with Utopian currents in social thought, not least in connection with colonial policy, Thomas More's *Utopia* having itself been described as marking "a watershed in the development of colonial theory".[85] One topical pamphlet in the Utopian genre, describing a mythical kingdom named 'Macaria', emanated from the intellectual circles in which Petty had moved prior to his arrival in Ireland. The "excellent government" of this mythical kingdom included a number of 'councils' handling the different aspects of state policy, one of these being a "council for new plantations [i.e. colonies]".[86] Petty greatly elaborated such ideas in his later writings, and, in his final scheme for the transformation of Ireland into a "kind of factory", he outlines the tasks of a proposed "council of fitting persons" in terms which vividly portray the transition from utopian speculation to the practicalities of administering a planned economy.

1. The lands and cattle are the same as now, wanting only a new application to each other.
2. A Council of Fitting Persons must make this application, by pitching the number of each species of cattle, for every sort of land within the whole territory of Ireland.
3. The same may pitch the number of cow-herds, shepherds, dairy-women, slaughter men and others, which are fit and sufficient to manage the trade of exported cattle, dead or alive, of hides, tallow, butter and cheese, wool and sea-fish, etc.
4. To appoint the foreign markets and ports where each commodity is to be shipped and sold, to provide shipping, and to keep account of the export-ation above mentioned, and of the imported salt, tobacco, with a few other necessaries.[87]
5. When the whole number to be left in Ireland is adjusted, then to pitch how many of them shall be English, or such as can speak English, and how many Irish, how many Catholics and how many others, without any other respect than the management of this trade, for the common good of all the owners of these lands and its stock indifferently.[88]

The power of the Council thus extends into the demographic sphere, or, to use Petty's phrase, "managing the multiplication" of the population,[89] and, since the entire population is to be "all aged between 16 and 60 years",[90] the Council will also be obliged to "carry away children and superannuated persons".[91]

Despite the normally positive connotations which the term 'utopia' enjoys today, there has, from Plato's *Republic* onwards, traditionally been, explicitly or implicitly, an associated 'dystopia' for those excluded from its highest privileges, and it is in this sense that Yann Morvran Goblet describes Petty's proposal as a system of "twin utopias".[92] The polarity between the two comes across vividly in Petty's writings as a whole: on the one hand, the variety and luxury of the glittering colonial metropolis of London; on the other, the dour homogeneity of Petty's scheme for a "new model Ireland":[93] housing that reaches a standard of basic habitability,[94] clothes that are "uniform"[95] and a humble country diet of potatoes and dairy products, enlivened only by foraging.[96]

In view of this sharp distinction between the metropolitan and colonial worlds as they are depicted in Petty's writings, it is disappointing to note the lack of attention hitherto paid to the fact that he accords the state a completely different political-economic status on either side of the divide; indeed, one otherwise perceptive study of his writings on government and administration totally omits any mention of colonies whatsoever,[97] while the same omission by Roncaglia is, arguably, even more remiss, in that his study is dedicated expli-citly to the relation of Petty's economic thought to development economics. It is evidently necessary, therefore, to underline the fact that, in Petty's writings, there is no assumption of political, administrative or political-economic equivalence between the role of the state in the colonies and in the metropolis; in political economy, such a concept was only to emerge a century later, in Smith's theoretical system, and, even then, it was effectively restricted to the North American colonies.[98] Petty's writings and practical involvements in state affairs thus usefully draw out the fact that his approach – especially as it concerns the issues now addressed by development economics – was based on the presumption of a dichotomy between a dominant and a subordinate status in all spheres of government, administration and political economy.

2.6 Conclusions

It may now be seen that a thorough search for the roots of the theoretical and methodological apparatus of today's development economics does not lead back, as is widely and complacently assumed, to the universalistic or progressive currents of thought commonly ascribed to the Enlightenment movement in eighteenth-century philosophy. Rather, the search for such roots leads back to Petty. Consequently, the urgent, difficult and soul-searching task of confronting and surmounting an intellectual heritage with roots in the unbridled phase of colonialism epitomised in his life and writings must surely be prioritised within development economists. Only by confronting this task without equivocation can a genuine assessment be made of the capacity of the conceptual apparatus prevailing within the subdiscipline to perform the progressive analytical tasks it claims to be capable of performing, whether in the sphere of policy formulation, or of contributing to the supersession of the colonialist attitudes of the past.

If indeed development economists have hitherto addressed these tasks on a theoretical and methodological basis whose intellectual roots stretch back to Petty, then it follows that some awkward questions must be faced. For, in his writings, the goal of development, to the extent that any anticipation of such an idea can be discerned there, is unequivocally given second place to the goals of colonial conquest and repression, international rivalry and predatory warfare. It is to such ends that, applying his pioneering quantitative method, he coldly calculates the advantages to the colonial power of the annihilation of the national life of the colonised people, their effective extinction as a demographic unit and the imposition upon their territory of an intentionally dependent, single-export economy, outlining a whole range of measures designed to obliterate the social, cultural and intellectual traditions indigenous to the colonised society – traditions which were assumed to constitute, by their very existence, a challenge to the unquestioned dominance of the colonial power.

The fact that historians of economic thought have hitherto largely turned a blind eye to this predatory colonialist character of Petty's pioneering writings reflects a wider incapacity, or unwillingness, of economists to surmount the traditions of colonialist thought embedded in the intellectual culture of the metropolitan countries in which the economics discipline has arisen and developed. Furthermore, as has now been shown, this is so even in the case of the subdiscipline which is, ostensibly, the one most directly concerned with superseding the intellectual legacy of the colonialist era.

In moving on to the second of the three branches of economic enquiry to be considered in the present study, namely the economics of taxation, Petty's colonialist assumptions and ambitions will not always be so explicitly and unmistakably expressed. By virtue of that very fact, however, it will become clear that the same colonialist assumptions and ambitions are inseparable from a far wider range of categories of economic analysis than those commonly associated with development economics alone.

Notes

1   Much of the text of this chapter is substantially the same as Goodacre 2005b, and is included with the kind permission of its publishers, Zed Books.
2   Meier 1984: 8; 1994c: 183–187.
3   Meier and Rauch 2000: 69.
4   Sen 1988: 10.
5   For example, Yang 2003, as cited further below.
6   Sen 1988: 10.
7   Meier 1994b: 7, citing Hicks.
8   Lewis 1988: 36.
9   Meier 1994a: 1.
10   See also Meier 1984: 3f.
11   See, for example, Meier 1994b; Meier and Rauch 2000: 72f.; and Yang 2003: 1.
12   For an example of such exaggeration in the development literature, see Yang 2003: 1, 31; and, for further discussion, Chapter 4.1.3 (ii); and Goodacre 2010c.
13   Sen 1988: 10, discussing PA: 242.
14   Lewis 1988: 28. This statement presumably reflects the fact that Lewis's source for his comments is Johnson 1937, who refers to Petty (p. 99) as "a man of peace", as discussed further in Chapter 3.2.2.
15   Clark 1940: 448f., 176f., 341, citing PA: 256, 267; see also Clark 1984: 70.
16   Pyatt 1984: 79.
17   Clark 1957: 492f. See also Pyatt 1984: 81. There is also an oblique reference to this advocacy of compactness in Yang 2003: 1, where it is termed "Petty's theory of urbanisation"; for further discussion, see Chapter 4.1.3; and Goodacre 2009 and 2010c.
18   Clark 1940: 448f., discussing PA: 296. See also Chapter 3.2.1.
19   Kurz and Salvadori 2003 [2000]: 42, in contrast, describe Petty as "an important author in the genealogy of input–output analysis", as further discussed in Chapter 4.1.5.
20   The force of Roncaglia's argument is weakened by his failure, all too characteristic of economists, to take account of conspicuously relevant branches of literature in neighbouring fields, including research by Ruth Thirsk and others on the 'drift' of manufactures to the countryside, as well as the entire debate over the concept of 'proto-industrialisation', and, for that matter, the substantial body of research by Barnard and others on Petty's own enterprises in Ireland, on which see note in Chapter 1.2.

21 Though this is not actually the terminology used in Lewis 1954.
22 Smith 1976 [1776]: 99.
23 See, for example, Meier 1994b.
24 See, for example, Cowen and Shenton 1995: 30–32; and, for the wider historical background, Perrotta 2003.
25 Cowen and Shenton 1995: 29, 31, a study subsequently elaborated in a 1996 monograph on the same theme. A prime example of a historical perspective limited to the post-1945 period alone is provided by the discussion of development economics in Krugman 1995: chap. 1. See Fine 2002: 2065, 2068 (note 25); and further discussion in Chapter 5.1.2.
26 See, for example, Smith 1976 [1776]: 87f. (rapid increase in population), 423f. (land is "to be had almost for nothing").
27 While Welch's study is the main precedent for what follows, there is also a briefer analogous discussion in Perelman 2000: 125–129. Welch's definition of 'Marx's theory of colonialism' is limited almost entirely to the discussions relating specifically to primitive accumulation at the end of the first volume of *Capital*. For a critique of such a restricted perspective on Marx's theory of colonialism, see Patnaik 2005.
28 See, for example, Meier 1994c: 182.
29 Marx 1970 [1867]: 762. On the state as 'agent', see note in Chapter 3.2.1.
30 Thus, while it may be justified to describe the original goal of the occupation to have been "something like an instant transition from feudalism to capitalism" (Wood 2002: 153f.), the further course of events had resulted in a more complex interplay of capitalist and feudal – or, at any rate, neo-feudal – interests.
31 It is disappointing that the debate among historians on the 'new feudalism' of the period has focused almost entirely on central and eastern Europe (see, for example, Brenner 1976: 50–60), despite the evident relevance of the situation in Ireland, as demonstrated by Morgan 1985: 274–278.
32 Wood 2002: 161.
33 This is not to dismiss the idea that the circumstances of his survey may have strongly influenced his labour theory in retrospect, as suggested by Hull 1899: lxxii, and further discussed in Chapter 4.1.1.
34 Andrews 1997: 147.
35 See, for example, VS: chap. 2; and, for further discussion, Chapter 3.1.3.
36 PA: 275, as further discussed in Chapter 3.1.4.
37 Morgan 1985: 278, much of whose discussion, though it concerns the Tudor period, remains relevant to conditions in Petty's lifetime.
38 Linklater 2013: 55–71 places Petty's writings in the context of a general survey of the ending of communal landownership internationally.
39 PA: 273.
40 PAI: 192.
41 PA: 273.
42 PAI: 201.
43 *Ibid.*: 189.
44 See Marx 1970 [1867]: chap. 33; and, for discussion, Rodriguez Braun 1987; and Welch 1997: 164f.
45 PA: 285.
46 As Cronin 2014 comments, Petty's goal was to transform the populations of the territories under England's into "a mobile, transnational labor force". See Chapter 5.1.

47 For further discussion, see Chapter 4.1.5.
48 See Chapter 3.1.3.
49 See Chapter 3.3.
50 Coughlan 1990: 216f.
51 Carlin 1993: 210.
52 PAI: 199, 164.
53 *Ibid.*: 198.
54 *Ibid.*: 201
55 *Ibid.* Petty's comments in the field of physical anthropology, particularly regarding the "several species of man" inhabiting other continents, have long been a topic for discussion among historians of anthropology, such as Margaret Hodgen 1964: 419–422. For a more recent and very thorough study of this question, see Lewis 2011, as discussed in Chapter 5.2.
56 PAI: 201f.
57 Carlin 1993: 219f.
58 PAI: 203.
59 *Ibid.*: 209.
60 For a detailed account of his workforce, see Barnard 1982: 4–11.
61 Quoted by Carlin 1993: 217. See also Coughlan 1990: 212f. Boate was a member of the circle of intellectuals centring on Samuel Hartlib, with whom Petty had also been associated prior to taking up office in the army of occupation in Ireland. See Barnard 1974: 58f.; 2000 [1975]: 214f.
62 Arndt 1981: 460–462.
63 PAI: 154f.
64 This idea was given wide currency by the English poet Edmund Spenser; see Coughlan 1990: 207. See also Morgan 1985: 268. Carlin 1993: 221f compares this "last twist of the knife" with "white South African claims that the black majority are late arrivals in the area".
65 PAI: 204.
66 Masson and Youngson 1960: 83 blithely express their approval of the contribution of Petty's survey of Ireland to "the civilising of nations".
67 PAI: 202.
68 *Ibid.*: 196.
69 *Ibid.*: 202.
70 *Ibid.*: 203.
71 *Ibid.*: 159f.
72 *Ibid.*: 202.
73 *Ibid.*: 208.
74 *Ibid.*
75 *Ibid.*: 202f.
76 TI: 573 §17. Petty's use of this concept, derived from premodern chemistry, is extensively discussed in McCormick 2007 (chap. 5 and *passim*), as well as in other works of the same author, including McCormick 2006, 2008 and 2016.
77 Though, even as his population transfer schemes were becoming further elaborated, another current of thought was increasingly preoccupying him, his 'populationism', and in his later writings he also wrote of the benefits of increasing Ireland's population. For an exploration of this contradiction in his writings on that country, see the discussion of Fox 2009 in Chapter 5.1.
78 See also Goblet 1930: II, 305, as further discussed in the Postscript.

79 PAI: 129; for discussion, see Coughlan 1990: 213–220; and Chapter 4.1.1.
80 Morgan 1999: 9. Similarly, Wood 2002: 160f describes Ireland as the "favourite test case or laboratory for English social theory and even natural science". The concept of 'laboratory' is also explored in relation to Petty's writings on Ireland by Harris 1998.
81 Hadfield and Maley 1993: 7.
82 See Bottigheimer 1971: 44; and Morgan 1985: 262–267.
83 TTC: 65 §5.
84 See PAI: 160f., with editorial note; PA: 299; and McCormick 2009: 158–160. See also Chapters 4.1.5 and 4.1.6.
85 Morgan 1985: 269.
86 Webster 1979: 67f.
87 TI: 575.
88 *Ibid.*
89 *Ibid.*: 605.
90 *Ibid.*: 563.
91 *Ibid.*: 576 §9.
92 Goblet 1930: II, 280–306.
93 TI: 567.
94 *Ibid.*: 577.
95 *Ibid.*: 569 §12.
96 PAI: 201, as quoted in Chapter 2.2. For further discussion of this polarity between variety and homogeneity, see Chapter 4.4.2 (iv).
97 Mykkänen 1994.
98 See, in particular, Smith 1976 [1776]: 624–626; and, for discussion, Stevens 1975.

3 Petty's economic thought and the fiscal-military state

3.0 Introduction: Petty and the historical roots of the fiscal-military state

Within the field of development economics, the search for the historical roots of the analytical categories of today has involved discussion of early modern colonialism in a particularly direct way. In turning to the second of the three subfields of economics chosen for exploration in the present study – the economics of taxation – much of the enquiry will be less inseparably and directly linked to the colonial context. This difference is signalled by a shift in the central focus of attention away from Petty's writings on Ireland to those which are concerned primarily with England. This transition is far from abrupt, since the fact that Petty moved freely between the colonial and metropolitan worlds represented, respectively, by these two countries is reflected in his economic thought no less than in the facts of his biography. This, in turn, reflects the fact that, in the case of Ireland, colonialism was not necessarily associated with the aspiration to begin a new life overseas, as was increasingly the case in the colonisation of America, but was more often perceived, rather, as a path to enhanced status within England.

There is, besides, a yet more profoundly significant respect in which the contrast between the colonial and metropolitan context is less pronounced in Petty's economic writings than it was to be in the work of subsequent writers. This is that slavery, the most extreme form of colonialist exploitation, was, in his writings, still conflated, both ideologically and conceptually, with wage labour. For, just as the great divergence in the economic fortunes of the countries of the world was still only in its very first stages, so also a corresponding conceptual divergence between wage labour and slavery had yet to open out; even Richard Cantillon, writing some four or more decades after Petty's death, used the word *esclave* indiscriminately to apply to slave and wage labourer alike. It was the conceptual distinction between the two, in the form of Smith's concept of the individual labourer in conditions of 'natural liberty', that marked the definitive transition to the age of 'Enlightenment' in the sphere of economic thought, just as it was the continuation of slavery, and, subsequently, indentured labour and all other forms of colonial super-exploitation, that revealed the apologetic – or unenlightened – features that fatally constrained the scope of that self-contradictory movement and ultimately confounded its claim to its high-sounding title.

In any event, enlightenment, however defined, was, as yet, at the most a subsidiary element in the economic thought of Petty's time, and the motivation of his economic writings remained much the same as that enunciated by his predecessor Thomas Mun, who listed the goals of foreign trade in the following ingenuously frank words:

> The great revenue of the king, the honour of the kingdom, the noble profession of the merchant, the school of our arts, the supply of our wants, the employment of our poor, the improvement of our lands, the nursery of our mariners, the walls of the kingdom, the means of our treasure, the sinews of our wars, the terror of our enemies.[1]

Within the field of economic history, much progress has been made in tracing the path through which the English monarchy progressed towards the realisation of such ambitions. A whole literature now exists on the development of the financial and other economic institutions through which, by the end of the seventeenth century, England's rulers had achieved the "widely feared fiscal-military power"[2] that was to carry the country through a "second hundred years war against France"[3] and the acquisition of England's first, or commercial, empire, and then onwards into the age of modern imperialism and the emergence of the pattern of global inequality as it exists today. For these momentous developments to be set on course, it was first necessary for a number of strands in the development of English society, economy and politics to become entwined together in the fabric of a new form of state structure, for which economic and fiscal historians have coined the term 'the fiscal-military state'.[4]

William Petty died the year before the 'Glorious Revolution' of 1688, which is commonly taken to mark the opening episode in this new stage of England's history. As in the case of all historical turning points, however, the significance of the revolution of 1688 is, paradoxically, belittled rather than truly appreciated if it is singled out for attention on its own, without reference to the developments of which it was a culmination. It has accordingly been argued that the advantages enjoyed by England in the years following 1688 were "path-dependent",[5] and that it was in the previous period – in other words, during Petty's lifetime – that "the constitutional and administrative foundations for a fiscal state were put in place".[6] Accordingly, the term 'fiscal-military' has come to be quite widely used in the context of the pre-1688 period,[7] a usage which accords with a more far-reaching call to counteract a tendency which "exaggerates the impact of the 'Glorious Revolution' [of 1688] as a discontinuity",[8] a standpoint which has been described as "truncated in chronology, narrow in conception, and insular in focus".[9] This admonition is particularly apt in respect of the wider social and ideological aspects of the new developments:

> The growth of the fiscal-military state created new social roles, justified by distinctive kinds of legitimisation; essential to an understanding of the phenomenon, therefore, is a discussion of the linguistic resources which justified and explained (and therefore enabled) the growth of fiscal-military power.[10]

As the foregoing account of his life and activities has already suggested, Petty's writings are, clearly, to be situated within this process of the ideological, cultural and linguistic resources for the developments which were to culminate in the consolidation of the fiscal-military state in the period following his death. There is consequently a need for a reappraisal of his contribution in the light of these discussions within the field of economic history. In what follows, an attempt will be made to undertake this task, and, in particular, to rectify the retrospective, and also pacific, perspective on his writings which has hitherto predominated in the literature on the history of economic thought.

3.1 Petty's fiscal theory and the history of economic thought

3.1.1 Introductory literature review

Taxation was, for Petty, "the window through which he saw the economic world".[11] Yet, despite this fully justified comment by a writer on the 'predecessors of Adam Smith', there has been hardly any attempt from within the literature on the history of economic thought to assess Petty's fiscal theory in the specific historical context in which it was formulated. Even the initial task of providing the basic historical background to his writings remains very largely where it was left over a century ago by Petty's editor and early biographers.[12] Furthermore, such progress as has subsequently been achieved in this task is almost entirely owed not to historians of economic thought but to historians of taxation[13] and economic historians,[14] or, rather, in the past two decades, to the "new subject called fiscal history"[15] which has effectively superseded the interdisciplinary boundary between those former historical subdisciplines, and whose attitude to the literature on the history of economic thought has, understandably, been unenthusiastic or even dismissive.[16]

Discussions of Petty's writings by historians of economic thought often pay little more than passing attention to his fiscal theory,[17] and in some cases make no mention of it whatsoever.[18] Those who have addressed the subject have, in most cases, focused on the conceptual resonance of his fiscal theory with that of their own period,[19] and it is seldom that they enter into the historical circumstances of the discussions in which Petty himself was engaged.[20] As for the great majority of general accounts of Petty's economic thought, no more comment is included on the fiscal background than is absolutely necessary to the task of outlining his theoretical legacy to what are perceived as wider aspects of economic theory, which are inevitably perceived as those which remain of central concern to economists today. In short, in this case, as in so many other fields of economic thought, the existing literature has hitherto remained blinkered by a retrospective approach.

A consequence of this retrospective approach is that most historians of economic thought have grossly underestimated, or even completely ignored, the military and conflictual background to Petty's fiscal theory. As a result, the relevant historical subdisciplines – 'fiscal studies' and economic history generally – have effectively come to constitute, in themselves, a critique of the history of economic thought as it is now commonly understood, being concerned, as they are, "less with the validity of an economic theory in terms of the modern discipline of economics than its historical importance at a given period of time".[21] A significant consequence of this insistence on a contextual approach is that, unlike historians of economic thought, they have fully participated in the "widening of the historian's view of warfare and its significance which has marked the writing of recent decades",[22] and which has resulted in a flourishing literature on 'war and society'. This literature was launched almost half a century ago by a seminal study which argued that a 'military revolution' had profoundly affected all aspects of European society in the century from 1550 to 1650,[23] a focus which was soon widened to include further such 'revolutions' in other periods, and which has addressed a wide range of social, political, administrative, technological and industrial topics.[24] This literature opens many avenues for a reassessment of Petty's thought and activities, including his contributions to science and technology,[25] as well as his economic thought.

The term 'fiscal-military' expresses, in itself, the essential truth that the vast expansion of scale in the military operations of the wars of the 1690s onwards – the most expensive conflicts that England had yet fought – was a process that was inseparable from the simultaneous 'financial revolution' which brought into existence the credit and banking systems as they have existed ever since.[26] Indeed, "nearly all that was 'revolutionary' about the years following 1688 was the product of war, not of some novel ideology",[27] and not only international war at that, since the outcome was linked to the "prior and bloody formation of a consensus among the political elite"[28] in the civil conflicts of the 1640s and 1680s.

In short, the distinction between what are now perceived as the military and civilian spheres had yet to emerge in its present form, and the economic and social thought of early modern writers such as Petty is, consequently, not susceptible to easy categorisation in such terms. Thus, on the one hand, it has been pointed out that there remained much in Petty's outlook that harked back to earlier writers, such as Machiavelli, who had perceived economic relations as subordinate to the political relations established by the ruler of the state, and as such capable of being expressed only in military terms.[29] On the other hand, it has equally convincingly been argued, from within the field of political science, that Petty was a "pioneer in the art of modern government", in that his writings explore the idea that the scope of state administration should be extended to embrace economic and other aspects of social life which had previously remained relatively untouched by state action;[30] it has consequently been described as ironic that someone so dedicated to the ideal of strengthening the absolute power of the monarch should have "provided the terms by which a civil society capable of challenging that authority could emerge in the early eighteenth century".[31] In the context of his time, there was no contradiction between these different currents of thought, and their coexistence in Petty's writings serves only to emphasise how anachronistic it would be to apply a military–civilian distinction, whether in the fiscal, technological, administrative or any other sphere. Indeed, developments in the military and general governmental spheres were so closely interlinked with each other that one commentator has put forward the paradoxical proposition that, in early modern times, "militarisation = civilianisation".[32]

Such is the background to Petty's fiscal proposals, designed as they were to apply to a form of state which has been described as a 'military-bureaucratic absolutism'[33] – a state whose structure was determined, in the first instance, by its continual waging of warfare, but also – and arguably to an even greater extent – by war finance: "The key to the rise of military-bureaucratic absolutism is not modernisation and warfare themselves, but the mobilisation of domestic resources to fund them".[34] Accordingly,

> [p]rotection, coupled with a powerful navy, a strong state, and the funding to prosecute war, became part of the 'inseparable connections' that combined successfully to forge England's (then Britain's) rise to global power over the course of the 'long' eighteenth century.[35]

In the sphere of economic thought, this led Petty to view "the economic concept of wealth…as the necessary foundation for military strength".[36] As a pamphleteer commented, in connection with the foundation of the Bank of England in 1694: "The wars nowadays seem rather to be waged with gold than with iron, and unless we pay well, we shall never be able to punish well."[37]

Writers on early modern economic thought have, with very few exceptions, allowed the entire literature on 'war and society' and the fiscal-military state to pass them by.[38] The consequences for the search for the roots of economics have been disastrous. The underlying motivation of Petty's economic writings – and, by extension, the motivation for the formulation of much of the conceptual apparatus still in use by economists today – has been brought into ever sharper focus within the neighbouring disciplines, and yet most historians of economic thought have hitherto quite simply allowed the nature of this motivation to pass under their noses unnoticed.

Once again, then, the history of economic thought is found to be suffering from the effects of its intellectual isolation, and a consequent failure to respond to a steadily expanding and directly relevant body of literature in neighbouring social science disciplines. For that literature provides ample opportunity to reassess Petty's writings in the light of the topical economic discussions of his day, and in particular to take account of the fact that those discussions were, overwhelmingly, centred on the question of how to finance the military–naval establishment. As has been rightly – and all too rarely – observed, this preoccupation lay at the heart of his economic thought as a whole, and, consequently, "it is important for modern scholars seeking to understand the nature of Petty's contribution to interpret those discussions within the context of that preoccupation".[39] For it was only by making an impact within this all-important fiscal–military sphere that his economic writings could serve their purpose of persuading the authorities to reappoint him to the high office to which he aspired to return.

Accordingly, in what follows, Petty's fiscal theory will first be outlined in its overall historical context. Next, illustrations will be provided of how historians of economic thought have, generally, restricted their treatment of this aspect of his writings to singling out his views on individual fiscal issues which present particularly striking analogies with elements of subsequent economic theory. This retrospective approach will then be shown to have obscured the fact that Petty's innovations in the field of economic analysis were formulated in the course of his paramount concern to justify the expansion of the fiscal base to include the labouring population.

3.1.2 The immediate aim of Petty's fiscal theory

Petty's writings on fiscal affairs address the whole range of taxes being levied or discussed during his lifetime, when the state was still "struggling to supply its coffers by forms of assessment that had come down from the middle ages".[40] In the resulting situation of "fiscal pluralism",[41] the forms of taxation included land tax,[42] duties levied on imports and exports (customs),[43] duties levied on goods produced domestically (the excise),[44] poll tax,[45] taxes on housing ('hearth tax'),[46] taxes on monopolies,[47] voluntary contributions ('benevolences'),[48] taxes levied by the Church ('tithes')[49] and other means of raising revenue, including sale of offices,[50] lotteries[51] and many other "smaller ways" besides.[52] It was around this "Heath Robinson"[53] fiscal system that Petty's kaleidoscopic concept spinning revolved. Indeed, he expanded the list of expedients rather than contracting it. For example, he pointed out that debasement of the coinage is effectively a form of taxation, and expressed disapproval of this "very pitiful and unequal way of taxing the people".[54] Furthermore, he saw compulsory service in the militia as a form of tax, and in this case not only enthusiastically endorsed it but also advocated its extension into the naval sphere, in the form of compulsory naval service for merchant seamen.[55] Despite all this diversity of reference, however, it is possible to discern in his fiscal thought a unifying guiding principle, which, since it is inherently absurd, may most fittingly be introduced by way of a parody.

In a satirical depiction of the activities of the early Royal Society, Jonathan Swift includes, among the strange lands described in his novel *Gulliver's Travels*, an island named Laputa, which its inhabitants, a community of crazy philosophers, have contrived to suspend in mid-air. There can be no prizes for guessing the inspiration for the individual who takes upon himself the task of devising the fiscal arrangements for this imaginary land – arrangements which, he claims, provide "the most commodious and effectual ways and means of raising money without grieving the subject". One of his schemes is that

> the highest tax was upon men who are the greatest favourites of the other sex, and the assessments according to the number and natures of the favours they have received, for which they are allowed to be their own vouchers. Wit, valour, and politeness were likewise proposed to be largely taxed, …every person giving his own word for the quantum of what he possessed.[56]

This parody captures, with uncanny accuracy, not only the diction but, more importantly, the fundamental guiding principle of Petty's fiscal thought, which is "how the causes of the unquiet bearing of taxes may be lessened".[57] The very idea of such a principle is, of course, essentially contradictory, since even the most loyal of populations, when faced with a tax demand, instantly become transformed into "the King's otherwise loyal subjects".[58] Petty's fiscal schemes thus constantly risked falling into the implausibility parodied in Swift's *reductio ad absurdum*, in which the payment of taxes is to be made positively titillating.

Like other writers on fiscal affairs in his time, Petty focused much of his attention on the excise, a form of tax whose contribution to total state revenue had risen rapidly in the Civil War period, resulting in a "structural shift"[59] from 'direct' to 'indirect' taxation – terms which Adam Smith was to introduce in the following century.[60] The excise principally fell on necessities, primarily beer, which, along with other alcoholic beverages, accounted for around 60 per cent of receipts, and which was a very significant element of the diet of the labouring population.[61] The rapid rise in excise revenue reflected the "commercialisation of English society, whose shops, breweries and distilleries provided the focal points for revenue collection",[62] and its extension consequently proceeded in step with the steady increase in the scale and accessibility of units of production and points of sale.[63] Even more relevant, in the present context, is the fact that, since necessaries had hitherto largely escaped the fiscal net (customs having principally fallen on luxuries), and since direct taxation on the income of the poor had effectively lapsed for a century,[64] the excise focused the issue of the extension of taxation to the poor in general. This became increasingly clear as the proportion of excise to total indirect taxation rose from 10 to 40 per cent in the Civil War period,[65] a trend that was to continue until it reached around 75 per cent during the eighteenth century.[66] After 1688 governments were to succeed in imposing universal taxation as a fundamental fiscal principle, underpinned ideologically by John Locke's contention regarding the state's protection of their right to "have and secure their properties", that "everyone who enjoys his share of the protection should pay out of his estates his proportion of the maintenance of it".[67] In Petty's lifetime, however, this principle of universal taxation was still contested.

The debates on these fiscal developments took place against the background of a popular conception that there could be a 'just tax', in the same way that there could be a 'just price', though, of course, "it is the latter which has been much better studied".[68] Petty contributed a new and more precise tone to discussions of this concept, addressing in detail such issues as public mistrust of the integrity of revenue officials, the levying of taxes at inconvenient seasons, and so on,[69] anticipating much of the content of the four 'maxims' of taxation formulated a century later by Smith.[70] In adopting such an approach, Petty was exceptional, however, since most writers of his time dressed up the discussion of fiscal affairs in more philosophical terms. The tone was set by Hobbes, who, though in essence he "did no more than repeat the Parliamentary justification of the excise",[71] presented his arguments in the high-flown language of 'equal justice', the debt owed by the individual to the commonwealth, the harmfulness of luxury and waste, and so on. Such a moralising and philosophising tone persisted among political philosophers well into the following century, with Montesquieu arguing that indirect taxation was "more natural to liberty" than direct,[72] and David Hume praising indirect taxation in terms "little short of an encomium".[73]

Underlying all this philosophising lay the much more down-to-earth issue of the danger of tax rebellion, and, beyond it, the ever-present fear that such rebellion might once again, as in the 1640s, culminate in civil war. In Petty's words, the problem was one of avoiding "great and ugly reluctancies in the people, and of involuntary severities in the prince, an eminent example whereof was the ship-money, no small cause of twenty years calamity to the whole kingdom".[74] Indeed, that period of conflict and civil war, which "originated as a tax revolt",[75] remained the fundamental point of reference for all economic, social, philosophical and political thought throughout the period in which Petty wrote.[76]

Seen in this context, it becomes clear that the deliberations of the philosophers on the merits of the taxation of consumption were, in reality, little more than a reflection of the parliamentary and other debates of the era, in which the real issue in question took on a more explicit and less philosophical aspect: here, what was central was the hope – or, more accurately, the wishful thinking – that the excise, being "levied on the outlays by households on goods and services",[77] would prove to be, by its nature, less provocative than direct taxes, due to its diffusion across the household budget and its comparatively even spread across time. For similar reasons, Petty at one point advocated a more widespread resort to the procedure, exemplified in the payment of tithes to the Church, of levying an 'aliquot' part of the agricultural product at the point of production. Tithes are, he stated in this connection, "the *modus* or pattern of a tax, …the most equal and indifferent which can be appointed in order to defray the public charge of the whole nation as well as that of the Church".[78]

The hopes of the advocates of the excise were to a considerable degree disappointed, however. First of all,

> their room to effect real changes in the balance between the contentious direct forms of taxation and less visible forms of duties on expenditures remained constrained…by ratios of marketed to total national consumption [and] the scale and concentration of units of production supplying accessible and regular markets located in towns and cities.[79]

Furthermore, and more importantly still, the excise had provoked, from the first years of its imposition, "many great tumults and great riots",[80] and the parliamentary authorities had consequently been forced to back down over its imposition on a number of necessities – or 'necessaries', a term which, along with its converse, 'superfluities', accordingly came into widespread currency in public debate, not least in the writings of Petty.[81]

Despite the fact that the excise had, thus, in modern terms, "already bumped up against local resistance and reached margins of diminishing returns",[82] it nevertheless continued to be perceived by the restored monarchy as possessing the advantage over taxation on income that it approached nearer to being 'insensible',[83] and this and other equivalent terms continued to run through fiscal debates well into the modern period. Petty's writings are no exception.[84] A distinctive feature of his presentation of the idea is that he gives it a characteristically quantitative form, implicitly specifying the level of 'insensibility' as 1/20 of income, expenditure or labour. No one, he contends, will rebel if the effect of a tax demand is merely that they must "work 1/20 more, and spend 1/20 less".[85] For, he muses,

> labouring men work 10 hours per diem, and make 20 meals per week, viz. 3 a day for working days and two on Sundays; whereby it is plain that if they could fast on Friday nights and dine in one hour and an half, whereas they take two, from eleven to one, thereby this working 1/20 more and spending 1/20 less, the 1/10 above mentioned might be raised, at least with more ease than to take up arms and resist it.[86]

Petty here takes up the concept of a threshold below which a proportional change becomes 'insensible', and applies it in explicitly numerical terms to the analysis of changes in economic variables. This gives his propositions the aspect of a kind of primitive form of the economic calculus that underlies the marginalist economics of today. While this analogy is admittedly tenuous, it nevertheless remains ironic that intimations of marginalism should be suggested in this context; for the methodology of marginalism is notoriously inseparable from its initial assumption of the absence of conflict, whereas Petty's policy guidelines are, in this case, designed precisely to avoid conflict in a world where it is assumed to be otherwise inevitable.[87]

In the case of his advocacy of compulsory service in the militia or navy, Petty could hardly apply the term 'insensible', and accordingly used the alternative term "gentle". The principle is advanced in similarly 'marginal' terms, however, his argument being that it is "a gentle tax upon the country, because it is only a few days labour in the year, of a few men in respect of the whole".[88]

In another formulation of his proto-marginalist approach to taxation, Petty argues that

> for men to pay a tenth of their expense…can be no hardship, much less a deplorable condition; for to bear the tenth part, a man needs spend but a twentieth part less, and labour a twentieth part more, or half an hour per diem extraordinary, both which within common experience are very tolerable, there being very few in England, who do not eat by a twentieth part more than does them good; and what misery were it, instead of wearing cloth of 20s per yard, to be contented with that of 19s, few men having skill enough to discern the difference.[89]

Such is the disarming frankness with which Petty exposes the ethics of sharp practice in the rag trade which underlie the stately prose of the author of *Leviathan*, a frankness not shared by subsequent writers on fiscal affairs, who preferred to emulate the latter.[90] Philosophers also continued to weigh in on the subject. Hume recycles the standard phraseology about how the taxation of consumption proceeds "gradually and insensibly", and, consequently, has the advantage of being "least felt by the people".[91] Montesquieu, who also uses the identical phrase "least felt by the people", argues that taxes on commodities have this property "because no formal request is made for them; they can be so wisely managed that the people will be almost unaware that they pay them".[92] Indeed, Adam Smith still advocates his 'maxims' in the same terms, claiming that they provide a solution to the problems posed by more provocative forms of taxation, which taxpayers might "feel very sensibly".[93]

Such, then, was the immediate aim of Petty's fiscal thought – to maximise revenue while minimising the danger of tax rebellion – and, though his quantitative formulation of the issues involved was distinctive, his espousal of this aim itself did not differentiate him from the philosophers of his own or the following generations, or indeed from the crazy philosopher in *Gulliver's Travels*. Nevertheless, while Petty was prepared to endorse the increasing resort to indirect taxation in similar terms as a "general principle",[94] he also went on to provide further elaboration and modification of this principle in a manner which anticipated the fiscal theory of a later period.

It has been stated that Petty was one of "not more than two or three men in the seventeenth and eighteenth centuries" who realised that, because of the nature of the goods upon which the excise could be levied, it imposed "a larger tax on the poor man, proportionally to his income, than on the rich man".[95] He also addressed the related problem of how to identify proxies, or indicators, which could be used for purposes of tax assessment, a question which engaged writers on fiscal affairs throughout the early modern period.[96] Petty's contribution to this discussion was to suggest the concept of an "accumulative excise", by which he meant an excise that would fall on an object the level of whose consumption would most closely reflect an individual's capacity or liability to pay tax, or that would, in other words, come "nearest the common standard of all expense". He correctly identified the reasons for the failure of beer to fulfil this function: as he pointed out, the poor 'accumulate' on their beer only "a little bread and cheese, leathern clothes, neck-beef, and inwards twice a week stale fish, old pease without butter, etc.". The rich, on the other hand, accumulate "as many more things as nature and art can produce".[97]

Petty evidently did not see this problem as open to solution. Instead, he suggested that the regressive nature of the excise should be accepted, and balanced by the progressive effect of retaining the existing taxes on the sources of the income of the rich.[98] In other words, he realised that any one tax "necessitates other ways than itself".[99] By thus discussing the incidence of taxes not in isolation from each other but as elements in an integrated and compensatory system of taxation as a whole, Petty was well ahead of his time, such a principle not becoming implemented in the English fiscal system for another two centuries.[100]

In short, "Petty stood alone"[101] in his pioneering formulation of some of the principal elements of modern fiscal theory, anticipating concepts which were subsequently to elude the minds of Hume, Montesquieu, Smith, and even David Ricardo. In seeking to account for this remarkable fact, it is necessary to bear in mind that, in Petty's time, "political violence and discord had been part of the common experience of several generations of Englishmen, including his own". He was consequently "not dealing with a world in which the sources of strife and discord were removable; he was providing guidelines for effective actions to contain conflict and disruption". In short, his economic analysis was "originally constructed as a way of dealing with inevitable conflict and strife, and predicated on a view of society as inherently disordered".[102] This perspective on the world was lost by the moral philosophers of the French and Scottish Enlightenment, who set their sights on the higher ideal of a world in which their societies and economies would be regulated by more benign forces. This was indeed to raise the science of society to a new level of more searching and fundamental analysis. At the same time, however, there was, by the same token, an inevitable loss in some of the more mundane aspects of strategy and tactics – aspects which had been second nature to the economic writers of the age they aimed to put behind them.

Just as the frankness and consistency of the political philosophy of Hobbes gives his arguments a continuing cogency which in many respects surpasses that of his more 'enlightened' successors of the following century, so also Petty's achievements are a reflection of his success in "pushing the political rationality associated with Hobbes toward a nascent economic rationality".[103] This rationality, combined with an unblushing adherence to the morality and outlook of the cynical and calculating world of pre-Enlightenment Europe, was what enabled him not only to cut through the moralising of the philosophers but also to devise a fiscal theory of such precocious sophistication.

3.1.3 Retrospective assessments of Petty's fiscal theory

The immediate motivation of Petty's fiscal thought was so clear to his contemporaries that Swift could safely assume that it would be understood by any reader of *Gulliver's Travels*. Yet historians of economic thought have, in general, displayed scant awareness of the issues involved, despite their widespread recognition that his writings were, in some general way, "practical rather than theoretical",[104] "prompted by the practical problems of his time and country",[105] directed towards "immediate practical objectives",[106] and that they contained "dozens of suggestions for doing something".[107] The actual nature of these 'practical problems', 'objectives' and 'suggestions' is customarily swept out of view, removing Petty's analytical concepts from their historical context, so that the focus may be shifted onto the analogies these concepts present with elements of subsequent economic theory.

There is no shortage of such analogy. To take one example, in expounding the principle of proportionality of taxation, Petty states that "the *ratio formalis* of riches [lies] rather in proportion than quantity",[108] or, as he goes on to explain:

> Let the tax be never so great, if it be proportionable unto all, then no man suffers the loss of any riches by it. For men…if the estates of them all were either halved or doubled, would in both cases remain equally rich. For they would each man have his former state, dignity and degree.[109]

It has been observed that there could be no clearer statement of the principle that taxes should "leave the relative distribution of wealth unchanged",[110] due to the assumption that "what matters to people is more their relative status than the absolute size of their wealth and income".[111] It has furthermore been noted that Petty associates this principle with disapprobation of luxury consumption, and he has accordingly been credited with anticipating the rationale underlying the concepts of conspicuous consumption and the 'demonstration effect' advanced by Veblen and Duesenberry, respectively.[112] Furthermore, following up ideas which had already been expressed by Hobbes, Petty displays what has been perceived as an "approbation of production",[113] since he relaxes the principle of proportionality in his discussions of fiscal measures to divert resources away from, in his own words, an "ill husband" to an "improving hand",[114] thus "transferring [riches and fortune] from the landed and lazy to the crafty and industrious".[115] He has, accordingly, been credited with advocating the use of fiscal means to encourage saving and investment, and thus anticipating arguments subsequently advanced by Mill, Marshall, Pigou, Fisher, Kaldor and Mead.[116]

These examples of the retrospective character of discussions of Petty's fiscal theory by historians of economic thought are paralleled in discussions of the

Table 3.1 England's national accounts

Expenditure	£m	Income	£m
Personal expenditure of 6 million persons at £6.67 per head	40	Rent of land	8
		Yield on "money and other personal estates"	7
		"The labour of the people"	25
TOTAL	**40**		**40**

Source: VS: 105–109, after Backhouse 2002: 69 (whose figures are taken from a different version of the calculation, however, in PA: 267).

wider context of public finance in general. In this connection, Petty presents a calculation, of which various versions appear in his writings, designed to quantify the respective contributions of land, labour and other sources to national income. In the earliest version of this calculation (see Table 3.1),[117] he begins by assessing annual income from rent as £8 million, and income from "money and other personal estates" as £7 million. He then goes on to state that average per capita expenditure in England, whose population he estimates at 6 million, is £6 2/3, from which he concludes that aggregate national expenditure must be 6 million times this amount – i.e. £40 million. From there, he moves on to conclude that, since land and other material property together account for £15 million of annual income, "the labour of the people must furnish the other 25" – i.e. £40 million less £15 million. This calculation has been described, in modern terms, as "Petty's method of indirectly estimating the wage bill, as the residue after deducting property income from national income".[118]

As a result of this calculation, Petty has almost universally been acknowledged as "the true originator of the concept of national income",[119] responsible for a calculation "quite similar to the present-day concept of national income and product at factor cost",[120] and so on. Not only the substance of the calculation but also its mathematical method has drawn comment from historians of economic thought. It has been pointed out, for example, that there was nothing qualitatively new about the conclusion which he here expresses, which is that labour produces a larger fraction of national income than land and other material property. What is new, however, is his quantitative expression of the issue. In his own words:

> The observations or positions expressed by number, weight, and measure, upon which I bottom the ensuing discourses, are either true or not apparently false, and which if they are not already true, certain, and evident, may be made so by the Sovereign Power, *Nam id certum est quod certum reddi potest* [For what can be made certain *is* certain], and if they are false, not so false

as to destroy the argument they are brought for; but at worst are sufficient as suppositions to show the way to that knowledge I aim at.[121]

This procedure amounts to establishing a "chain of deductive reasoning",[122] from premises (in the form of some common-sense approximate estimates[123]) to a conclusion expressed in quantitative terms (25 > 15), a mode of expression which has been described as one of "plausible relative values",[124] and which amounts to the claim that the conclusion "must be intellectually binding on anyone who accepted the premises and could find no flaw in the logic".[125] Petty thus detaches economic reasoning from the sphere of mere quantitative observation, on the one hand, and general qualitative assertion, on the other, and transfers it into the realm of deductive logic, thus opening up a whole world of conceptual elaboration which he was the first to explore, and earning effectively unanimous credit for the "anticipation of modern economics".[126] The reference to the ability of the "Sovereign Power" to bring truths into existence has been less often noted, or, indeed, is sometimes even omitted as a lacuna in the quotation; this element of Petty's statement does, however, bring these rather lofty comments on Petty's methodology back down to ground. As a recent commentator aptly puts it: "As with the [Down] Survey, in the end the truth of Petty's mathematics depended on the government's power and interest in making them true."[127]

This survey of some of the commentary by historians of economic thought on Petty's theory of taxation and public finance has been selective and impressionistic,[128] but it is enough to illustrate the overwhelmingly retrospective character of their discussions, in which his views are addressed almost entirely in their capacity as anticipations of the theories and methods of subsequent writers. The analogies which Petty's writings present with the economic thought of later periods – not least in the field of fiscal theory – are indeed striking, and his innovative mode of reasoning is of incalculable significance for subsequent methodological developments. As has now been shown, however, this phenomenon has also had the perverse effect that the attention of historians of economic thought has, as a result, been deflected from, rather than attracted to, the question of what significance would have been attached to the conclusions he reached in the historical context in which he put them forward.

It is not surprising, consequently, that there is a lack of consensus in identifying the general characteristics of Petty's fiscal thought. Petty has, for example, been portrayed variously as deciding against the kind of legislative programme being put forward at the time by Jean-Baptiste Colbert in France,[129] or, in contrast, of partially adopting it.[130] At a more general level still, his fiscal writings have been characterised as merely "throwing out hints and thoughts",[131] or, alternatively, as displaying a "unity of analysis".[132] Similarly, widely differing preconceptions have been expressed regarding the question of whether Petty's arguments merely reflected views already current or, on the contrary, exercised influence over them.[133]

As ever, these shortcomings of the retrospective approach are associated with a compartmentalisation of the analysis of different authors, according to their particular interests, standpoints and specialities. There is, in turn, a dearth of cross-reference between them, as well as, perhaps even more seriously, a general lack of reference to the work of economic and fiscal historians.[134] Thus depriving themselves both of a cumulative body of analysis of their own, and reference to empirical studies in the relevant neighbouring disciplines, historians of economic thought have hitherto failed to conceptualise the character of Petty's fiscal theory as a whole.

As Petty's editor long ago cautioned:

> It would be quite possible to take up the various economic topics discussed by Petty according to modern conceptions of them, and to do so would afford a ready-made standard for judging his economic notions. But it would also involve the risk of asking what he thought about problems concerning which it never occurred to him to think at all.[135]

What is more serious still, however, is that such an approach has obscured the issue of the questions to which his 'economic notions' *were* addressed, and it is this, as will now be demonstrated, which explains the disparate and unsatisfactory nature of assessments of his standpoint from within the history of economic thought.

3.1.4 Taxation and the labouring population

Petty's economic ideas, despite the wide-ranging and disparate nature of the 'anticipations' which have impressed historians of economic thought, were, at their point of origin, a cohesive and coherent body of doctrine, but only in the limited sense that they were all motivated by a single unifying goal: to regain for himself the kind of high office he had occupied under Cromwell. His economic writings are, then, attempts to convince the monarchy, in more credible ways than those proposed by the crazy professor in *Gulliver's Travels*, that he was capable of developing policies for increasing state revenue in a manner that might approach as near as possible to the Holy Grail of "commodious and effectual ways and means…without grieving the subject". Consequently, in his economic writings, he aims to display "a keen awareness of the relationship between the size of the fiscal burden [and] the taxable capacity of the state",[136] with a view to the "controlled development" of revenue.[137] In his own words, he claims to have developed a method that can bring "good method and order"[138] to affairs of state, and thus remedy the situation in which, "not knowing the wealth of the people, the prince [i.e. the state] knows not what they can bear".[139]

Thus far there is nothing particularly unusual in Petty's standpoint, which places him in a long line of would-be fiscal advisers who had, since Tudor times, sought royal favour by formulating arguments designed to show that the people were "grossly under-taxed" and that the fiscal net should be broadened.[140] Indeed, it has been said that he "was the epitome of the seventeenth-century 'projector'".[141] The degree of emphasis he places upon information is perhaps unusual, but, at any rate so far as fiscal theory is concerned, this is little more than a reflection of the pronounced growth in government information gathering which was already under way well before the Civil War period.[142] What is new in his fiscal theory, however, is that he disaggregates the potential fiscal base into its constituent elements, and, accordingly, claims to have found a method which can not only indicate opportunities for across-the-board tax increases but also, even more importantly, identify which particular sectors of the population are under-taxed relative to others. This is, in fact, the motivation for his national income accounts. As the German scholar Wilhelm Roscher observed as long ago as 1857:

> Since he estimates the yield of all England's capital items and landed estates to be 3/8 of the annual income of the people, and wages to be 5/8, he calls for taxes to be assessed at 5/8 for the people and 3/8 for land and stock.[143]

In 1899 Petty's editor elaborated this exposition, explaining that the aim of this calculation is to argue for the imposition of taxes in such a way that they "place upon the possessors of each source of income such a proportion of the aggregate burden as the capitalised amounts of their respective incomes may bear to the national wealth".[144]

Seen in this context, the analytically debilitating consequences of an excessively retrospective approach to the history of economic thought are brought into high relief. For almost every writer on Petty's economic thought has outlined his or her calculation of national income, and, by virtue of this, has been unavoidably confronted with the conclusion that labour produces a greater proportion of national output than land and capital combined.[145] The outcome has been that every conceivable kind of observation has been made on the nature of this statement: it has, for example, been discussed in terms of the complex relation it posits between the quantitative and the qualitative,[146] or, alternatively and more dismissively, categorised as a "metaphysical preconception";[147] the significance of its methodology has, as already discussed, been described as lying, variously, in its use of "conjectural rather than observed" facts,[148] "hypothetical variables"[149] or "plausible relative values";[150] the proposition has also been discussed, in general terms, as an anticipation of the concept of factors of production, and described as "a principle for which Petty contested"[151] and "central to Petty's claim about England's wealth".[152] Yet, amidst this plethora of comments of all kinds, there is one question which, with remarkably few exceptions, is ignored: why he should have wanted to 'prove' this particular proposition in the first place.

To answer this question, it is essential to view his calculation through "the window through which he saw the economic world", namely taxation. Only then does his intention become clear: to underpin the argument that "labouring people are under-assessed",[153] and, consequently, that it is labouring people who provide the primary frontier for the expansion of the fiscal base.

The literature on the history of economic thought has, then, almost entirely failed to appreciate what underlay Petty's pioneering achievements in the formulation of the fundamental concepts of modern fiscal theory, which was his advocacy of measures to counter what he explicitly describes as "shyness of taxing the poor",[154] who, he argues, "can and ought to pay their proportions".[155] The motivation behind the fiscal system he advocated was, in other words, "not the recognition of equitable taxation of the poor" but "the doctrine that the poor should share the burden of taxation".[156] Petty's fiscal theory was, thus, designed as a contribution to the debates which were to culminate in the doctrine of universal taxation, debates which were, as has been shown, largely unfolding around the subject of the excise, since the "chief distinguishing feature" of that tax, "as contrasted with traditional tax policy", was that, being levied on necessaries rather than just on luxuries, it "made the poor man regularly pay taxation".[157] The outcome of these debates has been described as "one of the landmarks in English political opinion", but is more fittingly described as the final defeat of the revolutionary ideology of the 1640s. For it was this principle, enforced by the victory of the 'Glorious Revolution' of 1688, which ensured that "the poor labourer, who hath threshed all day for a livelihood, should himself be threshed at night with unconscionable payment for things tending to the bare support of nature".[158]

Petty, unlike the philosophers of the eighteenth-century Enlightenment, was perfectly explicit about the issues involved here, which were to concede to the pressure from the propertied classes to alleviate the burden of direct taxation, and, by a 'structural shift' to indirect taxation, to increase the fiscal burden on the poor. Thus, in a proposition framed in terms of his method of 'plausible relative values', he criticises the current fiscal system, which, he argues, is one in which "¼ of the whole, paying needlessly four times too much, may be thereby so nettled as to do more mischief than the other unconcerned and thankless ¾ can allay".[159] This proposition shows how naïve it is to accept at face value Petty's claims to success in his "attempt to yoke numerical representation to impartiality";[160] for his appeal to quantification here stands revealed as a veil for an explicitly partisan standpoint. What lay behind the proposition was the fact that "tenacious and persistent political antagonism [towards taxes] from classes with money to spare did not extend…to indirect forms of taxation".[161] In that context, Petty's standpoint constituted an implicit endorsement of, or at any rate a surrender to, the threat of 'mischief' emanating from the 'quarter' whose interests would be threatened by the re-extension of direct taxation – mischief which would be unleashed if the fiscal burden was not shifted onto the shoulders of the 'three-quarters'.[162]

The extent to which the literature on the history of economic thought has obscured this underlying motivation of Petty's fiscal theory, and, beyond it, of his economic theory in general, is quite remarkable. The above-quoted exposition by Roscher, in 1857, had clearly noted the proportions of 3/8 and 5/8 for the contributions to national income of 'land and stock' and labour, respectively. Roscher likewise noted that Petty's aim was not to let the matter rest as a descriptive proposition relating to national income but to use his calculation as a prescription for the fiscal system – to advance it, in other words, as a call for action to impose taxes in the corresponding proportions. Despite the fact that, in a formal sense, he had thus clarified Petty's intentions, Roscher nevertheless did not draw out the fact that, in the context of the debates of his time, the proposition was not only prescriptive but polemical. Petty's editor, in his more elaborate exposition in 1899,[163] followed the same course, as also have subsequent historians of economic thought, who have by and large ignored advances within the field of the history of taxation, wherein the question was meanwhile fully clarified in a work published in 1913.[164] It was not until nearly 60 years later that, in a passing reference in a work first published in 1971,[165] the issue was again alluded to from within the history of economic thought. This was followed, in 1986, by a further study in which Petty's motivation was spelt out without any equivocation, along with the comment that the failure to appreciate this point provides an example of the adverse effect of lifting Petty's economic thought out of its historical context;[166] this observation was confined to a footnote, however, and, perhaps not least for that reason, has failed to attain currency in the work of subsequent writers. With these few exceptions, the relevant literature has, in general, provided little more than continuing obfuscation of the issue.[167]

There is a further range of issues in which the literature on the history of economic thought has hitherto suffered from its failure to perceive Petty's writings through the taxation 'window'; these issues lie in the field of his productivity theory. Here, as has already been seen, he saw taxation, at least implicitly, as a potential instrument of redistribution in favour of sectors of society which he perceived as productive; this was an innovative idea, at a time when it was effectively assumed that the purpose of taxation was exclusively to raise revenue. This idea did not involve any concession to the idea of an improvement in the life of the labouring population, however. On the contrary, he consistently held to the doctrine which has, in today's economics, become the concept of the 'backward-bending labour supply curve'[168] – in other words, the idea that labour supply decreases if wages are allowed to rise above a certain level – this level being perceived by Petty as one of bare subsistence, or "a subsistence to the workmen and no more".[169] This doctrine subsequently became current in arguments in favour of the taxation of necessities, and it has been suggested that Petty's views were influential in propagating this standpoint.[170] For example, one of his arguments in favour of a poll tax is that it stimulates child labour: "It seems to be a spur unto all men to set their children to some profitable employment upon their very first capacity, out of the proceed whereof to pay each child his own poll-money."[171]

It also appears that Petty had fiscal means in mind in his suggestion, based on the same logic, that corn supplies be restricted in years of plenty, since otherwise "the labour of the poor is proportionably dear, and scarce to be had at all, so licentious are they who labour only to eat, or rather to drink". He continues, in the same vein:

> It seems not unreasonable that this common blessing of God should be applied to the common good of all people, represented by their sovereign, much rather than the same should be abused by the vile and brutish part of mankind, …and consequently that such surplusage of corn should be sent to public store-houses, from thence to be disposed of, to the best advantage of the public… [Thus] a vast advantage might accrue to the common-wealth, which now is spent in over-feeding of the people, in quantity or quality, and so indisposing them to their usual labour.[172]

It is not clear whether he envisaged the appropriation of this surplus to be by purchase or by forced levy, but it would, in either case, clearly be consistent with his view that one of the "causes of error" in fiscal affairs has been "a fallacious tenderness towards the poor, …interwoven with the cruelty of not providing them work, and indulging laziness in them because of our own indisposition to employ them".[173]

In short, Petty's origination of national income accounting, his elaboration and development of debates on the taxation of consumption and of the principle of proportionality, along with all the associated theoretical by-products – from the labour theory of value to his anticipation in primitive form of the idea of factors of production – were not motivated by considerations of equity, whether at the social or the individual level, but, rather, by their very opposite. This truth, which would at the time have been unmistakable to his readers, has become obscured in the work of historians of economic thought, due to their almost exclusive preoccupation with those aspects of his thought, admittedly striking and numerous, which are of immediately evident relevance to the subsequent conceptual development of economy theory. The result is an impoverished appreciation of the circumstances in which his economic thought, and by extension modern economic thought in general, was first formulated.

There has, for example, been a failure to take account of Petty's perception of wage labour and slavery as a continuum. For him, if there is any distinction between the two, it is not a matter of a fundamental difference of social system but, rather, a question of relative profitability, as assessed in terms of 'plausible relative values'. For example, he argues that

> there can be no profit [in] slaves in such countries where a man can earn little more than he himself spends; but the contrary in East India, etc., where a man's victuals, etc., costs but 1/10 of what his work will be fit for abroad.[174]

Such a 'calculation' did not, however, deflect him from speculating on the possibilities for slavery in England as well:

Why should not insolvent thieves be rather punished with slavery than death? So as, being slaves, they may be forced to as much labour and as cheap fare as nature will endure, and thereby become as two men added to the commonwealth, and not as one taken away from it; for if England be under-peopled (suppose by half), I say that, next to the bringing in of as many more as now are, is the making these that are, to do double the work which now they do; that is, to make some slaves…[175]

Petty's system of national income accounting blends in the same seamless manner into the world of the slave trade, a further sharp reminder that the conceptual structure of modern economics largely originated in the same historical context as England's commercial and colonial empire – "an empire built on slavery".[176] The point of juncture lies in his concept of the "value of people".[177] This is an element of his general theory of the three sources of national income (land, "money and other personal estates" and labour), a theory which historians of economic thought have, inevitably, seen as his anticipation of the idea of the three fundamental 'factors of production'. All of these are represented by Petty as being, in modern terms, "linked by a common discount rate to the income received";[178] thus, in the case of labour, the value of people is calculated by "capitalising a stream of wage income…and treating the resulting valuation as a kind of capital asset price".[179] In formal terms, his calculation of the capitalisation of rent (R) to calculate the value of land (V_L) by means of the general discount rate (i) may be expressed as

$$V_L = R/i$$

Equivalently, the capitalisation of wages (W) to calculate the value of people (V_P) is

$$V_P = W/i$$

The value of the people of England, as they appear in Table 3.1, is, consequently, assuming a discount rate of 6 per cent, £417 million (i.e. £25 million/0.06), and, since the population is 6 million, their per capita value is £69.6, an amount he elsewhere calculates variously as £70[180] and "above £80".[181] This is strictly the value of an Englishman. An Irishman is, he considers, worth less than this. Those Irish who have been "destroyed" or sold as slaves are estimated to be worth as little as African slaves, or £25 for an adult and £5 for a child (£15 on average),[182] though "Argier [Algiers] slaves" are elsewhere valued higher at £60, this being about the same value as destitute Frenchmen.[183] Conversely, the value of an Irishman could be greatly increased if transferred to England, potentially rising by as much as 42 per cent (or "from 7 to 10") after seven years' residence.[184]

It has also been pointed out that, in a hitherto unpublished paper, Petty adds a further twist, by also giving estimates for the cost of raising a child – £4 for a one-year-old, £24 for a ten-year-old, and so on – in a calculation which

includes not only "victuals and clothes" but also what appears to be the opportunity cost at the prevailing rate of discount.[185] Such is the irony of the roots
of capitalist calculation, that they are first discerned not in the context of the
emergence of a new world of 'natural liberty' to supersede the restrictions of
feudalism but, rather, in the context of a reversion to the chattel slavery which
preceded it.

Once again, it is Swift who provided the most telling response to the predatory motivation underlying Petty's calculations, when, in his celebrated pamphlet
parodying Petty's political arithmetic, he proposes that Irish children should be
reared as livestock and eaten.[186] The image of the 'prince' as sheep shearer was
an old one;[187] Swift's merciless parody cleverly shows that such imagery must be
taken forward to a new stage, tantamount to cannibalism, if it is to fit with the
ideas advanced by Petty, who had indeed, in his population studies, frequently
used terms directly borrowed from the breeding of livestock.[188]

It is not possible to achieve an integrated and contextualised perception
of the rationale behind Petty's fiscal theory without taking into account this
predatory motivation underlying his fiscal and other schemes – a motivation
which, for Swift, was so clear and self-evident, and which indeed Petty himself did nothing to conceal. The adverse consequences of the shortcomings of
historians of economic thought in this respect are further illustrated when it
is considered that the effects of taxation "analytically cannot be separated from
the activities funded",[189] as will now be discussed.

3.2 Petty, public finance and warfare

3.2.0 Introduction

The background to the fiscal discussions in which Petty participated was a
massive increase in the revenue of the English state, an increase which continued
even more dramatically in the period that followed his death in 1687. To some
extent, this reflected an increase in the country's prosperity, but it was chiefly
due to an increase in the overall rate of taxation: "The proportion of national
wealth commanded by national government doubled in real terms during the
1640s and did so again in the 1690s."[190] Petty saw a proportion of 10 per cent
as desirable, and, while such a percentage was prophetically high in his lifetime,
it was surpassed within two decades of his death.[191] This "enormous growth in
fiscality"[192] was entirely the result of the state's "central preoccupation, namely
the waging of armed conflict";[193] the expansion was thus not 'fiscal' in the
sense in which the term is now customarily represented, but specifically 'fiscal-
military', a term which, as has already been noted, is now widely used by economic historians, but as yet barely current at all in the literature on the history
of economic thought. This lag in terminological usage reflects a wider failure
by historians of economic thought to appreciate the military roots of economic
theory and methodology, a shortcoming that is particularly debilitating for any
attempt to assess Petty's contribution.

In order to initiate a rectification of this inadequate approach, the nature of some of the categories of economic analysis forged by Petty will now be reappraised in the light of the conflictual context in which he forged them. Next, it will be shown that the spontaneous attempts of historians of economic thought to disown this aspect of their intellectual heritage have been aided by the fact that the military and conflictual aspect of Petty's work is not readily discernible in the text of his most widely regarded work, the *Treatise of Taxes and Contributions* of 1662. As an investigation of the historical background to this work will show, however, its apparently 'civilian' character does not reflect any fundamental repudiation of the military and conflictual motivation which is so characteristic of his other writings, but is, rather, a mere presentational feature, which can be explained by reference to the exceptional circumstances surrounding its composition.

3.2.1 Concepts and conflict in Petty's economic thought

Taxation was famously described by Hobbes as "the wages due to them that hold the public sword to defend private men in the exercise of several trades and callings".[194] Attempts to assess the degree of literal truth in this proposition in statistical terms, by specifying the percentage of state expenditure devoted to military and naval ends in early modern times, are inevitably largely conjectural, but it was certainly an "overwhelming proportion",[195] and is unlikely to have been much less than 80 per cent,[196] while Petty himself saw an even higher percentage as desirable (see Table 3.2, where his figures indicate that he recommended a proportion of 86.7 per cent). The remaining amount, whether a fifth or less of the total, was assumed – by Petty as by all early modern writers, including Adam Smith – to be devoted overwhelmingly to the maintenance of the monarchy in sufficient "splendour and magnificencies"[197] to sustain the state's prestige internationally, and, equivalently, to ensure that the monarchy lived in "greater visible splendour than others" domestically.[198] The state was, thus, perceived as a royal household,[199] and, to the extent that the power of its 'military-bureaucratic absolutism' was ever derogated, it was to parliaments, whose sessions were irregular, whose debates normally lacked real influence, and which, in any case, discussed little else apart from war finance. The state was, in effect, little more than an army with a particularly well-provided and gaudy high command.

Such is the context of Petty's sustained and single-minded efforts to devise, justify and promote means for expanding the fiscal base, so as to advance the cause of England's "naval, imperial, commercial and industrial hegemony".[200] This was a cause in which the commercial-industrial and military-naval spheres were utterly inseparable, not only as a matter of practice or expediency but in the very manner in which they were perceived and the terms in which they were conceptualised and analysed. For in Petty's lifetime, no less than in any other period since ancient times, there was a "correlation between economic perspectives and policies on the one hand and military

Table 3.2 Petty's recommended scale of state revenue and expenditure

Net state revenue	(£m)	Expenditure	(£m)	%
		Military:		
		Navy	2.0	↓
		Army	0.6	86.7%
Tax revenue net of costs of collection	3.0	Royal family	0.4	13.3%
TOTAL	**3.0**		**3.0**	**100%**

Notes: (1) These figures are very much greater than those actually prevailing at the time, being designed to show the supposed benefits that would result from Petty's proposed overhaul of the fiscal system.
(2) Income is shown net of the charge of tax collection, which he assumes to be 1/33 of gross revenue, which would thus be £3.09 million. The difference between the gross and net amounts – i.e. £90,000 – would, he suggests, allow a salary of £200 p.a. for a tax officer in each of 450 collection areas.
Source: VS: 116f.

perspectives, policies and technology on the other".[201] Awareness of such a correlation was instinctive and spontaneous for Petty, whose service in the navy and the army of occupation in Ireland had left him every inch the military projector. This is seen, most immediately, in his technological proposals, which ranged over all kinds of subjects from fortifications and ballistics to defensive sea barrages, and from the construction of armoured vehicles to a new method for the provision of fresh water on board naval vessels.[202] More substantially, his writings on ship building were explicit in defining their goal in terms of the dual-purpose nature of "shipping for war or trade".[203] Thus, all his writings and experiments in this field reflect the realities of his era, being preoccupied in the first instance with issues relating to "the gunnery, fireworks and other armatures peculiar to the sea and sea fights".[204] Such technical concerns blended seamlessly into what he termed his 'naval economics', by which he indicated the study of naval supplies, which was, in turn, a branch of his overall 'naval philosophy'.[205]

The retrospective approach prevailing among historians of economic thought, along with the associated compartmentalisation that has hitherto affected studies of the various different aspects of Petty's life and activities, has had the effect of isolating the analysis of his economic thought from any consideration of his directly naval and military schemes and proposals. This does not reflect a distinction in Petty's own thought, however, which no more recognises a frontier between the economic and the military-naval than between the civilian and military spheres in general.

Perhaps the most elaborate, though by no means the only, example of how Petty's 'naval philosophy' and political arithmetic are intertwined is his attempt to demonstrate that France could never expand its navy to the same size and strength as that of England.[206] His argument centres on the fact that the navies of his day were dependent on the merchant fleet to generate a body of trained seamen suitable for naval recruitment, through becoming "familiarised with hardship and hazards, extending to life and limb".[207] The size of a country's merchant fleet thus placed an upper limit on the potential size of its navy. He presents his argument in quantitative terms, in typical political-arithmetical fashion, without any conceptual boundary between 'economic' issues – notably the size of France's maritime commerce – and military-naval considerations, such as the number of years' training required for a naval seaman, personnel relations between different categories of recruits, the shortcomings of naval mercenaries, the characteristics of the harbours on France's coastline, and so on. This analysis is, in turn, linked with a proposal for a rolling programme for the training of merchant seamen for naval duties, with a rudimentary cost–benefit analysis.[208]

So inextricably interlinked in such calculations are Petty's 'political arithmetic' and 'naval philosophy' that his methodology has been aptly described as "quantitative modelling on behalf of the sovereign",[209] a term which more accurately captures its character than epithets which focus, more narrowly, on drawing out the extent to which it prefigures economics as it is now understood. His approach, in which the fiscal and military spheres are totally blended into a unified strategic perspective, enabled him to predict, with "astonishing accuracy", the state's future military and naval requirements and the corresponding costs.[210] Such a level of accuracy in prediction eludes the efforts of the economic ortho-doxy of today, which bases its analysis on the totally unrealistic initial assumption of a conflict-free economic sphere, or, as one commentator describes it, "the neoclassical theory of peaceful market economies".[211] Any attempt to force Petty's writings into such an unrealistic framework, by retrospectively presuming such a separation between the economic and military spheres, thus not only misses the essence of his intentions but also makes it impossible to appreciate the source of the analytical strength of his predictions, as compared with those of subsequent economics.

This military-economic character of Petty's mode of analysis may be compared with the work of some economists during the Second World War, of whom it has been said:

> Although they worked on technical problems, such as quality control in munitions production, making the best use of limited shipping resources, or even the design of gunsights, many of the techniques they developed and the attitudes they acquired influenced the discipline when the war was over.[212]

Once the all-pervasive military-conflictual aspect of Petty's thought is realised, it begins to become evident how far it dominated the formulation not only of those schemes which he explicitly directed towards military and naval goals but also the formulation of the analytical categories of his economic thought as a whole. This is illustrated, for example, in his perspective on rates of exchange, or, to use his term, 'local usury':

> As for example, if a man wanting money at Carlisle in the heat of the late civil wars, when the way was full of soldiers and robbers, and the passage by sea very long, troublesome and dangerous, and seldom passed; why might not another take much more than an £100 at London for warranting the like sum to be paid at Carlisle on a certain day?[213]

Similarly, he only grudgingly discards the long-outmoded view that customs duties represent a payment to the state "for protecting the carriage of goods... from the pirates", the proportion of 5 per cent being, he suggests, "pitched upon computation that the merchants, before the said undertaking and composition, had usually lost more by piracy".[214] He similarly presumes that interest rates were lower in countries free from social and political insecurity. This proposition is associated with his use of the concept of "years purchase" of land, which is defined as the inverse of the common discount rate prevailing in society. In formal terms, where V_L is the value of land, R is rent, i is the discount rate and Y is years purchase, we have

$$V_L = R.Y$$
$$R = i.V_L$$
$$\Rightarrow Y = 1/i$$

Thus, in England, land is valued at 20 or more years' purchase, or, in other words, at a discount rate of 5 per cent or so. In Ireland, however, "lands are worth but six or seven years purchase",[215] "by reason of the frequent rebellions",[216] implying that the discount rate could rise as high as 16 2/3 per cent. A further illustration of the conflictual element running through Petty's economic thought is that, as already noted, he associates times of 'scarcity and dearth' and times of 'plenty' with, respectively, times of war and peace, which, accordingly, play much the same role in his economic calculations as the trade cycle in subsequent economics; he holds, for example, that long-term revenue projections should be based on the assumption of "one year of war to three of peace".[217]

Perhaps most significant of all is the way in which Petty's military-naval perspective obscures the distinction, which he was, famously, the first to explore, between productive and unproductive labour. For he includes in the productive sector "husbandmen, seamen, soldiers, artisans and merchants", commenting, moreover, that the seaman is "three of these four [*sic*]", since he is not only a navigator but also a merchant and, significantly, "a soldier".[218] This inclusion of soldiers and, implicitly, of navymen in the productive category reflects the inextricable and self-reinforcing link between the waging of war and the increase of state revenue. This link had long been a commonplace in writings on economic affairs,[219] but was now coming to be perceived in definite and specific form as the proposition that only through "expenditure on the navy to safeguard markets overseas"[220] could the state increase its income from customs duties, a proposition which had become explicit in public debates at the time of the controversies over Ship Money.[221]

> Sustained increases in exports, imports and national production depended upon the government's commitment to the defence of foreign trade and to security within the realm. Were the revenues that accrued from tariffs on imported tropical groceries...unrelated to expenditure on the Royal Navy? Obviously not.[222]

In this way, a country's "trading capacity...depended on... [its] ability to dominate trade routes and ports".[223] The navy has accordingly been described as "an instrument of a national policy of commercial aggrandisement",[224] or "simply the military corollary of the Navigation Acts" (the legislative instruments regulating England's system of international trade protection), embodying the principle that "power should serve profit".[225]

In such a context, it is no wonder that Petty's pioneering attempts to formulate a productive–unproductive distinction should be hampered by the doctrine that soldiers and navymen are as productive as, if not more so, than husbandmen and artisans. Indeed, even the most undisguised piracy had a place in his national income accounts, including, as he does, the item "[t]he value of silver and gold taken from the Spaniards: sixty thousand pounds".[226] All this illustrates how the "distinctive kinds of legitimisation"[227] in whose formulation Petty was implicated all centred on fanning what has rightly been termed the 'chauvinism' of England's taxpayers, which enabled the state to exploit their resulting support for its "strategic, commercial and imperial objectives".[228]

We may now return to the main theme, which is the adverse effect on the history of economic thought of misconstruing the motivation underlying Petty's fiscal theory. It has already been seen that, in his time, the aim of fiscal policy was to handle the trade-off between maximising revenue and minimising the risk of tax rebellion.[229] Now, having examined the purpose for which that revenue was raised, it is possible to restate the nature of this trade-off in a yet more revealing form, as embodying the aim of "waging war without provoking tax revolts"[230] – or, in other words, maximising the capacity to wage predatory war internationally while minimising the risk of tax revolts and civil war domestically. It is precisely this policy problem which had been mishandled by the English monarchy during the 1620s and 1630s, resulting in the civil warfare of the 1640s, and it was to the task of devising more effective solutions to this problem that Petty's economic thought was, first and foremost, directed – explicitly so in the case of his writings on fiscal reform, and implicitly or indirectly in the case of practically everything else he wrote on economic affairs in general.

3.2.2 *Petty's* **Treatise** *of* **Taxes** *and the circumstances of its composition*

The picture that has now emerged of Petty's fiscal thought, and of his economic thought generally, is barely recognisable in the standard accounts provided by historians of economic thought, who routinely represent his motivation as a benign attempt to construct "elaborate schemes of social reform",[231] aiming "to increase the capabilities of a central government to manage resources for the general well-being of its citizens",[232] and so on. This impression of a welfare-oriented system is fostered by the fact that Petty's views on state expenditure are commonly discussed in aggregate, without taking account of the proportion devoted to warfare.[233] The focus of attention can, accordingly, be shifted to topics such as his call for public relief for the poor, which has, in turn, been assessed in retrospective terms; for example, one commentator suggests that this call is "indistinguishable from a negative income tax, a form of subsidisation of the poor found in Scandinavian countries".[234] Indeed, Petty is even described by one commentator as "a man of peace",[235] and, while such an extreme and bland epithet is admittedly exceptional, it is nevertheless possible to read most accounts of his economic thought without finding such a view seriously challenged.

The resilience of this misconceived notion of the philanthropic and pacific nature of Petty's thought is clearly due, in the main, to the predominant desire of historians of economic thought to represent the intellectual roots of economics in as favourable a light as possible. Nevertheless, there are also circumstantial issues surrounding the composition of his most highly regarded work which have helped to sustain this misconception. This work, his 1662 *Treatise of Taxes and Contributions*, besides being the first work devoted entirely to the subject of taxation,[236] is also, more significantly still, the source of the great majority of the economic concepts advanced by Petty that have subsequently attracted the attention of historians of economic thought,[237] who have, consequently, singled it out as Petty's "most important work",[238] his "major economic work",[239] his "most important work from a theoretical perspective",[240] "without doubt…his most important work",[241] "his most systematic work",[242] his "masterpiece",[243] and so on. While such assessments are understandable, given the preoccupations that predominate among historians of economic thought, their comparative neglect of Petty's other writings has resulted in a general failure to note that the 'civilian' pose adopted by Petty in this treatise is highly uncharacteristic of his work as a whole, and that this was the result of particular circumstances, as will now be explained.

Petty's involvement in fiscal affairs began in Ireland in the years 1657 and 1658, when he served as secretary to Henry Cromwell, head of the military-colonial administration, and, concurrently, as a joint clerk to the Cromwellian 'Council of Ireland'. It was long ago noted that among the official correspondence of the period is a letter from Henry Cromwell to the 'adventurers' in London, which is written in surveyors' jargon and refers in some detail to rules for the distribution of expropriated Irish land – rules which had evidently been drawn up (or at any rate encoded) by Petty, who, in his own writings, refers to them, collectively, as his 'perfect rule'.[244] In view of the detailed discussion of these rules contained in this letter, it has been reasonably suggested that, while the signature is Henry Cromwell's, "the language, however, is plainly Petty's".[245] The question therefore naturally arises as to whether it is possible to find the hand of Petty at work in the fiscal correspondence of the period as well, a question which is rendered all the more plausible by the fact that, as has also long been noted, he included, in a later work, some otherwise unrecorded statistical information on customs and excise receipts in Ireland during the same period.[246]

A reading of the principal source of relevant correspondence, the papers of Oliver Cromwell's secretary, John Thurloe,[247] suggests that Petty nowhere had such a direct influence over the drafting of fiscal and economic material as in the case of the 'perfect rule' letter, but that there are nevertheless interesting indications that he was very probably abreast of the contents of the correspondence on such subjects. It takes no very subtle stylistic analysis to be struck by the fact that the turgid and monotonous tone of Henry Cromwell's correspondence occasionally becomes enlivened, in this period, by bursts of flamboyant and occasionally ribald phraseology and ingenious rhetorical devices which irresistibly suggest Petty's influence.[248] The context in which these passages occur suggests that Petty himself did not actually draft the documents in question, however; rather, it may be suggested that his influence was indirect, perhaps through enlivening the table talk of Henry Cromwell's circle and thus giving the latter some choice phrases to include in his letters, or, indeed, through his involvement in their drafting, in his capacity as his secretary.

More substantially, a number of fiscal and other economic themes occur in the correspondence which give some idea of the topics which would have been under discussion during Petty's tenure of high office. For example, there is a tabular account of Ireland's revenue;[249] comments on foreign coins in circulation whose "intrinsic value" is much less that "what they pass for";[250] comments on Ireland's ports and trade;[251] dismissive remarks on its exports as consisting solely of "hides, tallow, pipe-staves and other coarse commodities";[252] and discussions of raising funds for "repairing the bridges, highways", etc.[253] The perennial fear of tax rebellion is also expressed in references to "errors in raising money [which] are the compendious ways to cause a general discontent".[254]

Following the restoration of the monarchy in 1660, Petty considered himself at liberty to enlarge on such themes without the restrictions imposed by his former position as a serving administrative functionary. Accordingly, his first attempt to regain high office consisted of a grandly conceived proposal, dated 1661, for a "[r]egistry of lands, commodities, and inhabitants" in Ireland, designed along the lines of a registry of such a kind which already existed in Holland.[255] In the document outlining this proposal, Petty displays a much more expansive and theoretically oriented approach than anything that can be discerned in the official correspondence of the Cromwellian period in Ireland. For example, the document discusses "not only the natural and intrinsic, but also the casual and circumstantial value of land", calls for taxes to be made "in their just proportions", advocates "sumptuary laws...to restrain exorbitant expense", urges "liberty of conscience", makes some general comments on the respective advantages of taxes on land, housing and religion, and of excise and poll tax, and calls for a general appraisal of the numerical strength of different sections of the population and the distribution of wealth among them.

In the course of advancing this proposal, Petty proudly announces that his scheme would be able to draw upon the fruits of "the several surveys and other inquisitions which hath been made within the seven last years in Ireland", prominently featuring "a geometrical survey taken by William Petty", of course. While, from a technical point of view, he was, no doubt, correct to feature his survey of Ireland as the outstanding item on his curriculum vitae, it was unwise in the circumstances, however; the new Irish colonial administration was not ready to contemplate a scheme based so explicitly on administrative continuity with its former Cromwellian opponents, and his proposal thus became the first in the long series of his unsuccessful career moves.

Petty accordingly changed tack, and, for a time, evidently immersed himself in discussions which focused more narrowly on "the great changes in the fiscal system"[256] embodied in the inaugural legislative instruments being drawn up at this time by the Restoration regime. It was these circumstances which surrounded the composition of his *Treatise of Taxes*, in which he uncharacteristically "made no reference...to his personal experience in Ireland",[257] let alone to his role in the Cromwellian military-colonial administration, and instead adopted the stance of a civilian 'consultant administrator'.[258] This explains the fact that, in this particular work, Petty is, most unusually, largely successful in creating the impression that he is "more interested in the fiscal well-being of the king and his subjects than in the financial health of William Petty".[259]

In any event, despite the fact that Petty's 1661 proposal had already broached many of the themes taken up in the *Treatise* published barely a year later, the latter work nevertheless constitutes a giant leap forward in conceptual elaboration, and it is consequently frustrating that so little research has been carried out so far on the relevant aspects of Petty's biography during the early Restoration years,[260] the more so since his simultaneous activities as a central figure in the establishment of the Royal Society are, in contrast, abundantly documented.[261] As a result, the *Treatise*, one of the seminal documents of modern economic analysis, is customarily discussed as though its ideas emerged fully fledged, and no attempt has been made to enquire into the manner in which its elaborate conceptual apparatus was formulated. All that is clear is that, in the period preceding its publication, Petty was intensely involved in an atmosphere of intellectual ferment, doubtless largely in "London's coffee houses and the intellectual and slightly bohemian society that flourished in them".[262] We get a glimpse of his participation in one forum of such discussions, the so-called Rota Club headed by the political philosopher James Harrington, whom Petty is said to have "troubled...with his arithmetical proportions, reducing polity to numbers".[263] Of the "admirable discourse"[264] that took place there, it has been said that "the arguments in the Parliament house were but flat to it",[265] and doubtless the same could be said of many other such forums of which no record survives. Thus, Petty's treatise clearly germinated in an oral rather than a written context, as he vividly indicates in his own words:

> What I have written…was done but to ease and deliver myself, my head having been impregnated with these things by the daily talk I hear about advancing and regulating trade, and by the murmurs about taxes, etc.[266]

A superabundant literature exists on the question of the extent to which Petty should be credited with joint authorship of John Graunt's celebrated work on London's 'Bills of Mortality', which were published in 1662, the same year as Petty's *Treatise of Taxes*.[267] General agreement has been reached that the principal author is Graunt, on the basis of the fact that Petty's subsequent endeavours in the field of statistics display no evidence that he has mastered the sophisticated analytical methods displayed in this work, which include "construction of ratios, time-trends in ratios, and identification of geographical and seasonal variations in births and deaths, [and] the technique of association".[268] In Petty's subsequent writings, all that remains of this sophisticated statistical apparatus is, on the one hand, an inexhaustible enthusiasm for the promotion of quantitative methods (leading one writer to remark that "seldom can a writer have said so much about his method of work and still had time for the work itself"[269]) and, on the other hand, a crude methodology whose only technical device is the use of simple averages.[270]

While this quite negative assessment of Petty's contribution to the history of statistics traditionally predominated in the secondary literature, a subsequent study, by Sabine Reungoat, puts a new twist on the discussion.[271] She acknowledges that Petty was on occasion far from scrupulous in his manipulation of his information; indeed, she wryly comments that some of his population estimates appear to have been reached by *tâtonnement*, by means of which he successively tries out different multipliers till he reaches an estimate that satisfies criteria "more political than scientific". She nevertheless finds, on the basis of a more detailed examination of the evidence than any hitherto conducted, that, when it was a question of satisfying *himself* as to the value and accuracy of his sources, Petty's efforts were meticulous in the extreme and pioneered methods of assessment that were subsequently to become familiar in the field of data collection. She also points out the pioneering nature of his proposal for the collection of the country's various disparate sources of statistical information, and their unification and critical assessment within a national institution. Reungoat's assessment might perhaps be taken to suggest that a mathematical-deductive bias within the history of statistics has elevated the achievements of Graunt in statistical manipulation at the expense of an appreciation of Petty's contributions.[272]

Just as Petty's participation in relatively sophisticated methods of statistical manipulation at the time of his collaboration with Graunt left little mark on his subsequent writings, so also an equivalent hollowing out is discernible in the case of his fiscal thought. As has been shown, it is the analysis of the regressive effects of the excise and the advocacy of a compensatory taxation system which so signally distinguish the fiscal thought of his 1662 *Treatise of Taxes* and its successor, his *Verbum Sapienti* of 1665. Yet these features disappear in his later works, being replaced by the crude assumption that aggregate state revenue rises in step with national income.[273] No one, however, has taken this equivalent debasement as cause to question the degree to which the ideas contained in the 1662 *Treatise* are attributable to Petty alone. Rather, its breathlessly colloquial tone gives much of it the character of a strongly biased transcription of public debates in progress ("daily talk", in his own words) – debates in which he evidently participated, but soon put behind him. The fact that he was tentative about identifying himself with much of the content of these debates is confirmed by the fact that the work was published anonymously, and not known to have been attributed to Petty by anyone until six years later, in 1668.[274] The first that is heard from Petty himself on the matter is ten years later still, in some correspondence of 1678, in which he appears to be happy to distance himself as much as possible from the work.[275] These circumstances might well be considered to be as worthy of discussion as the question of the extent of his involvement in Graunt's work, and at any rate throw into high relief the spectacular asymmetry between the amount of attention which the question of his authorship has received in each case. The truth appears to be, in fact, that this asymmetry has been generated primarily by a self-reinforcing tendency within the secondary literature to devote a vastly greater amount of attention to the history of quantitative methodology than to the history of fiscal theory.[276]

In any event, Petty clearly wrote his *Treatise* with the aim of representing himself as a fountainhead of innovative ideas in the field of fiscal reform, and of thereby securing appointment to a self-constructed official position by means of which he could implicitly, though not too overtly, draw upon his expertise and standing as surveyor of Ireland to undertake an overhaul of the entire revenue system. The same vision of an appointment as a supremo in the field of information gathering and revenue assessment continued to inspire him throughout his life, in the course of which his various proposals "encompassed virtually the whole spectrum of both Cameralism and the later cadastral reform movement of the eighteenth century".[277] Even in 1686, barely a year before his death, he still had not given up hope, and continued to press his ambitions in a disarmingly frank manner, drawing up an elaborate letter of appointment, and optimistically leaving a space at the end of the text for the monarch to sign![278] The title of his proposed position was to be

> Accountant General for all the Lands and People in the King's Dominions, Valuator General for all Lands, Houses and Tithes in Ireland, Regulator of Coins in Ireland, as also Licences for Selling Ale, Wine, and Spirit… [and so on].

These responsibilities were to be exercised not only in England and Ireland but "in all or any of Our [i.e. the monarch's] dominions throughout the whole world".

Thus, the *Treatise of Taxes and Contributions*, in one sense, sets the tone for all Petty's subsequent careerist endeavours, but is, at the same time, exceptional in its lack of military reference. Once he felt secure enough in his position in Restoration society, however, he reverted to his former military posture. Indeed, this reversion had evidently already set in even before the treatise went to press, for its preface, which summarises its arguments in a manner which clearly indicates that it was written subsequently to the body of the work itself, has a noticeably higher concentration of references to military requirements than the body of the treatise itself.[279] By 1665, three years later, his reversion to an openly fiscal-military stance was complete, his work *Verbum Sapienti* being directed explicitly to the fiscal requirements of the second Anglo-Dutch war, which was then in progress, with a torrent of naval-military statistics of a kind which had been totally absent from his 1662 treatise,[280] but which were to be such a prominent feature of his subsequent writings.[281] By the time he began his series of works on political arithmetic, from the early 1670s onwards, the civilian veneer was all but abandoned; the focus on raising revenue remained, but now the presentation was unabashedly, even stridently, military, with a strong naval bias, in such a way as to become, as has been seen, effectively "quantitative modelling on behalf of the sovereign", rather than being any longer confined, even ostensibly, to the narrowly fiscal, let alone the 'civilian', sphere.

In 1678, when asked to approve a reprint of his 1662 *Treatise*, Petty took the opportunity to dismiss that work, as based on the misguided calculation that it would accord with the current of opinion prevailing at the court at the time:

> You know I have no luck with my politics. Slight Court tricks have advanced many men, but the solid study of other men's peace and plenty ruins me. Wherefore let the Stationer do what he pleases with the *Taxes*.[282]

In other words, the preoccupation with peace and social welfare shown in that work had now become, so far as its author himself was concerned, a distant memory, a mere aberration from his otherwise single-minded dedication to schemes for militaristic enterprises to promote England's commercial and colonial hegemony, for military and naval confrontation with France, and for associated proposals for military and naval reorganisation. It was to underpin these warlike and predatory goals that the conceptual structure of his economic thought was forged, and not, as so many historians of economic would evidently prefer to believe, the pacific and welfare-oriented goals to which he had tactically – and highly uncharacteristically – given prominence in his 1662 *Treatise*.

3.3 Conclusions: state, natural law and military–bureaucratic officialdom

This survey of the influence of the fiscal-military context on Petty's economic thought has shown how the search for the intellectual roots of economics has hitherto been drastically constrained by a failure to centralise the conflictual issues that dominated the early stages in the formulation of the basic categories of economic analysis – issues that crystallised around the question of how to handle the trade-off between raising the revenue to wage war abroad and the danger of rebellion at home. Since the supreme task of economic policy was to seek solutions to this question, it followed that the crucial economic agent was regarded as, by definition, the state. Inevitably, therefore, Petty stood, as regards his overall social and political orientation, in the tradition of Hobbes, whose influence on his approach to economic and political issues has already been illustrated, and has long been recognised,[283] and with whom he shared an often extreme view of the rights of the state over the individual.[284]

This does not indicate, however, that there exists a simple polarity between Petty's state-oriented outlook and the Smithian approach based on the idea of a law-governed self-regulating market. Indeed, the concept of the operation of law, or 'natural law', in the flow of trade was already a "commonplace" by Petty's time,[285] and his writings abound in references to such laws governing economic life.[286] The role played by such supposed laws in the respective theoretical systems is fundamentally different, however. For Smith, economic law is represented as the inevitable and unintended outcome of the free interplay of market forces, operating like gravity in Newton's theory of planetary motion.[287] For Petty, in contrast, the operation of natural law is represented, more narrowly, as a constraint on the action of the state, whose task is to identify such laws and take account of them, in such a way as to ensure that its guidance of the economy proceeds aright;[288] in this connection, he constantly intones the slogan *Res nolunt male administrari*, or 'The world refuses to be governed badly".[289] There is, thus, a recurring tension in Petty's writings between his desire to ingratiate himself with the authorities – his schemes were invariably "very grateful to those who governed", as Davenant was to remark[290] – and his "efforts to speak truth to power",[291] a less accommodating tendency, which leads him to issue admonitions about "the vanity and fruitlessness of making civil positive laws against the laws of nature".[292] This ambivalent outlook, which typifies that of his time, has the effect that, in his political economy,

> he neither looks back to medieval concepts of hierarchically ordered societies, in which each person had a set place and rank, nor forward to eighteenth-century notions of self-regulating economic systems and invisible hands.[293]

This difference in the concept of economic law as it appears in the works of Petty and Smith is illustrated most clearly by their respective approaches to the concept of supply and demand in the market. For, while this concept is the hallmark of the Smithian theory of the market system, it plays only the most rudimentary role in Petty's economic thought;[294] indeed, the compiler of the most extensive list of Petty's 'anticipations' states bluntly that it is absent from his writings, leaving the one major gap in the list which remained to be filled by subsequent writers, from among whom he singles out Dudley

North and John Locke.[295] Elsewhere, it has been claimed that Petty's concept of finance, and, in particular, of interest, was "handled in terms of free-market theory", but, even then, it is acknowledged that it was only with Locke that such initial formulations reached their "culmination" and thus opened up the path that was to lead to the Smithian theoretical system.[296] Without a general theory of supply and demand, it is inevitable that Petty "has no conception of competition acting to eliminate inefficient production methods".[297] For him, it is a well-informed state, rather than the market, which can best function as a regulatory mechanism,[298] or "ultimate arbiter of resource allocation",[299] and he dismisses competition as a game of dice won "rather by hit than wit".[300] The organ of such state-imposed regulation was to be the military-naval and administrative bureaucracy, a world of officialdom which constituted precisely the opposite of the free market and the enlightened individual agency which were envisaged a century later by Adam Smith. Indeed, this was the very target against which Smith's argumentation was directed, aiming as he did for the replacement of the "guiding hand of the statesman"[301] by the "invisible hand" of the market, which was, he maintained, the sole guarantor of 'natural liberty'.

The same fiscal-military objectives which pervade Petty's writings continued to provide the underlying motivation which impelled the further development of economic analysis in the subsequent period as well. For example, the most notable of the following generation of political arithmeticians, Gregory King, compiled his extremely important statistical profile of England in the 1690s with the explicit aim of "reckoning how long England could go on fighting the war" with France which was then in progress.[302] Nor did the fiscal-military context diminish in significance with the subsequent emergence of the mature classical political economy; indeed, the proportion of state revenue spent on war "hardly changed before the reign of Queen Victoria",[303] and it was, accordingly, largely around the issues of war and war finance that the founding debates of modern economic thought as a whole took place. As one commentator puts it: "Classical political economy was forged on the anvil of war."[304]

This fiscal-military context might not, perhaps, be immediately obvious in the work of Smith, who relegates fiscal and military affairs to the second, and less often read, half of his *Wealth of Nations*,[305] and consciously strives, wherever possible, to sustain a homely, philosophical and 'civilian' presentation. Similarly, Ricardo's work *On the Principles of Political Economy and Taxation* can also largely be read as a 'civilian' document.[306] In contrast, much of the theoretical value of earlier writers such as Petty and King lies precisely in the fact that they are perfectly candid about the military and conflictual goals which motivate all their work, a frankness which has rarely been paralleled by later economists, even when their work responds to analogous situations.[307]

Yet it was precisely in this world of military-bureaucratic officialdom that Petty anticipated, or at least stumbled upon, not only many of the concepts of classical political economy but also much of the analytical apparatus on which the economic orthodoxy of today still relies. The 'recovery' of that context is, consequently, an essential task in the search for the roots of economics, revealing, as it does, that the nearer we approach those roots, the fainter becomes the enlightened tone of Smith's moral philosophy, and the more inescapably we are confronted with the world of office hunting, 'rent seeking' and corruption, the horrific realities of predatory colonialism, the ethics of piracy and the slave-trade, and the ever-present whiff of gunpowder.

Notes

1 Mun 1664: concluding paragraph. Though not printed till 1664, this work was in fact written around 1628.
2 O'Brien and Hunt 1999a: 57.
3 O'Brien 2002: 249.
4 Brewer 1989: xvii, 24. See further in Braddick 2000: 177–285; and, for a summary bibliography, Wrightson 2000: 353f.
5 O'Brien 2002: 264.
6 *Ibid.*: 246. So also O'Brien and Hunt 1999b: 198, 201 ("a hitherto buried corner-stone of what was to follow"), 223.
7 See, for example, Ertman 1997: 206.
8 O'Brien 2002: 246. So also Epstein 2000: 34–37.
9 O'Brien 2002: 245, who goes on to discuss the distorting effect of this 'Whig' per-spective on history as seen in the works of Douglass North and other historians.
10 Braddick 2000: 270f.
11 Johnson 1937: 97. So also Spiegel 1983: 132 (taxation was "closest to his heart").
12 The only treatments of a comprehensive character remain Fitzmaurice 1895: 189–216; and the editorial commentary by Hull on TTC (for example, at 5f., 7, 40, 41, 44, 59, 62, along with Hull 1899: lxix–lxxiv). The task had already been initiated by Roscher 1857: 84f. and Bevan 1894: 70–79, and was followed up by Pasquier 1903: 229–243.
13 See, in particular, Seligman 1910: 30–33, 49, 112, 256; and Kennedy 1913: 27, 63–67, 69–76, 80f.
14 See, for example, Chandaman 1975: 78; Jones 1994: 77–80; and Bonney 1995b: 176–181.
15 Bonney and Ormrod 1999: 1. Roseveare 2001: 291, reviewing literature in the field, declares that it "has now come of age". It has also been dubbed the 'new fiscal his-tory' (though in this case there is no affinity with the 'new' social science initiatives launched on the basis of 'economics imperialism', on which see Goodacre 2005b); for references, see Bonney 1999: 12 (note 61). A significant advance in establishing the status of this field was the publication of the trio of edited volumes Bonney 1995a, Bonney 1999 and Ormrod, Bonney and Bonney 1999. Other writers within this category include Braddick, O'Brien and Hunt.
16 Winch 2002: 4f expresses the guarded view of most economic historians towards "that much smaller tribe, the historians of economic thought". Morgan 2002: 190f is more explicit, breezily dismissing the leading neoclassical works on mercantilism as "some recent contributions from the US that are largely ahistorical". See also Bonney 1995b: 163, 223, as discussed further below.

17 For example, Whittaker 1960: 58–61; Letwin 1963: 114–146; Routh 1975: 35–46; Robbins 1998: 55–65; Landreth and Colander 2002: 5f.; Backhouse 2002: 68–72; and Brewer 2003: 83–85.

18 For example, Deane 1968; Thomson 1987: 231–235; and Vaggi and Groenewegen 2003: 29–36.

19 See, besides the above early studies, Schumpeter 1955: 209–215; Spiegel 1983: 132–135; Aspromourgos 2000: 63–66; and Finkelstein 2000: 114–121.

20 There is, for example, no specific fiscal contextualisation in the accounts of Petty's fiscal theory by Johnson 1937: 97–108; Roll 1973: 98–112; Roncaglia 1985 [1977]: 42–49; McNally 1988: 35–55; Hutchison 1997 [1988]]: 6–12; or Aspromourgos 1996: 30f., 69f. Exceptions are Hueckel 1986 and Finkelstein 2000: 114–121, though even these do not fully take up the train of thought opened up by earlier historians of taxation, as further discussed in Chapters 3.1.2 to 3.1.4.

21 Bonney 1995b: 223; see also p. 163.

22 Anderson 1998: 11.

23 Roberts 1956.

24 See, for example, Feld 1977; Tilly 1985; Parker 1996; Anderson 1998; Van Creveld 1991; Downing 1992; and Tallett 1992. For a brief assessment of this literature, see Sturdy 2002: 247–250, who points out that it has been slow to extend into the naval sphere.

25 Despite the documentation which was long ago made available by Lansdowne in PP and DB, the military aspect of Petty's scientific and technological activities remains underestimated, as in Webster 1975: 435–444 (an account of Petty's survey of Ireland) and Sharp 1977.

26 For relevant discussion, see Roncaglia 1985 [1977]: 47f.; Kennedy 1988: 76–86; Brewer 1989: 250; Tilly 1990: 87–91; Roseveare 1991: 1–51; Downing 1992: 180f.; Dickson 1993; Holmes 1993: 266–277; Jones 1994: 82–89; O'Brien 1998: 59–67; O'Brien and Hunt 1999a: 57, 62f., 69–72; O'Brien and Hunt 1999b: 218f.; Epstein 2000: 29; and O'Brien 2002: 248.

27 Epstein 2000: 29 (note 33), quoting a 1988 article by Roseveare.

28 O'Brien 2002: 263.

29 This is argued in Roncaglia 1985 [1977]: 50–60 and 1988: 168, citing comments on Machiavelli by Antonio Gramsci. Aspromourgos 1996: 71f comments that any influence of Machiavelli on Petty was doubtless indirect and transmitted through Hobbes.

30 Mykkänen 1994: 70, where the place of Petty's administrative thought is discussed in terms of Foucault's concept of 'governmentality'. Unfortunately, this study shares with the bulk of the literature on the history of economic thought a lack of reference to fiscal affairs. For other discussions regarding the applicability to Petty's writings of the governmentality concept, see Chapter 5.4.

31 Poovey 1994: 32.

32 Tilly 1990: 122–126 (section heading).

33 Downing 1992: 10–12. Compare Tallett 1992: 198–205.

34 Downing 1992: 14.

35 Morgan 2002: 165f., summarising O'Brien 1998.

36 Hueckel 1986: 45.

37 *Some observations upon the Bank of England* 1695: 18.

38 Among the exceptions are Goodwin 1991 and Coulomb 1998, both of whom are explicitly critical of the shortcomings of the history of economic thought in

this respect. Perelman has pointed out that Petty's focus on strengthening the navy contrasts with Smith's emphasis on the need for a peasant-based land army; he does not engage, however, in this connection, with the 'war and society' or 'military-fiscal' literature. See Perelman 2000: 126, 186–189, discussing Smith 1976 [1776]: 692f., 698.

39 Hueckel 1986: 41.

40 Bevan 1894: 85.

41 O'Brien and Hunt 1999a: 55.

42 TTC: 38–54, where Petty discusses its advantages over rent from royal estates (38f §3), and its effects under different prevailing lengths of lease (39f §5), on which see Pasquier 1903: 238f.; Seligman 1910: 30f., 112, 256; Kennedy 1913: 80 (who includes Petty's propositions on this subject among the "fancy theories" of the time); Roll 1973: 103; and Spiegel 1983: 132.

43 TTC: 54–61. For discussion of Petty's views, see Fitzmaurice 1895: 207f.; Seligman 1910: 31; and Kennedy 1913: 26–29.

44 TTC: 91–95. On the history of excise in this period, see Kennedy 1913: 63–75, etc.; Braddick 1994: 168–230; O'Brien and Hunt 1999b; and O'Brien 2002: 246f.

45 TTC: 61–64, 94 §8; VS: 112; PP1: 96f., 182–184. For discussion of Petty's views, see Kennedy 1913: 74; Braddick 1996: 105f.; and Finkelstein 2000: 115, 302 (note 70). For general background, see Braddick 1994: 241, 231–270; and O'Brien and Hunt 1999a: 77.

46 TTC: 64 §11, 94 §10–11. For discussion of Petty's views, see Seligman 1910: 31; Chandaman 1975: 78; and Bonney 1995b: 178. For general background, see Braddick 1994: 231–270.

47 TTC: 74f.

48 TTC: 65f. For discussion, see Bevan 1894: 76; and Jones 1994: 68, with reference to Chandaman 1975: 200–205.

49 TTC: 77–82; see also 25f., and index (p. 698), for further references. Petty describes tithes (TTC: 81) as "no tax", but "next to one", as discussed further below.

50 *Ibid.*: 75–77.

51 *Ibid.*: 64f ("a tax upon unfortunate self-conceited fools").

52 *Ibid.*: 82–84 lists a miscellany of new-fangled expedients proposed by 'projectors' in various countries. He ignores the many 'feudal' forms of taxation which still survived; see O'Brien and Hunt 1999a: 80f., where it is argued that these were now becoming "counter-productive".

53 Braddick 2000: 233.

54 TTC: 90f §19 (see also p. 84). For discussion, see Roncaglia 1985 [1977]: 47.

55 PA: 275–278. See further in Chapter 3.2.1.

56 Swift 1726: chap. 6.

57 TTC: 32 (heading of chap. 3).

58 O'Brien and Hunt 1999a: 75.

59 O'Brien and Hunt 1999a: 61f., with graph. So also O'Brien 2002: 261.

60 Smith 1976 [1776]: 869.

61 O'Brien and Hunt 1999a: 72. On beer in early modern times, see MacFarlane 1997: chap. 8.

62 Dickson 1993: introduction to the reprint.

63 O'Brien 2002: 261. Kennedy 1913: 61 makes the similar point that excise had the administrative advantage of being levied from few individuals, yet paid for universally.

64 Kennedy 1913: 20–22; O'Brien and Hunt 1999a: 77.
65 O'Brien and Hunt 1999a: 67f., 72. As a result of the introduction of the excise and
other fiscal reforms, O'Brien 2002: 246 states that the civil war period was "*the* con-
juncture in the realm's fiscal, as well as constitutional, history" (emphasis in original).
66 O'Brien 1988: 8f (with table); 2002: 253.
67 Locke 1689: II, §139–40. For the restatement of this same principle by Gladstone,
see Daunton 2002: 339. For the equivalent principle as advanced by Hobbes, see
Chapters 3.1.4 and 3.2.1.
68 Bonney 1995b: 165, citing works of Thompson and Root. See also TTC: 38 ("just
shares") and 94 ("natural justice" in taxation).
69 TTC: 21, 32–37.
70 Bonney 1995b: 165, 214f., citing Smith 1976 [1776]: 825–828. On the correspondence between TTC and Smith's maxims, or 'canons', see Bevan 1894: 101. For a
suggestion that Petty exercised an even wider influence on Smith's view of public
finance, see O'Brien 2003: 113.
71 Bonney 1995b: 170, discussing Hobbes 1651: 181. The correlation between the
views of Hobbes and Petty on indirect taxation was first pointed out by Roscher
1857: 85.
72 Montesquieu 1989 [1748]: 222. For discussion, see Bonney 1995b: 193.
73 Hume 1955 [1752]: 85. For discussion, see Bonney 1995b: 200.
74 TTC: 34 §11.7; see also 39, 55; and VS: 113.
75 O'Brien 2002: 246. See also O'Brien 1988: 4; and Epstein 2000: 28 ("the London
merchants' fiscal rebellion turned revolution").
76 Holland drew admiration for the fact that, despite having the highest rates of taxation in Europe, "it seems that the high taxes were willingly paid". Veenendaal
1994: 96.
77 O'Brien 2002: 261.
78 TTC: 81 §13.
79 O'Brien 2002: 261.
80 Parliamentary declaration of 1646, quoted by O'Brien and Hunt 1999b: 209; see
also 214. See further in Firth and Rait 1911: I: 916–920; and II, 1004–1007.
81 See, for example, TTC: 30 §38 ("necessary food and raiment"), 31 §39 ("bare
necessities of nature"), 37 §22, 43 §13 ("natural necessaries"), 43 §14 ("necessary livelihood"), 89 §17 ("all necessaries for life"), 90 ("necessaries of nature")
and 56 §2 ("all superfluities tending to luxury and sin"). See also Kennedy
1913: 29, 77; and O'Brien and Hunt 1999a: 68. Petty's use of the concept
of necessary consumption is, of course, of great significance in tracing the
emergence of the theory of surplus value; for discussion, see Aspromourgos
1996: 22–30, 104–107.
82 O'Brien 2002: 261.
83 See Kennedy 1913: 61, 62, 79f.; Chandaman 1975: 39; Bonney 1995b: 179 (note
108), 187; and O'Brien and Hunt 1999b: 217 (with further references).
84 His use of this terminology is of general reference, however, rather than specifically to excise; see, for example, TTC: 38; VS: 103 ("insensibly"); DPA: 129 ("almost
insensible"); TI: 549 §9 ("without being a sensible burden to the people"); and
572 §6 ("it will scarce be a sensible burthen").
85 VS: 113.
86 *Ibid.*: 110 §10. This passage is quoted by Marx 1970 [1867]: 273 in connection with
absolute surplus value and the length of the working day.

87 See also Braddick 1996: 150, discussing TTC: 53f., on "calming fears" over taxation. Other comparable passages are found at TI: 572 §6, §8 and 603.
88 PA: 275; so also 276.
89 *Ibid.*: 306.
90 See Beckett 1985: 304f., who surveys the views of Petty, Locke, Halifax and Davenant on this subject.
91 Hume 1955 [1752]: 85. For discussion, see Bonney 1995b: 200.
92 Montesquieu 1989 [1748]: 217. For discussion, see Bonney 1995b: 194.
93 Smith 1976 [1776]: 875f.
94 Aspromourgos 2000: 55.
95 Kennedy 1913: 69.
96 See O'Brien and Hunt 1999a: 79f for a list of examples, with references.
97 TTC: 91–95. For discussion, see Seligman 1910: 32f.; Kennedy 1913: 79f.; and Braddick 1996: 117. Petty saw the Hearth Tax as coming nearest to providing such an 'accumulative' standard; see TTC: 94 §10. The issue also prompts one of Petty's "interspersed discourses and digressions", in which he posits a distinction between those "actually and truly" rich and those who are rich "but potentially or imaginatively". For discussion, see Kennedy 1913: 64f. On beer, see further in MacFarlane 1997: chap. 8.
98 VS: 111f outlines an entire compensatory taxation system, which involves a poll tax as well as the excise and taxation on the income of the rich. For discussion, see Kennedy 1913: 74.
99 TTC: 56f §4, this particular comment referring specifically to customs.
100 See Kennedy 1913: 6, 75, discussing the system instituted in the period 1860 to 1880, for an account of which see Daunton 2002: 334–340. See also Bonney 1995b: 229, citing equivalent discussion in the French National Assembly. Hull (editorial note to VS: 120) does not appear to note this point, citing without comment a 1691 tract which wrongly complains that Petty proposed no such compensatory system.
101 Kennedy 1913: 74.
102 Buck 1977: 75, 76, 83, who fails to mention the fiscal context, however, as also does Endres 1985: 247, 251–255, in an equivalent discussion.
103 Poovey 1994: 27 (see also p. 17).
104 Sewall 1901: 70.
105 Schumpeter 1955: 213; compare also p. 31, cited by Bonney 1995b: 222.
106 Fitzmaurice 1896: 116b.
107 Greenwood 1928: 80.
108 TTC: 26 §26.
109 *Ibid.*: 32 §3.2.
110 Roll 1973: 102. For similar comments, see also Pasquier 1903: 230; Spiegel 1983: 132f.; Roncaglia 1985 [1977]: 44; Bonney 1995b: 179 (citing a proposal addressed to Arlington, 3 September 1671, Add. 72,865, ff. 24–28); Braddick 1996: 114 (discussing VS: 103, 115); O'Brien and Hunt 1999a: 78f.; and Finkelstein 2000: 120.
111 Spiegel 1983: 132.
112 *Ibid.*
113 Endres 1985: 252f.
114 Spiegel 1983: 133, citing PA: 269. See also Endres 1985: 252f.; and Aspromourgos 1998: 196.

115 TTC: 36 §21, as discussed by Braddick 1996: 230f. TTC: 56 §2 equivalently argues for the use of customs "instead of a sumptuary law".

116 See, for example, Spiegel 1983: 133 (all except Mead); Robbins 1998: 64 (Kaldor and Meade); and Pressman 1999: 6 (Kaldor). Roncaglia 1985 [1977]: 104 (note 12) adds references to equivalent discussions among Italian writers.

117 VS: 105–109. For other versions of this calculation, see PA: 267; DPA: 128f.; TI: 563f., 574.

118 Kiker 1967: 469, who comments that Petty's method is, "of course, very crude".

119 Studenski 1958: 11–13, 26–30. See also Hull 1899: lxxi; Schumpeter 1955: 213; Letwin 1963: 136; Kiker 1967: 468; Kendrick 1970: 284 ("the first estimate of national income"), 286, 289f.; Spiegel 1983: 126 (achieves "the conceptual derivation of the national income"); Endres 1985: 253f.; Mirowski 1989: 306; Olson 1993: 64; Erba 1998: 7–10; Backhouse 2002: 69–72; and Murphy 2009: 35–6, as discussed in Chapter 5.3. O'Brien 1997 [1992]: 154 is exceptional in cautioning that such credit has been accorded "perhaps generously". Finkelstein 2000: 119f., 304 (note 98), provides a valuable analysis of the accounting framework within which Petty formulated his calculation, with particular reference to his important note entitled "In merchandize" (PP1: 189–192). For a general discussion of the political context, see Lepenies 2013: chap. 2. For an authoritative account of the measurement of England's national income and its history, beginning with Petty, see Slack 2004, who cites the comment of Stone 1997: 30–31 that Petty's were "the first complete and consistent set of national accounts ever to have been made", and hence "a landmark in economic history".

120 Kendrick 1970: 286.

121 PA: 244f., a passage discussed by numerous writers, including Pasquier 1903: 109; Letwin 1963: 134 (who calls it Petty's "methodological credo"); O'Brien 1997 [1992]: 151f.; Lynch 2001: 228f.; and Backhouse 2002: 70.

122 Letwin 1963: 137.

123 "Petty's facts were conjectural rather than observed" (Poovey 1998: 123), or "hypothetical variables" (Lynch 2001: 227), accuracy being necessary only to the degree necessitated to establish the qualitative issue in question. Schumpeter 1955: 213 is thus more generous in his assessment than other commentators when he states that Petty "hammered out concepts from, and in connection with, statistical investigations"; a similar view is expressed by Kuhn 1963: 26f.

124 O'Brien 1997 [1992]: 151f.

125 Letwin 1963: 136f.

126 Lynch 2001: 228.

127 Attis 2014: 56–57.

128 A fuller survey would need to take into account important advances in the analysis of Petty's views on the taxation of consumption by Aspromourgos 2000: 63–66, who finds in a hitherto unpublished manuscript note (BL Add. 72,865 (ii), to which he assigns the abbreviated title '*Proportion*'), a primitive formulation of the principle of 'taxation of value added'.

129 Fitzmaurice 1896: 117b.

130 Roncaglia 1985 [1977]: 39. For further comparative study of the relation of Petty's fiscal writings to the "two rival systems" of taxation on the continent of Europe, see Fitzmaurice 1895: 190–192. On Holland as the epitome of fiscal 'decentralisation', see O'Brien 2002: 256.

131 Fitzmaurice 1899: 99b, citing *Edinburgh Review* 1895: 69.
132 Letwin 1963: 143. Similarly, Pasquier 1903: 243 describes Petty's thought as "un tout homogène [a homogeneous whole]".
133 Assessment of this question has been disparate and piecemeal. Chandaman 1975: 78 and Bonney 1995b: 178, commenting on TTC: 64 and 93f., note that the content of Petty's endorsement of a tax on housing corresponds closely with the provisions of the legislation which, at precisely the same time as the publication of his *Treatise of Taxes and Contributions*, introduced the Hearth Tax; this has led to the suggestion (most recently in Slack 2004) that Petty's opinions may have had a certain influence, though no evidence has been adduced to show that the line of causation ran in that direction. Kennedy 1913: 72 suggests reasons for the lack of influence of Petty's critique of the excise. Seligman 1910: 33 gives an account of how his ideas "gradually diffused themselves" in the period following his death. Jones 1994: 77f claims that Petty "heavily influenced" aspects of the political strategy of James II, and, though he provides no supporting evidence of this, new evidence put forward by Dale 2011 does indeed suggest that Petty's ideas carried more influence with that monarch than many commentators have hitherto assumed.
134 A lack of cross-reference also affects some of the work in these fields; for example, some of the literature of the new field of fiscal studies appears to have lost the thread of the discussions launched earlier by Seligman 1910 and Kennedy 1913. A rare exception is Braddick 1996: 117, 129 (referring to Kennedy 1913), 229f.
135 Hull 1899: lxix. Hueckel 1986: 64 (note 50) questions the extent to which Hull himself was successful in achieving such a break with the retrospective viewpoint.
136 Bonney 1995b: 178, who goes on to demonstrate that this was also connected with his views on the political constitution.
137 Erba 1998: 8.
138 DPA: 133.
139 TTC: 34 §10.
140 O'Brien and Hunt 1999a: 59, 67.
141 Bonney 1995b: 179.
142 O'Brien and Hunt 1999a: 85 argue that a powerful impetus was given to this development by the Ship Money reforms under Charles I earlier in the seventeenth century. It is also notable in this connection that the technique and presentation of Petty's Down Survey of Ireland had a closely analogous precedent in the 'Strafford survey' in Ireland in the 1630s. See DS: 54–63; and Andrews 1985: 60–63. On the wider implications of Petty's insistence on the efficacy of knowledge in strengthening governance, see Mykkänen 1994; and Poovey 1994: 26f.
143 Roscher 1857: 85. The proportions are given in this fractional form in VS: 110 §8.
144 Hull 1899: lxxii. Petty's argument is thus distinct from, though not inconsistent with, the more general principle advanced by Hobbes (and also by Petty, at, for example, TTC: 91) that people should pay tax in proportion to their "share and interest in the public peace". For discussion, see Kennedy 1913: 64–66. The principal passages in which Petty advances his 'proportionality' concept are TTC: 26 §26, 32 §3.2, 65, VS: 110, 114, 116; and DPA: 127–134.
145 See, for example, Hull 1899: lxx–lxxii; Letwin 1963: 136f.; Roncaglia 1985 [1977]: 44, 104 (note 10); Endres 1985: 254; and Backhouse 2002: 69.
146 See, for example, Endres 1985: 254; and O'Brien 1997 [1992]: 151f.
147 Endres 1985: 254.

148 Poovey 1998: 123.

149 Lynch 2001: 227.

150 O'Brien 1997 [1992]: 151f.

151 Letwin 1963: 136.

152 Backhouse 2002: 69.

153 Spiegel 1983: 127. Hueckel 1986: 57 (note 6) similarly comments that labour "in Petty's view bore a disproportionately low share of the tax burden".

154 DPA: 127f.

155 *Ibid.*: 131.

156 Kennedy 1913: 75, whose own opinion, however, is that such a disregard for equity was a characteristic of vulgarisers of Petty's fiscal theory, rather than of Petty himself.

157 *Ibid.*: 66f.

158 'Philodicæus' (1647): 116 (§14). For discussion, see Kennedy 1913: 76f.

159 VS: 114.

160 Poovey 1998: 124. Olson 1993: 58 provides an example of precisely such naïveté in his comment that Petty "seem[s] to have been genuinely concerned not only to appear but to *be* disinterested" (emphasis in original). Such an assessment may be set against the more realistic observation by Lynch 2001: 249, who tellingly contrasts the promotion by the Royal Society of "the ideology of a science free from politics" with the reality that natural science "became linked to technical solutions for the state".

161 O'Brien 2002: 246.

162 The underlying truth that taxation is a tug-of-war between different social interests subsequently provided the basis for the development by Locke, Davenant and others of the theory of 'incidence'. See Seligman 1910: 101–109, *passim*; and Kennedy 1913: 80f.

163 Hull 1899: lxx–lxxii.

164 I.e. Kennedy 1913, as already discussed.

165 I.e. Spiegel 1983: 127, as already quoted.

166 Hueckel 1986: 57f (note 6), whose conclusion is evidently reached independently, there being no reference to Kennedy 1913.

167 Kendrick 1970: 284 is typical, remarking that Petty was responding to "the need to build quantitative bases for analysis of the effects of proposed tax policies", without even raising the issue of what policies he was advocating. Finkelstein 2000: 118 states that Petty's aim was "an equitable taxation policy", and that he calculated the proportions of national income from various sources so "that they should be taxed accordingly", thus following Roscher's precedent of correctly interpreting Petty's immediate purpose without drawing out its polemical significance.

168 This term is used, with specific reference to Petty, by Spiegel 1983: 130; Hueckel 1986: 42f.; Hutchison 1997 [1988]: 21; and O'Brien 1997 1992]: 153. Ghosh 2001: 52 (with diagram) uses the term in relation to the economic thought of the time, but without specific reference to Petty. Bowley 1973: 179f discusses the issue in connection with Petty's wage theory as a whole.

169 TTC: 55 §4; see also 52 §15, where he urges that "the price of labour must be certain" – i.e. that the wage level must be held constant – and expresses approval for the statutes limiting wage rates. (As already discussed in Chapter 3.2, he was also confronted with the limitations of such a concept of labour supply in conditions in which potential wage labourers have the alternative choice of withdrawing from the labour market in favour of subsistence cultivation.)

170   This is the view of Seligman 1910: 49–52, who cites the equivalent views of Petty's contemporary John Houghton, as well as William Temple and the eighteenth-century writer Josiah Tucker (though he omits to mention that the same concept reappears in Hume 1955 [1752]: 83, who holds that taxes on the poor "increase their industry"). Seligman's view is contested by Kennedy 1913: 81, however, who considers that it is "a strained interpretation of Petty to attribute Houghton's policy to him". Furniss 1920: 134 draws attention to the "greater practicality" of thus lowering real rather than nominal wages by increasing the price of necessities – a point that was subsequently to be elaborated, in hardly less blatant terms, by Keynes 1936: 257–271.

171   TTC: 63 §6.

172   PA: 274f. Conversely, in 1686, the German 'cameralist' Wilhelm von Schröder proposed a public granary to meet times not of plenty but of dearth; cited by Bonney 1995b: 185. For further discussion, see Furniss 1920: 123, 134; and Hueckel 1986: 60 (note 60).

173   VS: 114.

174   PP2: 231 §83.

175   TTC: 68f §12. For discussion, see Hueckel 1986: 59 (note 13); and also Olson 1993: 67.

176   Morgan 2002: 180.

177   See Hull, editorial note to *Bills*: 454; Olson 1993: 47, 64f (who finds an anticipation of this concept in Hobbes); Roncaglia 1985 [1977]: 59, 108 (note 32); Aspromourgos 1996: 94f., 198 (note 7); Finkelstein 2000: 124; Aspromourgos 2000: 60; and Backhouse 2002: 69f. For references to equivalent calculations by Gregory King, see Laslett 1992: 23f. The account by Kiker 1967: 468f relates Petty's calculation to the subsequent concept of 'human capital', and points out that he made widespread use of it "in attempts to demonstrate the power of England, the economic effects of migration, the money value of human life destroyed in war, and the monetary loss to a nation owed to deaths", citing respectively EW: 505–513 (the *Two essays in political arithmetic, concerning…London and Paris*), PAI: 192, PAI: 152 and VS: 108–110.

178   Backhouse 2002: 70. In fact, Petty does not always assume a discount rate that is constant across all these 'factors of production'; see, for example, VS: 108, where he assumes it to be higher (6 per cent) in the case of "money and other personal estates" than in the case of the rent of land (5 8/9 per cent, apparently a slip of the pen, since he estimates the value of land and rent to be £144 million and £8 million, respectively, a yield of 5 5/9 per cent). On the relation of interest rates to returns on land in this period, see Finkelstein 2000: 302 (note 62).

179   Aspromourgos 2000: 60, on which the following formal presentation is based.

180   PAI: 152f., the 'Proportion' manuscript (cited by Aspromourgos 2000: 61), *Bills*: 469; PAL: 476; PP2: 55f.; TI: 563f.

181   PA: 267, though here he states that this is an average, and that "adult persons" are worth "twice as much". Petty's disaggregation of population into age cohorts is commonly vague, and into sexes even more so, as discussed by Poovey 1994: 30.

182   PAI: 152f. At TI: 600 he gives yet another set of estimates, stating that "able-bodied Irishmen…are worth here above £80 per head, at Algier above £40, and as negroes [*sic*] above £20 per head".

183   In *Two essays in political arithmetic, concerning…London and Paris*, EW: 512. For comments on this passage by Rousseau, see Postscript.

184 TI: 576f §4 (from £70 to £100), 603 §5 ("from 7 to 10"). Such an increase in value through naturalisation accords with Petty's aim that the Irish should be "transmuted into English", as discussed in Chapter 2.4.

185 Aspromourgos 2002: 61, discussing the '*Proportion*' manuscript. Spiegel 1983: 129 also sees "echoes of the concept of opportunity costs" in Petty's doctrine of a 'par' between land and labour.

186 Swift 1729, on which see further in Goodacre 2010a, and in the Postscript.

187 Bonney 1995b: 185 cites Mun 1664: chap. 18 as an example, and also traces the use of this image in German cameralist writings.

188 For example, he regularly denotes women of childbearing age by the term 'breeders', which was normally used for livestock; its use for women carried overtones of ribaldry, as for example in Shakespeare's *3 Henry 6*: II, i. For examples of Petty's people-breeding principles, see PP2: 47–58; and, for discussion, Chapter 4.1.6.

189 O'Brien and Hunt 1999a: 65.

190 Braddick 2000: 213.

191 For estimates of the corresponding absolute amounts, with discussion and a graph, see O'Brien and Hunt 1999a: 54–58, 60. See also O'Brien 1988: 1–5 (with table); O'Brien 1998: 68; Wrightson 2000: 258; and O'Brien 2002: 249f.

192 Tallett 1992: 178.

193 O'Brien 1988: 1.

194 Hobbes 1651: 181.

195 O'Brien and Hunt 1999b: 198.

196 O'Brien 1988: 2 suggests a figure of 79 per cent for the decade following Petty's death (1689–97). For general discussion, see Braddick 1996: 21–48. Relevant statistics are being accumulated on the website of the European State Finance database, edited by Bonney.

197 PA: 295.

198 TTC: 18 §4.

199 For discussion, see Bonney 1995b: 226f.

200 O'Brien 2002: 258.

201 Lowry 1991: 7, as further discussed in Chapter 4.4.2 (i).

202 See, for example, PP1: 25–42; PP2: 51–84, 141–6.

203 PP1: 178 §3. So also PP1: 233 §5, and, similarly, *ibid*.: 181 §6 ("shipping of all sorts, comprehending the Navy").

204 *What a Complete Treatise of Navigation Should Contain* §18.

205 He divided the science of navigation ('naval philosophy') into three branches: (1) the 'physico-mathematical' aspects – i.e. ship building; (2) naval policy, which included naval intelligence, maritime geography, fishing and maritime trade opportunities, and maritime law; and (3) naval economics, which included the acquisition of supplies at minimum cost, measures to ensure self-reliance for strategic supplies, depreciation of vessels, maintenance costs and provisioning. This division into three branches is outlined most comprehensively in his *Treatise of Naval Philosophy*, of which the above-quoted briefer document (*What a Complete Treatise...*) appears to be an initial draft. For further discussion, see Chapter 4.1.4.

206 PA: 276–284.

207 *Ibid*.: 259.

208 *Ibid*.: 276f. This proposal is classified as a "gentle tax", as discussed in Chapter 2.1.2.

209 Lynch 2001: 228f. Similarly, Finkelstein 2000: 107 comments that "Petty's purposes were not confined to those of economics *per se*".

210 Brewer 2003: 84. Compare, for example, VS: 116, DPA: 129f. and PA: 305 with the table in Holmes 1993: 439.
211 Coulomb 1998: 315. See also Chapter 1.4.
212 Backhouse 2002: 291. This aspect of the history of economics is extensively discussed in Mirowski 2002.
213 TTC: 47f., on which see Hull's editorial note. As Petty remarks, in such a formulation, the bare transport costs constitute a minimum, possible only on the assumption (utterly unrealistic in his time) of absolute security, as further discussed in Chapters 4.1.5, 4.2.1 and 4.4.2 (i).
214 TTC: 54 §3. For discussion, see Kennedy 1913: 26–29.
215 TTC: 7 §8.
216 *Ibid.*: 45f §19–23, where this argument is overlaid by a separate theory that the length of an individual's perspective on property is generally limited to three generations. On years purchase in Ireland, see also PA: 228f.; and TI: 559 §5, 562, 565, 583 §1, 590, 606; compare also 560 (on interest rates).
217 TI: 567. See also PP1: 173 §14; and Chapter 1.3.
218 PA: 259. Marx 1963–71 [1862–63]: I, 179f., comments that the inclusion of soldiers in this passage weakens Petty's conception of productive labour; this observation is not enough, however, for Hueckel 1986: 61 (note 25), who contends that Marx takes insufficient note of the context of Petty's comment, stating that it was, in effect, merely an aside in an extended discussion devoted entirely to military matters.
219 See, for example, Bodin 1962 [1576]: 655f., as discussed by Bonney 1995b: 167f.; and the words from Mun 1664 on "the means of our treasure", as quoted in Chapter 3.0.
220 O'Brien and Hunt 1999a: 65.
221 *Ibid.*: 85, citing Laud.
222 *Ibid.*: 66.
223 Tribe 1978: 87.
224 Brewer 1989: 11.
225 Kennedy 1976: 536. Historians of the period more often describe England's naval goals in more anodyne terms, such as the "defense of the domestic economy from external aggression": O'Brien and Hunt 1999a: 65; see also p. 53.
226 PA: 296, as already noted in Chapter 2.1.
227 Braddick 2000: 270f., as discussed in Chapter 3.0.
228 O'Brien 2002: 264, as discussed at greater length in O'Brien 1998: 70–74.
229 The use of this convenient neoclassical terminology is not intended as an endorsement of the view that the nation state can adequately be represented, in any wider sense, merely as a maximising agent within the same 'rational choice' behavioural framework as an individual 'household' or 'firm'. See Fine and Milonakis 2003: 557, discussing North 1981: 143–157. It may be noted, in this connection, that Mirowski 1989: 306 considers that "the notion that a nation as an entity could be thought of as possessing a wealth or an income is an old idea, dating back to William Petty and Gregory King in late seventeenth-century England".
230 O'Brien and Hunt 1999a: 63.
231 Aspromourgos 1996: 106; so also 123.
232 Olson 1993: 3; so also 193.
233 See, for example, Robbins 1998: 59; and even Aspromourgos 1996: 52.

234 Spiegel 1983: 133f., commenting on TTC: 29–31. See also Lynch 2001: 223f., commenting on *Bills*.

235 Johnson 1937: 99, as already noted in Chapter 2.1. For Petty's critical reflections on "offensive war", see TTC: 21–23; and, for an invocation to "peace and plenty", see DPA: 37.

236 Seligman 1910: 30.

237 For example, in the list of 'anticipations' provided by Routh 1975: 36 (see Chapter 1.0), two-thirds of the references cited are in this one work.

238 O'Brien 1992: 147; and Aspromourgos 2001: 12.

239 McNally 1988: 35.

240 Aspromourgos 1996: 16.

241 Kurz and Salvadori 1998: 195.

242 Bevan 1894: 70; and, similarly, Hull 1899: lxi.

243 Hull 1899: lxx.

244 The letter was sent in connection with Petty's mission to London during 1658, on which see Chapters 1.1 and 4.1.1.

245 Prendergast 1870: 243, commenting on a letter from Henry Cromwell to Methusaleh Turner and others, 27 January 1658 (Thurloe Papers: VI, 759f.).

246 Ashley 1934: 92f., commenting on PAI: 197, says that these were figures that Petty "should have been in a position to know".

247 For general background to the Thurloe Papers, see Aubrey 1990, where his correspondence with Henry Cromwell is discussed on pp. 134f., etc.

248 Prime examples are two letters from Henry Cromwell to Lord Fauconbridge, 10 and 17 February 1658 (Thurloe Papers: VI, 789, 810). The quasi-medical metaphor of 'sweetening the pill' of unpopular measures might also be taken to indicate the influence of Petty. See Thurloe Papers: VI, 759f., 820.

249 Council of Ireland to the Protector, 10 June 1657, to which is appended "An account of the annual present revenue of Ireland for one year, ending the 1st of May 1657, etc." (Thurloe Papers: VI, 340f.).

250 Letter from the Council of Ireland to Thurloe, 4 March 1657 (Thurloe Papers: VI, 96). The term 'intrinsic' was later to be used in the same context by Petty in TTC: 86 §6, 87 §12; *Quantulumcunque*: 445, 447; and, in a more light-hearted context, in a letter quoted in Fitzmaurice 1895: 155.

251 Letter from Henry Cromwell to Thurloe, 15 July 1657 (Thurloe Papers: VI, 404).

252 This list is, in fact, employed only as a metaphor for a supposed lack of interesting news to 'export' to a correspondent in England. Letter from Henry Cromwell to Lord Fauconbridge, 10 February 1658 (Thurloe Papers: VI, 789).

253 Letter from Henry Cromwell to Thurloe, 24 February 1658 (Thurloe Papers: VI, 819f.). This letter is quoted at length by Ramsey 1933: 221f.

254 Letter from Henry Cromwell to Thurloe, 24 February 1658 (Thurloe Papers: VI, 819f.).

255 PP1: 77–90. The proposal was directed to the first duke of Ormonde, the leading figure in the Irish colonial administration during much of the Restoration period. See Strauss 1954: 121f., who quotes correspondence from the Ormonde papers. See also TTC: 26f §27–28 (and editorial note) and 49f. For discussion, see McNally 1988: 48f., who draws out the relevance of the text of Petty's proposal for his subsequent primitive formulation of the labour theory of value; and also Roseveare 1991: 27; and Finkelstein 2000: 113, 126f. On Holland as model for institutional reform, see Chapter 4.1.2.

256 Hull 1899: lxx.
257 Poovey 1998: 125.
258 This term is used by Schumpeter 1955: 209.
259 Poovey 1998: 125, who warns, however, that the reader "should not be taken in".
260 As Aspromourgos 2000: 58 points out, "little light" is cast by the British Library archive of Petty's papers on the development of Petty's economic thought in this period.
261 The Royal Society was founded in 1660, and incorporated by royal charter in 1662.
262 Downs 1977: 129.
263 Aubrey [1971]: 91. See also Hull, editorial note to TTC: 23 §13; and Strauss 1954: 93f. The Rota Club functioned only for less than four months, between autumn 1659 and 20 February 1660 (Downs 1977: 129).
264 Pepys 1970 [1665]: I, 14, records that Petty was a participant on 10 January 1660.
265 Aubrey [1949]: 125 (in brief life of Harrington). For discussion of the influence of Harrington on Petty, see McNally 1988: 120–125, though evidence of direct discussion between the two is very limited (*ibid.*: 128).
266 TTC: 9.
267 Bevan 1894: 42–52 was the first to consider seriously the idea that there was a major input by Petty into this work, on which he accordingly conducted a textual analysis, including a list, in tabular form, of parallel passages in *Bills* and TTC. This was followed by Hull 1899: xxxiv–liv, and a partisan defence of Petty's claim to authorship by Lansdowne in PP2: 273–284 and PSC: xxiii–xxxii. For a brief account of this initial debate, see Strauss 1954: 187–189. Groenewegen 1997 [1967] adds some new references from the literature of Petty's time. Keynes 1971: 75–77 provides a further account of the steadily expanding body of literature on the subject, usefully summarising the views of a number of writers, including Greenwood, Willcox, Westergaard, and Glass, followed by Lynch 2001: 197–119, 221f., and Finkelstein 2000: 300 (note 38), and now, in the most thorough assessment yet, in Reungoat 2004, on which see further below.
268 Endres 1985: 249, a list of technical features which is greatly expanded, with particular reference to time series analysis, by Klein 1997: chap. 2. On the status which has accordingly been conferred upon the work as the founding document of statistics and demography, see Kendrick 1970: 289 ("the beginning of the discipline of statistics"); Roncaglia 1987: 853b ("the birth of the science of demography"); Brewer 1992a: 714; and Schurer and Arkell 1992: 8.
269 Letwin 1963: 128. See also Finkelstein 2000: 110f.
270 Spiegel 1983: 125. A similarly negative assessment is given by Laslett 1992: 9–11, with citations from the work of Willcox and others.
271 Reungoat 2004.
272 *Ibid.*: 133 ("tâtonnement"), 79–80 (a national institution). For further discussion of Reungoat's work, see Chapter 5.1. Rohrbasser 2008 adds to the discussion of Petty's contribution to the history of statistics, in a study of the debt to his work of Süssmilch.
273 See, for example, PA: *passim*; and TI: 566.
274 See Hull's editorial note to TTC: 4.
275 See PSC: 61, as discussed further below.
276 Any further consideration of the authorship issue would need to remain sensitive to the fact that it is precisely the preservation of the interchange of numerous

different views in a predominantly oral culture which constitutes much of the value of a document such as Petty's *Treatise*, which is, in this respect, analogous to the diaries and gossip of Pepys, Evelyn and Aubrey.

277 Bonney 1995b: 180.

278 As his editor remarks, Petty "left nothing to chance" (PP1: 253). The text of this document, along with an accompanying note, are transcribed at PP1: 258–260.

279 The Preface is in effect, though not in form, a dedicatory letter to Ormonde (on whom see note 255 above), and its relatively martial tone thus also reflects the return of Petty's ambitions to the Irish theatre.

280 VS: 116; see also Hull's editorial commentary; and Bonney 1995b: 179.

281 See, for example, PA: 305f.; DPA: 127–129; and TI: 572 §10.

282 PSC: 61. He had included similar remarks in a letter to the diarist Aubrey written some months earlier (transcribed in Fitzmaurice 1895: 258).

283 The correspondence of much of Petty's thought with that of Hobbes was first pointed out by Roscher 1857: 85 (in connection with the advocacy of taxation of consumption), and was then taken up by subsequent writers, including Bevan 1894: 87–94; Fitzmaurice 1899: 113, etc.; Hull 1899: lxi–lxii; and Pasquier 1903: 239–242. For a later discussion, see Aspromourgos 1996: 64–70. On Petty's association with Hobbes in Paris in 1645–46, see Christensen 1989: 697; and, in much detail, McCormick 2009: 36–39. On the significance of Hobbes to economic theory in general, see Backhouse 2002: 74f., 88.

284 Bevan 1894: 91 ("no limit to its [the state's] interference"); Hull 1899: lxii ("no account whatever of the rights and sensibilities of the citizen"); O'Brien 1997 [1992]: 153 ("Hobbesian ruthlessness", "étatism"); and Brewer 2003 ("his policy proposals were designed to strengthen the state, almost regardless of individual rights or interests"). His overall constitutional stance is sufficiently indicated in his characterisation of the Irish rebellion of 1641: "That which the Irish did amiss in was, as I apprehend, the changing of the English monarchy into a democracy" (TI: 618).

285 Chalk 1951: 339. See also Jones 1994: 80f.

286 See Chalk 1951: 343f for references. See also Spiegel 1983: 134f (in relation to Petty, Hobbes and Grotius); Routh 1975: 44f.; Buck 1977 (in relation to Hobbes, Graunt, Petty and Boyle); Ekelund and Tollison 1981: 7; Hueckel 1986: 60 (note 24); Olson 1993: 67–69, 193 (with particular reference to the influence on Petty of homoeostatic ideas in medicine); and Montes 2003 (on Smith and Newton).

287 See Thomson 1984 [1965]: 332–335; Wightman 1975: 59–64; Buck 1977: 83f.; and, for further references, Bonney 1995b: 164 (note 2). On the concept of Smith's theoretical system as 'moral Newtonianism,' see Chapter 1.4.

288 Parel 1997: 122, who refers to this as a "royal task".

289 This translation is that of Spiegel 1983: 135. See Hull, editorial note to TTC: 9, with references to possible derivations from Aristotle and Bede.

290 Davenant [1771]: I, 129. For discussion, see Fitzmaurice 1895: 203; and Routh 1975: 45.

291 Lynch 2001: 229.

292 TTC: 48 §3. So also *ibid*.: 60 ("resisting of nature, stopping up the winds and seas, etc.").

293 Buck 1977: 75.

294 Fitzmaurice 1899: 101a, citing Petty's *Dialogue of Diamonds* (see EW: 624–630). See also Aspromourgos 1996: 157–162. Petty was worsted in a discussion of supply

and demand by his correspondent Southwell; see PSC: 148, 151, 153, 163f.; and, for discussion, Finkelstein 2000: 305 (note 121).

295 Routh 1975: 47. Groenewegen 1973: 505, in contrast, suggests that the concept (though admittedly not the actual phrase) was present "since at least the middle of the seventeenth century". See also Finkelstein and Thimm 1973: 68f.

296 Chalk 1951: 344.

297 Aspromourgos 1998: 196; and, similarly, Aspromourgos 1996: 50f.

298 For example, Roncaglia 1985 [1977]: 48 notes that Petty advanced a number of proposals for "the elimination of excessive public expenditures", and comments that "there is no substantial difference between this objective and that of reducing direct costs of production to a minimum". See also TTC: 28 §32, where Petty advocates state action to 'retrench' the number of retailers; for discussion, see Hueckel 1986: 44; and Finkelstein 2000: 125–127, who wryly asks (306 (note 137)), in the light of today's experience, "if this man so determined to streamline government payroll ever really considered the size of the bureaucracy needed to gather and sort all that information".

299 Finkelstein 2000: 120.

300 TTC: 52f §17. Hueckel 1986: 55 comments that Petty displayed "a profound mistrust" for prices that were determined by supply and demand. Similarly, Finkelstein 2000: 127, 129, comments that "the sole target of all Petty's efforts was to keep the anarchy of those 'market relations' at bay", with "nothing left to chance or the disruptive self-interest that fuelled the market".

301 Bonney 1995b: 227f.

302 Laslett 1992: 18. See also Bonney 1995b: 182, who cites an equivalent calculation by Davenant [1771]: I, 265f.

303 O'Brien and Hunt 1999a: 198.

304 Goodwin 1991: 23.

305 See Goodwin 1991 and Coulomb 1998 for discussion.

306 The principal exception is chapter 19 ("On sudden changes in the channels of trade"), which is devoted to problems of the transition between war and peace. For discussion, see Goodwin 1991: 30f.

307 A rare exception is Stone 1988, who, in an account of his work for the British war Cabinet during the Second World War, relates how, just like Gregory King before him, he undertook calculations on how long the country could continue to finance its war expenditure. Compare the discussion by Backhouse 2002: 292 of the wartime economics of the US economists Simon Kuznets and Robert Nathan. For further discussion of King in this connection, see Laslett 1992: 19.

4   The spatial economy from Petty to Krugman

4.0 Introduction

In exploring Petty's economic thought in connection with the search for the roots of development economics, the focus was primarily on his writings on Ireland. In turning to the economics of taxation, the centre of attention shifted to his writings on England and its fiscal-military ambitions. Now, in addressing the third and last of the three branches of economic enquiry to be considered in this connection, namely spatial economics, the focus returns once more to Ireland, and, by the same token, to Petty's population transfer schemes. For, as will now be seen, Petty's writings display as direct and pronounced a resonance with this third branch of economic enquiry as they have been shown to have with the first.

In what follows, an account will be provided of Petty's approach to spatial-economic analysis, a branch of economic thought whose field of enquiry has been described as "the three-way interaction between increasing returns, transport costs, and factor mobility".[1] This formulation suggests the threefold division of the subject matter which will here be adopted. This arrangement conveniently lays the basis for bringing the conceptual structure of Petty's approach to these issues into apposition with the spatial economics of today, while at the same time demonstrating how the logic of his spatial-economic analysis drew him inexorably towards his conviction in the benefits to be reaped from the transfer of Ireland's population into England.[2]

Next, the subsequent history of spatial-economic analysis will be traced, with particular reference to the crucial achievement of Johann von Thünen in laying the basis for the transition from the classical to the marginalist approach to spatial-economic issues, and, beyond them, to economic issues generally. This will be followed by an outline of the most prominent current initiative within neoclassical spatial economics, Paul Krugman's 'new economic geography'. This initiative will, in conclusion, be placed in direct confrontation with Petty's writings on analogous issues, providing an opportunity to assess what has been achieved, and lost, in the passage from the world of Petty to that of the economic orthodoxy of today.

4.1 Petty's spatial-economic analysis

4.1.1 Surveyor's metromania

Abundant illustration has already been provided of Petty's commitment to expressing economic relationships in quantitative terms. This mode of expression came easily to him, due to what one commentator describes as his "enthusiasm for counting everything in sight",[3] as a result of which he always had suitable numbers at hand for any purpose. As he himself put it, in more lofty terms:

> The method I take is not yet very usual; for instead of using only comparative and superlative words and intellectual arguments, I have taken the course – as a specimen of the political arithmetic I have long aimed at – to express myself in terms of number, weight, or measure; to use only arguments of sense, and to consider only such causes as have visible foundations in nature; leaving those that depend upon the mutable minds, opinions, appetites, and passions of particular men to the consideration of others.[4]

Almost every historian of economic thought who has commented in any detail on Petty's writings has cited this passage, which has been described as his "methodological refrain".[5] More critically, it has also been perceived as an example of the "arrogant frenzy of enthusiasm for quantitative and mathematical study of social life" that was sweeping through intellectual circles in his time, a proclivity which has also been described as a symptom of 'quantophrenia' and 'metromania'.[6]

But, while a great deal of attention has been paid to Petty's place in the origination of quantitative methods in economic analysis ('terms of number'), historians of economic thought have hitherto failed to take account of the additional fact that his use, in this context, of the terms 'weight' and 'measure' had, in his time, a literal significance that would have been immediately evident to his readers. For he wrote at a time when there was increasing access to information on social and economic affairs, and those fields of information which were open to expression in 'terms of number' concerned not only financial and demographic units but also (for example, in the case of import and export data) units of weight, and units of physical space ('measure'). In this last respect, a demand for estate and county maps, as well as local information generally, had swept the landowning classes since the previous century, and there was now both a demand for, and an increasing supply of, the equivalent aggregate information at national level as well. Thus, from 1669 onwards, a "kind of yearbook"[7] was published, entitled the *Present State of England*, compiled by Edward Chamberlayne.[8] Not only does Petty refer to this work in his own writings,[9] but there are also connections of a more direct kind: Petty's *Political Anatomy of Ireland* was, apparently, originally designed as a companion volume or supplement to Chamberlayne's yearbook,[10] while the 1683 edition of the latter includes the whole of *Political Arithmetic* as a supplement.[11] As for information on import and export statistics, Petty draws on another current reference work, the *Discourse of Trade* by Samuel Fortrey, a fertile source of data in 'terms of weight'.[12]

Once it is realised that Petty uses the terms 'weight' and 'measure' with specifically physical and spatial reference in this way, the spatial aspect of his economic thought becomes conspicuous, particularly if, as is widely accepted, the roots of his economic methodology are taken to lie in his survey of Ireland.[13] In that case, his "not very usual" affliction can be diagnosed as a particular occupational variant of metromania affecting practitioners of data gathering and, in particular, surveying – 'surveyor's metromania'.

Above all, Petty repeatedly returns, throughout his writings, to the theme of his survey of Ireland, marking, as it did, the high point of his official career. In order to convey a suitably awesome impression of the enormous scale of this undertaking, he quantifies the distance "measured by the chain and needle" in terms of multiples of the Earth's circumference; it was the equivalent, he claimed, to "the measuring of as much land-line as would have near four times begirt the whole earth at its greatest circle",[14] a multiple which he subsequently revised upwards to "near five times",[15] "above five times",[16] "near six times",[17] and finally "eight times".[18] This progression has aptly been described as 'Falstaffian', after Shakespeare's character whose tales similarly grew in the telling;[19] it may also justly be cited as a symptom of acute surveyor's metromania, and, certainly, the clank of the surveyor's chain never ceased to sound in Petty's ears, inducing him to take every opportunity to invest economic categories with a spatial element, often expressed in terms of a specific distance or area.

Such spatial specification is seen in its most explicit form in Petty's discussions of the agrarian economy, both internally and in its relation to the economic influence of London. This is illustrated (along with relevant citations) in Tables 4.1 and 4.2, where the measurements in question – originally an assortment of radii, circumferences and areas (square, circular and 'oval') – are all reduced, for comparison, to terms of radius. The perspective this reveals – which has, in recent decades, re-emerged in studies of market areas in the agrarian economy[20] – is one in which each spatial measurement or unit is associated with a particular economic category, concept or function; to use the jargon of the economic geography of today, Petty's units of analysis are not 'scale-independent'.

For example, the parish, though obviously, in the first instance, a unit of ecclesiastical administration, is frequently identified by Petty with the range of transactions within the subsistence economy, the terms 'parish' and 'village' being effectively used interchangeably in this context.[21] He consequently sees the optimal dimensions as being the same in both cases: the ideal organisation of parishes should be such that "none need go two miles to church", while he discusses the agrarian economy at base level (whether in terms of 'parishes' or

Table 4.1 Dimensions of the agrarian economy

Spatial unit	Petty's description	Dimensions (standardised to radius in miles)	References
Actual size of parishes	"The largest parishes I know being not more capacious than of three or four miles square"	[1.7–2.26]	TTC: 24 §18
Large parishes in "some wild countries"	"Lest it be said that in some wild countries a thousand people do not live in a less scope of ground than of eight miles square…"	[4.5]	TTC.: 24 §18
Optimal size of parishes	"None need go two miles to church"	< 2	TTC: 11 (subheading)
Range of subsistence economy	"People living within a market day's journey"	[> 2, < 5?]	PAI: 180
Tax official	"Without ever going five miles from the centre of their abode"	< 5	VS: 116 (see note in Table 3.2)
A "man's country"	"A man's country is the circuit of land whose radius is half a day's journey from his house".	[> 5?]	PPI: 209 §6 (see also Goblet 1930: II, 260f.)
Protestant parishes in Ireland	"They [i.e. the Protestant clergy] must have precincts of near 13/14 miles square, and consequently they must be itinerants…"	[7.33–7.9]	PAI: 148 (and editorial note)
Cash sale	"Farmers must first carry their corn perhaps ten miles to sell and turn into money"	10	TTC: 35§15.10

'villages') as consisting of "people living within a market day's journey", which suggests much the same optimal range of around two miles – or, at any rate, less than about five, given that allowance must normally be made for porterage (carriage by foot), as well as time for transactions. A cash sale, in contrast, has a range of anything up to ten miles. The optimal range for tax collection is the intermediate distance of five miles – longer than that of the subsistence economy, since transport of goods is not involved, while, at the same time, short enough to allow for a return journey within a day. This latter concept, once again, forms the basis for a definition – a person's 'country'.

Table 4.2 London: its size and the range of its economic influence

Spatial unit	Petty's description	Dimensions (standardised to radius in miles)	References
Size of London: built-up area (1)	"An oval piece of ground… [which] contains about 7500 acres, whereof about 1500 is built…"	[0.86]	PPI: 30 §2; also PAL: 471 §1 (first edition)
Size of London: built-up area (2)	"The present City of London stands upon less than 2500 acres of ground"	[< 1.11]	PAL: 471 §1 (second edition)
Size of London (2): 'field'	"[A]nd 6000 [acres] field"	[1.73]	PPI: 30 §2
Petty's proposed wall round London (1)	"A wall of 12 miles or 65,000 foot about will fortify the said ground artificially"	[1.91, 1.96]	PPI: 30 §10
Petty's proposed wall round London (2)	"A wall of 100,000 foot in circumference"	[2.45]	PPI: 32
Impact of London on grain prices (1)	"The shires of Essex, Kent, Surrey, Middlesex and Hertford next circumjacent to London"	[about 18]	TTC: 51f §13
Agricultural area necessary to provide London at seven times its current population	"A circle of ground of 35 miles semidiameter will bear corn. garden-stull, fruits, hay and timber for the 4,690.000 inhabitants of the said city and circle. so as nothing of that kind need be brought from above 35 miles distance from the said city"	35	PAI.: 471 §2
Impact of London on grain prices (2)	"If the corn which feedeth London. or an army, be brought forty miles thither"	40	TTC: 48 §5

It is not only at the base level of the agrarian economy that Petty provides his categories of economic analysis with such explicit spatial specifications; he also traces the various grids and subgrids of economic activity all the way up to the metropolis, London, once again specifying each of them in terms of scale-specific economic (and, in this case, military) considerations, as shown in Table 4.2. For example, he considers that the defence of London can be secured by a wall of 12 miles' circumference (later expanded to around 20 miles), which would be adequate, he remarks, evidently with an eye to siege conditions, "to plant necessary garden stuffe [for] food, milk and cows".[22] Outside this zone, London's impact on grain prices may extend for a considerable distance, specified, variously, as a radius of around 18 or 40 miles. He also speculates on a hypothetical situation in which London's population is increased to seven times its present size; in that case, he calculates, its agricultural provisions could be grown within a radius of 35 miles.

The roots of Petty's spatial-economic perspective can be traced even further back than the performance of his survey, to his negotiations over the 'small print' of the contract under which he was to perform it. It is characteristic of his account that he not only exposes the abuses to which the proposed system of payment was open but also unblushingly reveals how he benefited from them. He explains that the survey's procedure was to calculate the area of units of land by the measurement of their perimeter,[23] pointing out that, under this system, payment by area, rather than perimeter, allows the surveyor to "gain exorbitantly". What he indicates here is, in formal terms, the fact that, as the area surveyed approaches a circle, the proportion in which perimeter and area increase approaches the ratio $2\pi r: \pi r^2$; accordingly, measurement increases in arithmetical, and payment in geometrical, progression. Yet he subsequently relates, in grandiose terms, how he paid his measurers by 'linary contents', while he himself was paid by 'superficial content', an arrangement which, as the context makes clear, shows that he secured for himself precisely the system of payment he had so painstakingly exposed as 'exorbitant' a couple of pages earlier![24]

The payment of a map maker according to the extent of land mapped constitutes the purest and most elementary form of the transformation of spatial into economic categories. In this transaction, the act of summation of the extent of land measured (whether area or perimeter) is identical with the act of drawing up an account of payment due for work performed; thus, the tabular listings which Petty provides of the land he surveyed are, simultaneously, both geographical and accounting documents, a dual nature which is reflected in the term he uses to describe them: "accounts of lands admeasured".[25] Furthermore, the fact that the allotments of land to the soldiery were in lieu of pay was, in a sense, the beginning of his lifelong quest for "a par and equation between lands and labour".[26] Thus, it was second nature for Petty to perceive monetary units as identically interchangeable with units of the measurement of land, and to equate these, in turn, with units of labour; in other words, from his point of view, the fundamental categories of economic life could be immediately correlated with those of spatial measurement. Furthermore, in the course of drafting documents during the negotiations between the colonial administration in Ireland and the City of London speculators ('adventurers'), Petty extended the spatial-economic implications of his survey from the micro to the macro level, and, moreover, forged for the purpose an amalgam of surveyors' and financiers' jargon which has never ceased to defy elucidation.[27] Indeed, it is tempting to believe that it was concocted precisely for that purpose; certainly,

Petty had, as has been seen, every interest in keeping the process of land distribution "shrouded in obscurity".[28]

To emphasise the formative influence of Petty's survey of Ireland on his approach to spatial-economic analysis is not to deny that other intellectual influences were also at work in this connection. His medical training was evidently one such influence, and his frequent use of anatomical imagery, and, of course, his adoption of the term 'political anatomy',[29] exemplify the fact that "economic geography easily lends itself to the metaphor of anatomy/body",[30] both subjects being open to discussion in terms of equivalent categories of analysis at "opposite ends of scales of size".[31] Besides medical influences, Petty's involvement with the promotion of experimentation by the Royal Society is also reflected in his spatial-economic analysis, as will be seen in the case of his approach to the mechanics of transport.[32]

But, while medical, mathematical, technological and mechanical influences gave form and character to Petty's spatial-economic analysis, it was, undoubtedly, above all his survey of Ireland which first set him on his lifelong course of "grounding his economic and political theories on the facts of the map".[33] Goblet long ago observed that this aspect of his work had received remarkably little attention from historians of economic thought, who, being, in general, "strangers to geography" and seizing on his use of the term 'political arithmetic', had preferred to regard his method as an "abstract economic science", concerned with observed facts whose content is "reduced to a strict minimum" – that is, voided of specific content and abstracted from their context, in order to render them susceptible to quantification. By the same token, as Goblet goes on to argue, that specific content cannot be properly identified without taking due account of the essential fact that Petty explicitly, and most meticulously, took care to situate his economic ideas firmly within the context of the geographical environment of human activity.[34]

Having now brought to the fore the deeply rooted spatial referencing that pervades Petty's economic writings, the next task is to explore his approach to the first element of the 'three-way interaction' at the heart of spatial-economic analysis: the range of issues which fall within the category of 'scale economy', or, rather, more broadly, the 'benefits of agglomeration'.

4.1.2 Holland and the advantages of its 'situation'

> Envy and wonder stimulated a great deal of economic thinking in England during the middle decades of the seventeenth century… [In particular,] the sustained demonstration of…Dutch commercial prowess acted more forcefully upon the English imagination than any other economic development.[35]

Accordingly, the topic of Holland's industriousness in the fields of commerce, technology and manufacture inspired numerous treatises and pamphlets in

Petty's time;[36] he even claims to have written an essay on this theme himself, while a student in Holland in 1644, and, though he records that this particular item was "lost at sea",[37] his writings of the following decades repeatedly return to the subject. For him, Holland exemplified the principle that

> a small country and few people may, by their situation, trade, and policy, be equivalent in wealth and strength to a far greater people and territory.[38]

Holland's advantages were, then, classified by Petty into the three categories of 'situation', 'trade' and 'policy', and, in each case, he drew out what he saw as the lessons that England could learn from that country's exemplary experience.

In the sphere of 'policy', Petty called for the emulation of Holland's land register,[39] its public bank and other financial institutions,[40] its imposition of the excise,[41] its use of mercenary land forces[42] and its concession of liberty of conscience to religious heterodoxies.[43] One commentator even goes so far as to state that "his social and economic plans...were in many ways an adaptation of Dutch institutions to English conditions".[44] Likewise, in the sphere which he termed 'trade', Petty upheld numerous aspects of Holland's economic life. For example, he applauded its concentration of manufacture and commerce in its own hands, through international division of labour in relation to the agrarian economies of its inland neighbouring states.[45] He even extended his endorsement of the exemplary practices of Holland in the sphere of trade into the principle that "the model of the greatest work in the world...is the making of England as considerable for trade as Holland".[46]

Of more immediate relevance in the present context, however, is the category of Holland's advantages which Petty identified as those of 'situation' – or, in other words, its geographical advantages. A commentator – not, it may be noted, a historian of economic ideas, nor for that matter an economic geographer – has concisely summarised his arguments in this respect as follows:

> The Dutch soil was better; the population, although much smaller, was less scattered and, together with the protection offered by the dikes, made defence much easier in consequence; the level countryside and the damp climate were favourable to the use of windmills and irrigation; living as they did at the point where three great rivers had their outlet to the sea, the Dutch were able to develop the trade and commerce which was more profitable than manufacturing; nearness to navigable waters made for cheap commerce; ships could be harboured easily and at small expense; the facilities available for the fishing trade were great and the results lucrative; so were those of the trade in naval stores made possible by Holland's shipping advantages; and so on.[47]

In short, Petty's approach to this subject provides a prime example of the single-minded manner in which he developed geographical themes into spatial-economic analysis; indeed, for him, Holland's advantages of 'situation' came to overshadow all the other factors which he adduced, under the headings of 'trade' and 'policy', to explain that country's disproportionate 'wealth and strength'.

Such a spatial-economic approach provided Petty with an unparalleled opportunity to apply his principle of considering "only such causes as have visible foundations in nature", a principle which he elaborates in this context as follows:

> Many writing on this subject do so magnify the Hollanders as if they were more, and all other nations less, than men, as to the matters of trade and policy, making them angels, and others fools, brutes, and sots, as to those particulars; whereas I take the foundation of their achievements to lie originally in the situation of the country, whereby they do things inimitable by others, and have advantages whereof others are incapable.[48]

Nor do the attractions of this theme, for Petty, end here, for it also has the further advantage that it provides opportunities for the use of 'terms of number, weight or measure', an advantage which he naturally exploits to the full, as, for example, in the following formulation:

> Though France be in people to Holland and Zealand as 13 to 1, and in quantity of good land, as 80 to one, yet it is not 13 times richer and stronger, much less 80 times, nor much above thrice.[49]

In thus broaching the question of the source of the respective strengths of the leading European powers of his day, Petty was, politically speaking, entering deep waters. In the context of the European power politics of his day, his standpoint carried with it an implied challenge to the French-leaning international policy of England's monarchy. For, if indeed England were to learn from the experience of Holland, and thus to grow in 'wealth and strength', it would inevitably raise the question of whether it could, in that case, come to rival, or surpass, the power of France. As his editor puts it: "The moral of the *Political Arithmetic*, implicit but clearly implied, is that Charles II may, if he will, make himself independent of the bribes of Louis XIV."[50] It was not until 1688, the year after Petty's death, that the tension within the English ruling establishment over its international alignment was settled definitively in favour of Holland, when England "secured the services of a Dutch monarch"[51] and embarked upon its "second hundred years war against France".[52] In Petty's lifetime, however, these issues remained unresolved, and his inflexible adherence to the logic of his spatial-economic argumentation, with its inevitably anti-French implications, was doubtless a significant factor in his failure to recover high office in the state.[53]

4.1.3 Productivity and 'living compactly'

Petty's reflections on the 'situation' of Holland converged with his experience as surveyor of Ireland to suggest a polarity between the advantages and disadvantages of, respectively, a "thick-peopled" and a "thin-peopled" country, or, equivalently, between "living compactly" and living "far and wide dispersed".[54] Holland and Ireland were, in other words, two "polar cases"[55] which exhibited the effects of high and low population density in their most pronounced form. As for England and France, these lay somewhere in between: "England is four or five times better peopled than Ireland, and but a quarter so well as Holland"[56] – or, equivalently, England, Wales and Scotland had 4 acres per head, England alone 3 acres, and the United Provinces of Holland "not above 1 or 1½"[57], and so on.

The significance of Petty's concept of the advantages of 'living compactly', not only for his spatial-economic analysis but for his political economy as a whole, is hard to exaggerate. While, in many respects, compactness, as he sees it, is analogous to the concept of the 'benefits of agglomeration', as these are now understood in spatial economics, some important qualifications need to be made in this analogy to take account of the historical context in which he wrote. In particular, his concept is by no means always associated with the urban context which might be assumed to be implicit, and so cannot be described simply as "Petty's theory of urbanisation".[58] In fact, identifying the locational context of Petty's discussions is not at all straightforward.

In his earlier writings, Petty normally appears to associate the advantages of compactness with what would now be termed a 'rural–urban continuum', a term which has been defined as

> [t]he merging of town and country, a term used in recognition of the fact that in general there is rarely, either physically or socially, a sharp division, a clearly marked boundary, between the two, with one part of the population wholly urban, the other wholly rural.[59]

It was precisely in the context of such a blurring of the rural–urban divide that manufacturing regions were, in many cases, coming into existence in England and Holland in Petty's time, as described, some decades after his death, in the classic account by Daniel Defoe of cloth-manufacturing districts in the Yorkshire Dales.[60] Petty writes, for example:

> Suppose some great fabrick [i.e. factory] were in building by a thousand men, shall not much more time be spared if they lived all upon a thousand acres, than if they were forced to live upon ten times as large a scope of land.[61]

He clearly cannot have envisaged an urban context in this case, since an area of 'a thousand acres' is out of all proportion to the scale of towns in his time;

by his estimate, even London covered only "about 7500 acres, whereof about 1500 is built".[62]

In subsequent works, Petty begins to add increasingly specific urban reference, and, eventually, this urban reference narrows down almost exclusively to a metropolitan context, or, more specifically, the context of London and the other capitals of Europe. It is, in particular, in connection with London that his pioneering contributions to urban theory are to be found – his careful use of the category of suburb, his observations on the relation of both town and suburb to surrounding boroughs, his specification of the agricultural area required to provision the town, his use of the category of built-up area, the relation of that area to the city wall, and so on.[63]

There is, in addition, a further locational context, which is the military one. This is illustrated in one of Petty's most explicitly spatial-economic propositions on price:

> If the corn which feedeth London, or an army, be brought forty miles thither, then the corn growing within a mile of London, or the quarters of such army, shall have added unto its natural price, so much as the charge of bringing it thirty nine miles doth amount unto.[64]

The spontaneous manner in which Petty here assumes the equivalence between urban and military demand reflects the realities of the period of international and civil war through which he lived, in which armies were, in themselves, extremely significant concentrations of population, whose presence and movement not only were of strategic significance but affected all aspects of economic and social life in general. For the scale of military recruitment, relative to population, was such as to rank it as a major demographic phenomenon, particularly in the poor areas of Europe, such as Scotland, where, at the height of the Thirty Years War of 1618–48, perhaps a tenth of the entire male population was engaged in military employment in continental Europe.[65] Furthermore, as Petty would have needed no reminding, the economic significance of armies extended far beyond the narrowly military sphere itself; for example, as he himself had witnessed, the Cromwellian army in Ireland took upon itself the immediate organisation of much of the country's agricultural production for a period of several years, following the invasion and preceding the distribution of the land.[66]

From the point of view of general economic theory, the outstanding feature of Petty's compactness concept is that those forces which are now identified as falling within the category of 'productivity' cannot, in his view, be separated from their spatial context. The forces of productivity are, for him, quite simply not effective independently, abstractly or aspatially. This is seen throughout Petty's observations on productivity, which may be divided into the three categories of scale economy, division of labour and the diffusion of technical knowledge. Each of these is represented in his writings as an advantage of compactness, to which they are all, in other words, conceptually subordinate.

(i) *Economies of scale* are chiefly identified by Petty in the sphere of government administration, his approach having been paraphrased, in today's terms, as the argument that "population growth is attended by increasing returns, since the overhead, the cost of government, does not rise nearly so fast",[67] or, alternatively, that there are "real economies of scale in the costs of the unproductive apparatus necessary to the proper functioning of the economic system"[68] – or, more widely still, economies in "the 'overheads' of organised social life".[69] In Petty's own words:

> A nation wherein are eight millions of people, are more than twice as rich as the same scope of land wherein are but four; for the same governors, which are the great charge, may serve near as well for the greater as the lesser number.[70]

Petty elaborates this principle in ingenious ways. In the case of the justice system, for example, he argues that the efficiency of the administration of justice varies inversely with the distance of summonses and directly with the social visibility of criminal activity:

> The charge of the administration of justice would be much easier, where witnesses and parties may be easily summoned, attendance less expensive, when men's actions would be better known, when wrongs and injuries could not be covered, as in thin-peopled places they are.[71]

Militarily, an increased concentration of England's population in London would make it more easy for that city's governors to control the population remaining "scattered without it", while "a few men in arms" could in turn easily govern those within.[72]

Petty did not scruple to extend the same train of thought into the sphere of religion, arguing that there was ample scope for economies of scale in the provision of clergy, and, in particular, in the delivery of sermons, an argument which he expressed in quantitative terms, to devastating ironic effect. The maximum size of a parish, he suggested, should be such that its congregation can fit in a single church. The maximum size of the church should be, in turn, "that unto which the voice of a preacher of middling lungs will easily extend".[73] This would require a corresponding reduction in "supernumerary ministers", which could be achieved by the restoration of celibacy, so as "not to breed more churchmen than the benefices, as they now stand shared out, will receive"[74] – "quite a different 'population theory' from Malthus", as Marx was later to observe with approval.[75] Petty's argumentation deftly negotiates the transition between the quantitative and qualitative aspects of this issue:

Whereas in England there are near 10,000 parishes, in each of which upon Sundays, holidays and other extraordinary occasions there should be about 100 sermons per annum, making about a million of sermons per annum in the whole, it were a miracle if a million of sermons composed by so many men and of so many minds and methods should produce *Uniformity* upon the discomposed understandings of about 8 millions of hearers.[76]

Petty goes on to point out that a rational reconfiguration of parish boundaries, to bring them into correspondence with the demographic facts, would, allowing "a thousand sheep under every shepherd", enable the number of parishes to be reduced from the present 10,000 to 1,000 only, the ideal size being such that "none need go two miles to church".[77] Even if the reduction in parishes, and accordingly of priests, was not such as to decimate them in this way, but merely to halve them to 5,000, the saving "would, reckoning the benefices one with another but at £100 per annum a piece, save £500,000"; nor would this be the only saving, since it would also open up the possibility of an equivalent halving of "bishops, deans and chapters, colleges and cathedrals, which perhaps would amount to two or three hundred thousand pounds more".[78]

Thus, while the rationalisation of parish boundaries is not a simple matter of compactness as such, both issues provide Petty with an opportunity to draw out the same essential point: that, in his eyes at least, the benefits of economies of scale are conceptually subordinate to, or a result of, a favourable spatial configuration of social life, due either to given demographic conditions or rational social organisation, or both.[79]

This underlying affinity between Petty's observations on parish boundary reform and his compactness concept is further strengthened by the fact, already noted in connection with Table 4.1, that he habitually assumes the parish to be identical with the basic unit of the subsistence economy. He does not extend the principle of scale economy into his analysis of the process of production, however. The nearest approach is that the principle enters, somewhat obliquely, into his discussions of commercial issues, in the form of some passing reflections on storage and carriage. As regards storage, he sees those living compactly as having advantages of economy of scale by comparison with "those who live in solitary places", since the latter "must have their houses stored with necessary provisions, like a ship going upon a long voyage".[80] In connection with carriage, he argues that the concentration of manufacture and maritime trade in a large manufacturing-town-cum-port (the reference, naturally, being to London) results in economies of scale in the lading of ships, since they can take their entire cargo on board in the one location.[81]

Finally, it is notable that, in the case of Ireland, Petty also displays a further perspective on the question of administrative economies. For any administrative benefits to be derived within that country, that country's depopulation would obviously not be those associated with 'living compactly'. But he ingeniously introduces a new emphasis on what might be termed economies of homogeneity, or of simplicity. For example:

> There will be little pomp or expense in the Chief Governor, etc., the only business being to regulate the simple cattle trade to the best common advantage... The Courts of judicature may be much abated, for that there will be little or no variety of cases or actions... The officers of ports will need only to keep an account of exportation, where there are no importations, or very little or simple.[82]

In the related sphere of efficiency in the operations of the Church, his emphasis likewise shifts from economies of scale in the supply of sermons to the economies that may be derived from the supposed simplicity of the tasks of churchmen in Ireland, for, he supposes, "the work of the clergy will require little intricate learning or school-divinity".[83] Likewise, in the political sphere, as he sneeringly comments:

> Whereas there are disputes concerning the superiority of Parliament, now there will need no Parliament in Ireland to make laws among the cowherds and dairy-women; nor indeed will there be any peers, or free-holders at all in Ireland, whereof to make a Parliament.[84]

Such, once again, is the way in which Petty's analytical apparatus goes through a fundamental modification when transferred from the metropolitan to the colonial context.

(ii) *Division of labour*, unlike scale economy, is a concept which Petty explicitly pursues into the heart of the productive process. It is an exaggeration, however, to claim that "his account of the advantages of division of labour lacks none of the ingredients of Adam Smith's celebrated interpretation",[85] an assessment which grossly underestimates the significance of Smith's concept of the role of the market in this connection. As I have elsewhere discussed,[86] it is indeed the case that both writers were concerned with the question of how to increase productivity, and that in this connection they both discussed the advantages of the division of labour. The distinctive features of their respective discussions of the subject are completely different, however. Petty represented it as one of the advantages of spatial compactness, whereas for Smith, of course, it proceeded in step with the extension of the market.

There are also other respects in which Petty's use of the concept displays primitive features. First of all, the examples he gives show that he has not yet decisively broken with the approach – characteristic of comments on the division of labour by ancient writers – of placing the emphasis on the advantages it provides for the improvement in quality of the output, rather than increase in its quantity;[87] only in one passing remark does he break, and then only indirectly and inconclusively, with this standpoint, in the observation that division of labour may result in "better and cheaper" products.[88] A further distinction between the concept as it appears in the work of Petty and Smith is that, for Petty, it lacks the abstract character which Smith was to give it, a character which marked the culmination of a process which may be traced through the writings of a succession of writers in the decades after Petty's death.[89] The subsequent destiny of the division of labour concept is not the central concern in the present connection, however; rather, what matters here are the spatial connotations it receives in Petty's writings.

As regards the spatial unit at the lowest relevant level of scale, the workplace, Petty's examples do not unambiguously indicate whether he envisages division of labour, in any given instance, as taking place in a single workshop or between independent tradespeople trading in intermediate goods.[90] His earliest example concerns the making of surveying instruments for use in his survey of Ireland, where his account suggests that this manufacturing enterprise drew on preexisting skills – those of the wire maker, the watch maker, the turner, the pipe maker and the founder.[91] If this example is indeed taken to represent division of labour within a single workshop, then it provides an unusually explicit account of a particular early stage in the workshop's history, when practitioners of formerly independent crafts are first grouped together, prior to the subdivision of their respective crafts into detail operations, and with each craft retaining its identity and original name. The other two manufactures for which Petty mentions division of labour are cloth, in connection with which he habitually listed a number of different trades and technical operations,[92] and watch making.[93] In both these cases, the workplace context is ambiguous; examination of the operations he lists indicates that they would normally have been performed partly in subgroups in a number of workshops, and partly by independent tradesmen.

At a higher level of scale, Petty's examples of division of labour conveniently illustrate three aspects of his concept of compactness. In the case of the surveying instruments, he indicates that the craftsmen on whose skills he drew were members of the Cromwellian army; his account thus provides a valuable example of the role played by the military as a forcing house for the development of the division of labour, and also, more generally, for the emergence of a "factory culture".[94] In the case of cloth manufacture, his detailed listing of no fewer than 17 operations,[95] combined with the fact that he wrote a paper on dyeing,[96] shows that his background in the family of a clothier and dyer had left him with a specialist knowledge of the subject. This personal background also suggests the kind of locational context he might have had in mind in this case. For the clothing and dyeing establishments in his home town of Romsey in Hampshire extended into the neighbouring countryside, along the banks of the multiple tributaries of the river flowing through that town,[97] which must, thus, have presented the aspect of a rural–urban continuum, or even a 'little Holland'.[98] In the case of watch making, in contrast, Petty unambiguously takes this manufacture as an example of the advantages of an urban, or – even more narrowly – metropolitan, context, explicitly categorising it among the advantages of "so vast a city" as London.[99]

(iii) *Diffusion of technical knowledge* is the third component of Petty's productivity theory, and, of course, the one which reflects most directly his life-long concern for "the advancement and propagation of useful learning".[100] Once again, this concept becomes, in the course of his writings, increasingly subordinate conceptually to the benefits of compactness, and, by the same token, increasingly associated with the urban, and eventually metropolitan, context.

When, at the age of 24, Petty wrote his early treatise on educational and technological reform, *The Advice of W. P. to Mr. Samuel Hartlib*, he had relatively little experience of urban society, as it is now understood. Neither residence in his native Romsey, nor even in the towns where he had studied in Holland, would have been, in this sense, a fully 'urban' experience. He had, it is true, stayed for some months in Paris, and perhaps a few more in London, but this had evidently left him with no particular propensity to associate the advancement of learning with cities as such. At any rate, there is, in this early treatise, no reference to an urban context whatsoever. On the contrary, much of the treatise takes the form of a proposal for an educational and techno-logical institution whose characteristics are, throughout, suggestive of a rural setting.

The proposed institution would have, Petty suggests, not only a 'garden' for cultivating pharmaceutical products but also "large pieces of ground for several experiments of agriculture" and "ponds and conservatories for all exotic fishes", while "all animals, capable thereof, should be fit for some kind of labour and employment", and detailed information would be compiled on agricultural, as well as manufacturing, technology.[101] Much of the treatise is clearly influenced by the system of education applied in the Jesuit colleges of continental Europe, at one of which, at the University of Caen in Normandy, he claims to have studied in his early teens.[102] Most of these colleges were situated in what would, today, be regarded as a rural setting. The college at Caen was, it is true, atypical in this respect, that town, with around 25,000 inhabitants,[103] being a relatively large population centre, with a flourishing cultural life. At the same time, how-ever, the town was the hub of the cattle trade of the region, and much of the ethos of the place would certainly have been, by today's standards, rural rather than urban.

Even in his 1662 paper on dyeing, delivered to the Royal Society, the processes Petty describes continue to suggest the context of the 'rural–urban continuum' of Romsey, where he must first have gained his experience of the techniques he details. That same year of 1662, however, also saw the publication of Graunt's work on the population of London, which represented, in itself, a step forward in the development of urban culture, and Petty's participation in that work, whatever it did, or did not, entail in respect of its contents, must cer-tainly have marked the stage in his own intellectual trajectory when he took on board the idea of a specifically urban society.

Graunt's work does not, however, have cause to mention the subject of tech-nical knowledge, and the association of such knowledge with towns was only to emerge somewhat later in Petty's writings. It was, perhaps, the increasing prosperity and development of London, and the impression its dynamism created upon him during his successive visits during the following two decades, which caused him, increasingly, to associate technical knowledge with urban society. This association may well have been intensified by the fact that it was, of course, these visits which enabled him to participate in the work of the Royal Society, particularly during his prolonged stay of nearly three years from 1673 to 1676, when he was to the fore in revitalising that organisation following a period in which its activities had effectively lapsed.

It is also noteworthy that the Royal Society's sister organisation which Petty headed in Ireland was named after the capital rather than the country as a whole – the Dublin Philosophical Society. Furthermore, in a 1676 lecture to the equivalently named Dublin College of Physicians,[104] he makes it plain that his aspiration is to promote learning specifically in that capital city, so that it could join "the great cities of Europe", and he gives no indication that he is concerned to raise the level of learning in Ireland as a whole.[105]

Finally, in his writings on London during his last years, Petty provides a full elaboration of the advantages of metropolitan society for the diffusion of technical knowledge. Among the features he mentions in this context are dissecting theatres, hospitals, gardens, laboratories, linguistic skills, collections of 'rarities', the Royal Society, with its improvement of "mathematical, mechanical and natural learning", and, not least, the technology of "shipping and gunnery".[106] These advantages are here explicitly related to his concept of compactness:

> For in the great vast city, there can be no so odd a conceit or design, whereunto some assistance may not be found, which in the thin, scattered way of habitation may not be.[107]

Such, then, is the conceptual dominance of compactness in Petty's approach to productivity issues. The concept functions, in effect, as a central organising principle, subordinating to itself, as specific instances of its own potency, the advantages of scale economy, division of labour and the diffusion of technical knowledge.

The insistently spatial – or 'metromanic' – character of Petty's political economy was, of course, to be lost in the passage from Petty to Smith.[108] Contrary to appearances, however, this does not reflect any fundamental retrogression by Smith from attention to spatial issues. On the contrary, Smith's spatial-economic analysis achieves a substantial advance upon Petty's in almost every particular; Smith addresses, for example, the question of the origin of towns in their rural context, the relation of urbanisation to the growth of the national economy, the spatial implications of sectoral shifts, the urban hierarchy, the distinction between government towns and commercial towns and the relation of city size to profit rate, the cost of living and the wage rate.[109] This underlines the fact that the distinction between the spatial-economic analysis of the two writers lies deeper than the question of whether or not a 'metromanic' presentation is adopted, and extends to embrace a far more fundamental difference; this is that, for Smith, what provides the impulse to productivity – as exemplified, in the first instance, by the division of labour – is the extension of the market, whereas, for Petty, whose attitude to the market is dismissive, the route to productivity, in all its aspects, is, above all, the compacting of the population.[110]

4.1.4 Transport costs

Petty's involvements in transport issues embraced the fields of technology, information and mechanical experiment.

In the first of these fields, that of transport technology, Petty's principal contribution was, of course, in the maritime sphere, in which his aim was to persuade the naval authorities to adopt the construction of ships with twin hulls. His enthusiasm for this project acknowledged no bounds: "Noah", he points out, "did mankind in one bottom save; what then in such a case would he do with two?" In a similar vein, he suggests that "if Columbus lived [he] would as much wonder at this vessel going to America as at its [i.e. America's] finding".[111] There was, in short, much more to his vision of the 'double bottom' than a mere technical innovation, for it embodied Petty's entire 'naval philosophy',[112] representing, for him, "a grand new principle transforming navigation".[113] Not least of its supposed advantages was, in accordance with this 'philosophy', its capacity to accommodate ordnance, and his writings on the subject, accordingly, return repeatedly to the vessel's firepower and other features relating to "sea fights".[114] The same orientation can be seen in all his writings on maritime affairs; for example, in the field of commercial accounting, he estimates that one-eighth of the cost of sea freight is due to "the charge of guns, ammunition and extraordinary men for the defence".[115]

As for Petty's writings on inland navigation, these display the seaman's prejudice against what he saw as a primitive form of navigation, reflecting "the infancy of shipping";[116] the use of twin hulls would, he argued, stand at the opposite extreme, as the culmination of millennia of development, progressing through the stages of poles, oars and sails.[117] His 'double bottom', in short, epitomised the age of ocean travel,[118] and was designed, no less than his economic writings, as a means to strengthen England's capacity "to gain the universal trade of the whole commercial world".[119]

Ironically, it was precisely those who took Petty's invention most seriously who scuppered its chances of being taken up in earnest by the English navy. For the fact that the vessel drew so little water made it highly suited to navigating "harbours, bays or creeks",[120] and Petty's opponents at court raised the scare that, if the Dutch got their hands on the design, it would be of vastly greater advantage to them than to the English, due to the particular characteristics of the Dutch coastline.[121]

Turning from the technology of navigation to that of land carriage, Petty's contribution is best viewed in the broad historical framework of the shift in emphasis of early modern 'headline economics' from the maritime and the mercantile to the inland and the industrial. In the field of political economy, a milestone in this process is Adam Smith's expression of preference for inland manufactures whose growth is "the offspring of agriculture" over those which are "the offspring of foreign commerce".[122] Despite the emphatically maritime orientation of Petty's writings, it is also possible, paradoxically, to discern indications of the emergence of the more inland-oriented perspective that was to culminate in Smith's standpoint, though his steps in this direction are admittedly hesitant, and his maritime and mercantile outlook finds ways to assert itself even in writings devoted specifically to land issues.

One example of the hesitant nature of Petty's attempts to focus his attention on wheels rather than waves is a project which he drew up and costed for the construction of armoured vehicles, or "war chariots". This was by no means an innovative idea in itself,[123] but Petty gave the project his own distinctive character by discussing the vehicle's equipment and manning, and even its potential tactical manoeuvres, in such unmistakably naval terms that it reads very much like a prospectus for a naval vessel.[124]

A further example which displays Petty's complex and contradictory orientation to matters back on shore is provided by his only technical paper dedicated exclusively to the subject of land carriage. This time, his focus is diverted from his stated objective not so much by a maritime bias as by another of his enthusiasms. His paper begins by listing the vehicles under consideration:

> Land carriage by draught is by wheel-barrows, straddles, carts of two wheels, sleds, wagons of four wheels, by cars on two high wheels, drays on two small wheels, Irish cars of two very small wheels.[125]

While this appears a promising beginning to a consideration of the subject of wheeled transport in an agrarian economy, the ensuing discussion soon veers off into technicalities which, in his time, at any rate, arose only in the context of luxury carriage construction. This interest was characteristic of the period, not least among the members of the Royal Society, a 'coach craze' having at one time absorbed much of that institution's attention for a period of almost three years.[126] Petty's contribution was the construction of what he termed his "pacing saddle". This was a hooded vehicle, or 'calash', a distant precursor of the 'Surrey with the fringe on top' in the musical *Oklahoma!*, though a heavy-duty version, designed alike for the mountainous Kerry countryside and for the London–Holyhead route.[127]

Besides these involvements in transport technology, Petty also addressed transport issues in the field of information. For example, in his proposals for a "register of lands", he calls for the collection of topographical information on transport routes and related spatial-economic issues – on "roads, postages, fairs, markets, ports, harbours, streets, cities, corporations, etc.", on stages along the relatively new system of stage routes then spreading across

England[128] and on inns.[129] Similarly, he argues that the valuation of Irish land requires a knowledge of its "distance from church, market, place of Assizes and Sessions, as also from Dublin, and other ports or navigable rivers".[130] As always, the conflictual and military dimension, while less conspicuous than in his writings on maritime affairs, is nevertheless never far from his mind, and he calls for the information to include not only "horses fit for war"[131] but also all features relevant to the "quartering and victualling of armies, whether they stand or march".[132]

Besides his involvements in the fields of technology and information, there is also a third field in which Petty addressed transport issues, which is that of experimental mechanics. His endeavours in this field clearly grew out of his experience in naval technology, and survive only in the form of a number of schemes which he devised for experiments 'in small', mostly relating to carriage by water, but some also to land carriage, as well as to comparative land–water issues.

This last topic – especially as it concerns the land–water transport cost ratio – is one which gave early modern writers on economic subjects an easy opportunity to provide a matter of common observation with the apparent authority of being expressed in quantitative terms, and Petty was naturally to the fore in exploiting this opportunity. The actual ratio he gives varies, and is, unfortunately, never provided with any particular explanation or empirical substantiation. In a set of notes which were apparently drafted in connection with his preparatory work for writing his *Political Arithmetic*, he states that "vecture by water is but from 1/12 to 1/20 cheaper than by land *caeteris paribus*".[133] In *Political Arithmetic* itself, this is modified into the statement that "the charge of water carriage is generally but 1/15 or 1/20 part of land carriage".[134] In 1675 his correspondent Robert Southwell, who would, by this time, have been acquainted with Petty's manuscript of this work, provides a more specific formulation of this issue, in which he appears to be attempting to rationalise these same ratios:

> The ordinary proportion between ship and wheel carriage is about one to twenty, and of inland water-carriage to wheel carriage, as one to twelve. Wherefore we may generally say that land to water carriage is as about sixteen to one.[135]

Adam Smith was later to discuss these issues, though in terms of time rather than cost, primarily in connection with coastal navigation between Scotland and London.[136] Interestingly, his discussions suggest a very similar ratio of 17:1, and it may well be that Petty and Southwell also had such coastal, or short-run, navigation in mind in suggesting ratios in the 12 to 20 range, since, when it comes to long-distance maritime trade, the ratios they suggest are of a very different order. For example, Petty begins his paper on land carriage in grand style, with the claim that

[t]he water carriage of goods round about the globe of the Earth is but about double to the price of land carriage from Chester to London of the like goods.[137]

The ratio which he here implies – taken literally, around 140:1 – is perhaps not intended entirely as a mere rhetorical flight of fancy, since Southwell's paper explicitly suggests, in similar contexts, ratios of 60:1 and 75:1.[138]

Of particular interest is the fact that Petty breaks, to some extent, with this tradition of offhand quantification in a further statement, that "one horse can carry upon wheels as much as five upon their backs, and in a boat or upon ice, as twenty".[139] This statement is distinguished, above all, by the fact that, whether or not it is actually based on empirical evidence or experimentation, it is presented in a form which, at least implicitly, appeals to the authority of such 'scientific' methodology.[140] This highlights the fact that Petty's approach to the land–water cost ratio is exceptional in his writings on spatial-economic issues in the degree to which it assumes an abstract, or, at any rate, mechanical, character – an aspect to which we shall return in connection with his theory of locational rent.

4.1.5 Labour as a 'mobile factor of production'

Petty's spatial-economic analysis has now been placed in apposition to two of the components of the 'three-way interaction' at the heart of today's spatial economics, namely economies of scale (or, more broadly, the benefits of agglomeration) and transport cost minimisation. We now come to the third and final element, the movement of productive factors.

As already discussed in other contexts,[141] any attempt to establish an analogy between Petty's concept of the "principles of wealth" and the subsequent theory of factors of production has to be hedged around with so many qualifications that the term 'analogy' is strained to breaking point. Nevertheless, elements of the two bodies of thought retain one particular element of correlation even when all the more profoundly distinguishing characteristics are taken into account, and, as it happens, this remaining element of correlation comprises what is central in addressing their respective approaches to spatial-economic issues. This is the division of the components of the productive process, however conceived, into the categories of mobile and immobile, a division which is, naturally, of greater concern in the spatial-economic than in other fields of economic analysis.

The centralisation of the mobile–immobile distinction in the spatial analysis of both Petty and today's spatial economics has, despite the enormous differences in theoretical context, an attendant consequence which affects them both. This is that, despite the fact that both acknowledge, in principle, a threefold distinction of factors or 'principles' – labour, land, capital – the third element, capital, becomes, in practice, marginalised, resulting in a retreat from a threefold to a twofold perspective, in which labour and land embody, effectively almost exclusively, the properties of mobility and immobility.

The threefold approach in Petty's political economy has already been discussed in connection with his pioneering system of national income accounting;[142] his twofold approach is epitomised in his celebrated statement that "labour is the father and active principle of wealth, as lands are the mother".[143] While there was nothing particularly new in this last statement,[144] it is characteristic of Petty that he took it up and elaborated it in new ways; in particular, he attempted to define a 'par', or common standard of measure, between these two 'principles of wealth',[145] which have been termed, in this connection, "the two original factors of production".[146]

That the nature of capital is indistinctly conceptualised by Petty is unsurprising, given that this was to remain a problem in production theory for a further century and more. Capital was emphatically categorised as 'unproductive' by the Physiocrats; it was to a considerable degree conflated with inventory by Smith, as indicated by his continuing use of the term 'stock';[147] and even much of Ricardo's economic analysis can be plausibly represented in single-factor (labour-only) terms.[148] As for Petty's writings, it takes some searching even to locate capital at all, let alone to see how he perceives its role in production in relation to the primal pair of labour and land. His category of "money and other personal estates", in his national income accounts, combines rent on housing with items such as "money, plate, jewels and fine furniture".[149] Such lists, of which there are a number of examples,[150] thus exclude capital in production. For instance, they exclude the eponymous element of capital, namely cattle, despite the prominence which they and other livestock occupy in his writings.[151] Only in his final *Treatise of Ireland* is there a clear reference to physical capital in explicit association with the process of production, in his category of "goods not fit to be brought into England or to be used in the cattle trade".[152]

Turning from physical capital to Petty's perception of the credit system, it has already been seen that his views on interest and exchange were linked with the level of, and expectations of, conflict rather than with the degree of exploitation of factors of production.[153] He displays the same conflictual perspective in his concept of a bank, a term which, for him, is synonymous with a war chest, or a "stock for war".[154] This reflects the fact that the 'banking' of large sums of money remained, in his time, closely identified with the state's fiscal-military arrangements, as was to be confirmed seven years after Petty's death by the formation of the Bank of England in 1694, the stated purpose of whose funds was "the carrying on the war against France".[155]

Petty had, in short, "only a vague conception of capital".[156] This has led to the character of his economic thought being described as "pre-capitalist",[157] on the basis that he showed "no systematic conception of capital and profitability",[158] capital and accumulation playing "no clear role" in his thought.[159] Further research has, to some extent, modified this conclusion, finding elements of capitalistic calculation in his primitive concept of opportunity costs, or "stock lying dead".[160] It is even possible to find, with some imagination, the concept of circulation of capital, in his plan to pay workers at his iron foundry in Ireland in iron ore, which has been aptly dubbed an 'ore model';[161] the term 'ore-ore' model would be even more appropriate. All such intimations of the category of capital, whether in production or circulation, are, clearly, secondary, however, and, in effect, Petty's economic analysis focuses almost entirely on land and labour alone.

The same effective adoption of a twofold, rather than a threefold, approach is, naturally, reflected in the distributional categories corresponding to Petty's 'principles of wealth'. The most immediate manifestation of this is the conflation of profit with rent, two categories whose differentiation was as yet indistinct in the "emerging agrarian capitalism" of the time.[162] As a consequence, it is "characteristic of early classical political economy, both in England and in France, that surplus is first clearly seen in the context of the rent yielded by agricultural land",[163] and, consequently, a separate distributional category of profit is as yet indistinctly identified; profit is "not yet separated from rent",[164] or is, at any rate, "eclipsed by rent".[165]

Both capital and profit are, thus, largely absent from, or, at the most, peripheral to, Petty's discussions of production in general, an absence which is clearly a consequence of the embryonic stage of the development of capitalism itself in his time. In the spatial economics of today, in contrast, the assumption of a two-factor world without capital, and in many cases a single-factor ('Ricardian') world with labour alone, is adopted, as will be seen, explicitly and avowedly, for the sole purpose of facilitating the procedure of mathematical modelling, with labour and land doubling up as 'metaphors' for mobile and immobile factors in general.

In any event, the outcome is the same: capital is elided from the analysis, resulting in a twofold, rather than a threefold, categorisation of the factors of production, or 'principles of wealth'. Those that are mobile are thereby reduced from two to one, and the question of the 'movement of productive factors', however conceived, becomes identical with the question of the movement of labour only.

4.1.6 The spatial-economic logic of Petty's population transfer scheme

Petty's spatial-economic analysis has now been placed in apposition to all three elements of what is represented, in today's spatial economics, as the 'three-way interaction between increasing returns, transport costs and factor mobility'. This 'three-way interaction' may now be reviewed as a whole, in the form in which it appears in Petty's writings, showing how relentlessly the logic of this interaction drove him towards ever greater conviction in the potential benefits of his population transfer scheme.

Petty was not the first early modern writer to raise the question of extending spatial-economic analysis into the field of policy, and as early as

1650 his proposal for a compacting of England's population had already been anticipated by a pamphleteer named Henry Robinson, who suggested it as a means to counter the waste of transport resources in the clothing trade. Robinson called attention to the fact that wool was being conveyed to London for sale as a raw material, then out to the various cloth-making districts for processing and weaving, only to be transported back to London again as cloth for sale as a final good. He suggested, as an alternative to the transport of intermediate goods "to and fro" in this way, "that the people set up their habitations in such places, where these unwrought materials are to be had cheapest", and went on to draw more general conclusions on the advantages of compactness:

> To make all things alike plentiful with all people throughout the land, it is necessary to reduce, as much as may be, all straggling tenements, villages and towns, together into so many cities, nearer to one another, that there may be people enough of each trade, calling and occupation, for supplying one another's occasions within themselves, with whatsoever shall be commodious and necessary both for their own sustentation, and in order to advancing the inland trade of the nation.[166]

Furthermore, Robinson associated such compactness with the advantages of Holland, drawing attention to that country's dense inland navigation network, and calling for improvements to that of England in terms almost identical to those used by Petty in his *Treatise of Taxes*, written a decade later.[167] Petty's policy proposals for compacting the population were thus, like so many other aspects of his economic thought, an elaboration of ideas which were already 'in the air' in his time.

The spatial-economic logic underlying Petty's population transfer scheme is represented in tabular form in Table 4.3. This table reflects the fact that, for a given unit of a commodity, the minimisation of total transport costs, which will here be defined as T, can be broken down (by the 'multiplication rule') into the two separate problems of, first, minimising the cost of transport per unit of distance, or mileage cost, defined as t, and, secondly, minimising the distance across which the commodity is transported, defined as d, thus:

$$T = d.t \Rightarrow min\ (T) = min\ (d.t) = min\ (d).\ min\ (t)$$

The first problem, then, is to minimise mileage cost, whether in respect of land or water carriage, which will now be defined, respectively, as t_L and t_W. The first means to this end is, as indicated in Table 4.3, the improvement of means of conveyance. As already discussed, inland navigation vessels and, to a lesser extent, wheeled vehicles were the subject of considerable attention from Petty from a technological point of view. In this, they are different from porterage (i.e. transport on foot), the droving of livestock and packhorsing, since he does not regard any of these as susceptible to improvement. Accordingly, the mileage

Table 4.3 The spatial-economic logic of Petty's final scheme

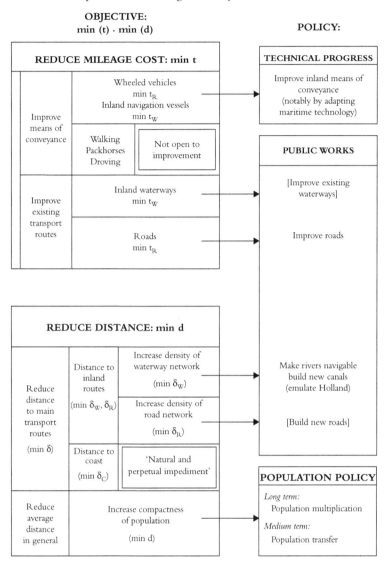

cost is here defined, differently, as τ, whose value is constant in each case. Even these modes of conveyance did not escape Petty's relentless theorising, however. For example, he contends, on the basis of some rather laborious geometry, that "man in his motion or gression…supporteth a greater weight upon less footing than any other sort of animal".[168] As for the droving of livestock, he interestingly assumes it to be costless (τ = 0); indeed, in the case of a horse, transport costs are negative (τ < 0), since it is "such a commodity as will carry both himself and his merchant to the market, be the same never so distant".[169] He also includes packhorsing in some of his discussions of the mechanics of transport,[170] though with no indication that he regarded this or any other of these more humble means of conveyance as open to technological improvement.

The second means of minimising mileage cost (min (t)) is to improve inland transport routes, both in respect of roadways (min (t_R)) and waterways (min (t_W)). In this connection, Petty repeatedly calls for "employing our idle hands about mending the highways, making bridges, causeways and rivers navigable",[171] his concern for such improvements being, more than once, linked to the facilitation of the import of livestock from Ireland.[172] Here, Table 4.3 makes a distinction, which is logically present, though not made explicit, in Petty's writings, between, on the one hand, improving existing routes (i.e. contributing to the minimisation of t) and, on the other hand, constructing new ones (i.e. contributing to the minimisation of the average distance to main transport routes), a distance which will now be defined as δ, and differentiated, in the case of the waterway and roadway networks, respectively, into $δ_W$ and $δ_R$.

The prominence which Petty gives, in his discussions of fiscal priorities, to the call for the improvement of the inland waterway network has led one commentator to include him among the pioneers of the 'canal lobby' which was to motivate the large-scale canal-building projects of the following century.[173] Petty's calls for transport route improvement are somewhat perfunctory, however, by comparison with other elements of his approach to spatial-economic issues. In particular, he displays no interest in the technology of canal and road building, despite the topicality of these issues in his time,[174] in strong contrast to his close involvement in the technological aspects of maritime transport, and, to a lesser extent, the technology of inland means of conveyance. Nor does he provide the kind of cost–benefit analysis that is characteristic of his more enthusiastic policy proposals. His only comment on the immediate economic aspects of the matter is a passing allusion to the fact that "in some places tolls are taken upon passage over bridges, causeways, and ferries built and maintained at the public charge".[175] Such tolls are, he states, among the "smaller ways [of taxation] which I have observed in several places of Europe", though he does not explicitly advocate their imposition in England, as Smith was later to do.[176]

This half-heartedness in Petty's approach to the improvement of inland navigation routes may perhaps reflect a conflation of this issue with the closely related subject of the advantages of Holland, bringing the whole question, in his eyes, almost entirely into the natural – in other words, geographical – sphere. For, although he nowhere explicitly mentions Holland in connection with his calls for the improvement of inland waterways, they must clearly have been encouraged, if not inspired, by the memory of that country's "rivers, dikes, bridges, wharves, cranes, carriage",[177] and, however much $δ_W$ was, in this case, reduced by the artificial means he lists, its initial low value was clearly a natural endowment.

An associated issue which preoccupied Petty, and which also inevitably suggests comparisons with Holland, is the question of how to quantify a country's average distance to the coast, which will now be defined as $δ_C$. This question effectively overlaps with that of the density of the inland waterway network, since, "from the point of view of inland navigation, the sea becomes merely a river round England",[178] while, in the case of Holland, the two questions coincide to an even greater degree, due to the peculiar nature of that country's irregular coastline, with its inlets and inland seas. Indeed, Holland's coastline, taken together with its situation on three major navigable rivers and its dense canal network, gives it such an advantage in respect of waterborne transport that Petty comments that, in that country, "there is scarce any place of work or business one mile distant from a navigable water".[179]

Petty thus suggests that, in the case of Holland, the maximum value of both δ_W and δ_C is one mile. This value is clearly not related to any actual calculation, but, nevertheless, the mere fact that this aspect of its advantages could be expressed in quantitative terms in this way was evidently enough to suggest to him the idea of devising a calculation that could quantify the equivalent situation in England and France. In the case of δ_C, he suggests the method of dividing the area of the country (A), in square miles, by the length, in miles, of its shoreline (C), thus:

$$A / C = \delta_C$$

His conclusion is that "every part of England, Scotland and Ireland is one with another but twelve miles from the sea", with the equivalent distance (i.e. δ_C) in the case of France being about 65 miles.[180] It has been suggested that this form of calculation was in fact devised by Petty's correspondent Southwell, who included it in a paper on water transport delivered to the Royal Society in 1675,[181] but by that time Southwell would have been acquainted with Petty's formulation,[182] and it is most likely the product of the discussions between Petty and other members of the Royal Society which had already resulted in the publication, in 1674, of his *Discourse of Duplicate Proportion*.[183]

In any event, Petty's calculations draw attention to the inescapable realities of physical geography and the limits these set on a country's water transport possibilities (thus, for France, $\delta_C = 65 = $ const.), and it is here that he sees insuperable obstacles to the further development of France's sea power, due not only to its high δ_C but also, to make matters worse, to a lack of deep water ports on the northern coast, and other negative features of its maritime geography with both commercial and strategic consequences.[184] For such obstacles to a country's 'greatness' he coins the term "natural and perpetual impediments", in contrast to the impediments faced by England, which, he argues, are "contingent and removable".[185]

Of Petty's calculations, it has rightly been observed that "it is not the accuracy or inaccuracy of these statements that matters, but the very fact that they were made",[186] reflecting, as they do, the increasing topicality of coastal navigation among writers on economic affairs. Indeed, the same assessment applies, equally, to the associated topic of inland navigation, and Petty's writings reflect a dawning awareness of the possibilities for the transformation of England's transport system that could be realised by an extension of its network of inland waterways, a development whose subsequent course was to lower δ_W substantially in some areas of England, though constrained by the 'natural and perpetual impediments' of its geography, as illustrated in Figure 4.1.

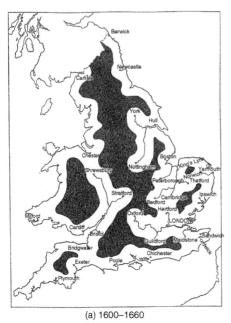

(a) 1600–1660

(b) 1660–1700

Figure 4.1 Reduction in distance to navigable water

Note: The shaded areas, where the distance to navigable water is more than 15 miles, decrease substantially in parts of England in the seventeenth and eighteenth centuries.

Source: Willan 1936: frontispiece and 32. By permission of Oxford University Press.

In short, all possible means for minimising t_W, t_R, δ_W and δ_R were, at one time or another, of interest to Petty. They presented little possibility for a medium-term, let alone a short-run, impact on the overall transport cost minimisation problem, however, and it was this which impelled him to turn, instead, to the alternative solution of compacting the labouring population.

As Goblet comments, in a statement with wide-ranging theoretical resonance:

> Petty, who was, at the same time, both economist and geographer, and a precursor of anthropogeography as much as of political economy, recognised that the constant obstruction placed by nature in the way of the development and efficiency of human activity is distance. And, since he sees no practical mechanical means to lessen the duration of transport, to bring nearer in time the parts of the state which are dispersed across space, to place in easy contact the producer and the consumer, the factory and the market, he seeks to suppress or deflect the effects of this insurmountable obstacle.[187]

Goblet adopts the term 'anthropogeography' from the nineteenth-century German nationalist geographer Friedrich Ratzel, whose work had subsequently been reformulated in unrestrainedly populist terms by the founders of Geopolitik, notably Karl Hofhauser, and, eventually, incorporated into the propaganda of Nazism.[188] Goblet's aim was to recapture what he saw as the positive achievements of Ratzel for the liberal intellectual tradition. The outcome of this project was, ultimately, disappointing theoretically,[189] and remains stranded in these intellectual episodes of the past. The fact that his *magnum opus* on Petty was never translated into English doubtless contributed to this lack of impact of his work within the field of geography in general. What is most regrettable in the present context, however, is one particular consequence associated with the neglect of Goblet's work, which is that it has resulted in a missed opportunity to bring the legacy of English colonialist thought into consideration in the context of issues lying at the interface between geography and economics; the concept of 'space-time compression' is one obvious example.[190]

Such wider theoretical implications must, here, be set to one side, however, in order to sustain the focus on the immediate logic which brings Petty's writings into apposition with today's spatial economics. To return, then, to the problem of how to compact economy and society, one solution, for Petty, was to search for ways to raise the population through increased fertility, and he accordingly displayed great interest in the problem of how to devise policies for such 'multiplication' of the population.[191] Such policies clearly remained a long-term measure only, however. It was in this way that the entire logic of his spatial-economic analysis drew him steadily towards what, thus, appeared as a comparatively short cut to achieving the same goal: the policy of the inward transfer of population from Ireland to England.

In retrospect, this spatial-economic logic underlying Petty's population transfer scheme might be assessed as a mere assertion of what is inescapably obvious, given his perception of the relation of productivity to compactness. To make such an assessment would be to draw too close a parallel, however, with the economics of today, when 'assumptions' and economic principles are simply a matter of formal, or mathematical, logic. For Petty, in contrast, the scheme was founded upon a number of assumptions which were, in fact, by no means simple to formulate, let alone self-evident, in his time, and both his writings and their biographical background show how deeply rooted were the problems with which he had to wrestle, over a period of decades, before he could eventually arrive at the solution offered in his *Treatise of Ireland*. Of these problems, three may be singled out for particular attention.

First of all, the scheme is based on the idea that the labouring population can, or should, be perceived as a mobile 'principle of wealth' (or 'factor of production') separate from the land. This was no mere formal assumption, in the manner of today's modelling devices, but, on the contrary, was an element in his gradual shift from a neo-feudal to a proto-capitalist perspective.[192]

Secondly, his scheme involved, of course, a reversal in direction not only of the Cromwellian 'transplantation' policy but of the entire drift of England's colonial policy in Ireland, since Tudor times and before. Despite the increasingly evident fact that the requisite body of adequately capitalised colonists was never going to materialise, it seems that, even for so determinedly eccentric a thinker as Petty, these traditional colonialist habits of thought died hard, and slowed down the process whereby he turned to his scheme in earnest.

A third idea was also necessary for his scheme to take its final form; this was that the agrarian economy can, or should, be susceptible to 'splitting' into its two basic components, the agricultural and the pastoral. The process through which Petty arrived at this idea was just as prolonged and contradictory as in the case of the other habits of mind which weighed down on his spatial-economic analysis. It was only gradually that he abandoned the initial assumption that the agrarian economy may be regarded as a single-product, single-sector homogeneous whole, with an output assumed to be, simply, corn. The convenience of this assumption for his efforts to construct a theory of value and distribution may also have contributed to obscuring, for him, the agriculture–pastoral distinction, familiar though it had been in much of the English writing on Ireland since Tudor times,[193] and, as his papers show, it was not until within a year of his death that he hit upon the idea of exploiting this distinction in connection with his scheme.[194]

It was, above all, it seems, this last principle – the application of the agriculture–pastoral distinction – which, for him, finally clinched the logic of his scheme. For, by providing this distinction with the new twist which it now received, he considered that he had found a solution to the problem of what to do with Ireland once it had been vacated of the Irish. He could now represent his scheme in terms of what Goblet describes as the "two utopias of Ireland-ranch and greater London, the most remarkable diptych of human geography of any that was contrived prior to the twentieth century".[195]

Thus convinced that his scheme could, at last, be definitively divested of the character of a 'dream or reverie' and reformulated "on lines which he hoped would secure the Royal approval",[196] Petty was thrown into the final frenzy of calculation that was to occupy the last months of his life, as preserved in the text of his *Treatise of Ireland*, that grizzly swansong to a lifetime of metromanic theorising.

4.2 From Petty to von Thünen

4.2.1 Petty and locational rent

The foregoing outline of Petty's approach to spatial-economic issues has provided ample illustration of his practice of embodying economic concepts in concrete and immediate form, a prime example being the embodiment of his compactness concept in the advantages of a specific country, namely Holland. Furthermore, it has also been illustrated how this approach places constraints on his economic thought, in the sense that it ties down his analytical method to such a low level of abstraction that decades of wide-ranging and determined analysis were required to struggle through to the formulation of propositions which, in retrospect, appear self-evident and non-problematical – notably that labour could be transferred, in the manner of a 'mobile factor of production', that the direction of the Cromwellian 'transplantation' scheme could be reversed and that the agrarian economy could be 'split' into its two basic subsectors, the agricultural and the pastoral.

All this seems to contradict the suggestion that Petty be credited with "the isolation of economic factors from their broader context",[197] and, certainly, this suggestion does not apply to his economic thought as a whole. As has already been noted in the case of his approach to the land–water cost ratio, however, there are cases when he finds it more straightforward to detach his economic analysis from the broader social context and formulate it in terms of abstract, logical relationships derived from mechanics. In what follows, this other, more 'deductive', face of Petty's economic thought will be further explored, first in connection with the same example of the land–water transport cost ratio and, secondly – and more significantly – in the case of his spatial-economic perspective on rent.

It is, of course, only in the most hypothetical sense that generalisations can be made regarding the land–water transport cost ratio ($t_L : t_W$), and, accordingly, the occasions when Petty turns to mechanical formulations in this connection are precisely those in which his mode of analysis is seen at its most abstract. For to express the ratio in this way implies, first of all, abstraction from the facts of geography; for example, in the above formal presentation, the subscript W does not differentiate between maritime, coastal and inland navigation. Secondly, there is abstraction from the conflictual and other 'real-life' aspects of economic relations – aspects which are, elsewhere, as central to his discussion of transport costs as they are to any other aspect of his economic thought, as has been seen in his frequent allusion to the impact on transport of the prevailing situation of mercantile warfare internationally and domestic insecurity. Such a conflictual context clearly makes it impossible to assume that $t = \underline{t} = $ const. Consequently, distance alone (d) cannot serve, to any reasonable extent, as a means of calculating total transport costs (i.e. $T = t.d$).

It is true that, in formal terms, there is nothing to stop us simply adding a parameter for the level of conflict, κ, where $\kappa \geq 1$, and $\kappa = 1$ indicates zero conflict, so that

$$T = \kappa.t.d$$

Petty does not regard the economic effects of conflict as open to expression in quantifiable terms, however; as he states in another context (a discussion of the Restoration land settlement in Ireland), his conclusions are reached by "omitting the angry part of the efficient and final causes of this settlement, as not reducible to number, weight, and measure".[198] It is, in contrast, precisely on the basis of the omission of "the angry part" that he addresses the issue of the land–water transport ratio, effectively making the hidden assumption of a zero conflict situation, where $\kappa_L = \kappa_W = 1$, so that

$$\kappa_L.\ t_L.d:\ \kappa_W.\ t_W.d$$

is reduced to simply

$$t_L:\ t_W.$$

The same result is obtained, of course, even when $\kappa_L = \kappa_W > 1$ (in other words, a situation in which domestic and international conflict levels are equal at a non-zero level). To bring such a hypothetical situation into consideration, however, is to strain the logic of his discussions of the land–water cost ratio too far, since conflict is nowhere raised by Petty in this particular context; rather, this is clearly an issue which induces him to make a no-conflict assumption pure and simple. Thus, when he equates the cost of land transport from Chester to London with "water carriage round about the globe of the earth",[199] he is evidently abstracting both from civil insecurity in England[200] and from a host of international maritime issues relating to the respective sea power of the rival European powers. In what follows, then, we follow Petty in thus abstracting transport issues from their conflictual and other immediately contingent context, and pursue further some of the more formal and deductive elements of his spatial-economic analysis.

General abstract statements on the transport cost component of price, particularly as they relate to the land–water cost ratio, were 'in the air' in Petty's time. The French Jesuit geographer Georges Fournier writes in his 1643 work on 'hydrography':

If we had to go by land to the Moluccas to fetch spices, or even just to Spain to get raisins, olives and figs, they would reach us as a more costly item than the gold of Potosi or the pearls of the Persian Gulf, and an orange brought from Portugal by land would cost more than a capon.[201]

In formal terms, singling out just the case of the orange and the capon, Fournier's proposition may be represented as a simple additive relation between the price of an orange in Portugal (p_{OP}), the price of a capon in France (p_{CF}), the mileage cost of the transport of an orange by land (t_{OL}) and the distance from Portugal to France (d_{PF}); thus

$$p_{OP} + t_{OL}.d_{PF} > p_{CF}$$

Petty's correspondent Southwell makes a comment that is similarly replete with possibilities for deductive spatial-economic analysis when, in the course of a light-hearted, though theoretically fascinating, exchange on the price of fish, he states: "If Wat Waller's sturgeon were caught in the Thames, I dare say it was worth more than 5 taken in the Elbe, or 15 taken at Archangel."[202] This proposition neatly illustrates what is perhaps implied by Fournier, but not in such an explicit manner, which is that the transport cost element of price may, more conveniently, be expressed in multiplicative terms, so that, with subscripts T, E and A representing the Thames, the Elbe and Archangel, respectively, we have

$$p_T = 5p_E = 15p_A$$

The quantities 5 and 15 may, alternatively, be represented in reduced form by the parameter T, in which case we can use the following general function for the price at location r of a good produced in I locations:

$$p_r = T_{ir}p_i$$

Thus, in the case of the sturgeon caught in the Thames, there are zero transport costs, a situation that is represented by $T_{TT} = 1$. One caught in the Elbe has a high value of T ($T_{ET} = 5$), and in Archangel it is higher still ($T_{AT} = 15$).[203]

It is typical of Petty that he does not rest content with discussing the transport cost component of price in such general terms but also extends his analysis into issues of more general significance for economic theory, notably rent. In particular, he addresses the issue subsequently expressed by Smith in the statement that "land in the neighbourhood of a town gives a greater rent than land equally fertile in a distant part of the country".[204] Accordingly, the concept now indicated by the term 'locational rent' has been widely attributed to Petty, as yet another in the list of his 'anticipations'.[205]

A prime example of Petty's approach to this issue is contained in his elaborate proposition on the conditions for profitability of agricultural production around a central town. The town he selects is, unsurprisingly, London, the agricultural area being the five surrounding counties, "the shires of Essex, Kent, Surrey, Middlesex and Hertford next circumjacent to London", an area which may, for convenience, be assumed to have a radius of about 18 miles.[206] "Provisions," he states, effectively homogenising these to a single agricultural product (implicitly corn[207]), "must be cheaper or dearer as the way to London was more or less long, or rather more or less chargeable." In other words, the distance from London of, say, location r is d_{rL} ("more or less long") and unit transport cost per mile t_i ("more or less chargeable"). Thus, if the price obtaining at r is p_r, the price of that location's product in London (P_{rL}) is

$$P_{rL} = p_r + t_r.d_{rL}, \text{ where } d_{rL} \leq 18$$

He then extends the discussion to embrace a further area lying beyond the five 'circumjacent' counties, which may be represented as the J locations, such that $d_{jL} > 18$. If, he now goes on to ask, the five-county (18-mile radius) area "did already produce as much commodity as by all endeavour was possible, then what is wanting must be brought from afar, and that which is near advanced in price accordingly". Here he confronts the equalisation of prices, such that, for example, in the case of locations r and s in the five-county and further area, respectively, we have

$$p_r + t_r.d_{rL} = p_s + t_s.d_{sL} = P_L'$$

and, since $d_{sL} > d_{rL}$, we have (assuming $t_s \geq t_r$)

$$P_L' > P_L$$

Thus far, we have not addressed the question of how the multiple prices P_{iL} are unified into a single price P_L (and, similarly, how P_{jL}' are unified into P_L'). Unification of prices is made possible, however, by Petty's introduction of the element of quantity – i.e. in the phrase "as much commodity". This allows prices in each location in each area (p_i and p_j) to be weighted by the quantity produced there (q_i and q_j), where total output is

$$Q = \Sigma q_i + \Sigma q_j$$

giving a weight in the case of, say, locations r and s of q_r/Q and q_s/Q. This gives us a new definition of P_L' as follows:

$$P_L' = 1/Q \left[\Sigma q_i.(p_i + t_i.d_{iL}) + \Sigma q_j.(p_j + t_j.d_{jL}) \right]$$

There is an alternative to such 'imports' and the concomitant rise in price from P_L to P_L', however. This is to increase the productivity of the land within the five-county area itself by means of 'improvements'; he gives a list of these, all of which are achieved by increasing the input of labour, or "by greater labour than now is used",[208] namely

> digging instead of ploughing, setting instead of sowing, picking of choice feed instead of taking it promiscuously, steeping it instead of using it wholly unprepared, and manuring the ground with salt instead of rotten straw, etc.

Petty goes on to stipulate two conditions for the profitability of introducing such improved methods. To express these conditions in formal terms, we begin by noting that labour and land are effectively the sole 'factor' inputs to cultivation, whether by unimproved or improved methods; assuming constant returns to scale in both cases,[209] this allows the amount (i.e. the price or wage) of labour required in location i to be expressed as the simple multiplicative expression

$$l_i.w_i$$

where w_i is the locational (hourly) wage and l_i is the amount of labour (in hours) required to cultivate one acre of land. The value of l_i, in the case when no improvements are made, is defined as l_o. Now, wages are, he strongly argues, to be held constant: "[T]he price of labour must be certain."[210] In other words, where unit locational wage costs are w_i and w_j, we have

$$w_i = w_j = \underline{w} = \text{const.}$$

We can now, accordingly, normalise $\underline{w} = 1$, so that $l_i.w_i$ becomes simply l_i.

The first of the two profitability conditions Petty stipulates is that the outcome must be such that "then will the rent be as much more advanced as the excess of increase exceeds that of the labour". Though phrased in an ungainly manner, this can be expressed, for location r, as the increase in rent (ΔR_r) due to the rise in yield per acre from q_{io} to q_i' as a result of the improved methods, thus:

$$\Delta R_r = p_r.(q_i' - q_{io}) - (l_r - l_o)$$

Petty then goes on to define a second and more elaborate profitability condition:

> The touchstone to try whether it be better to use those improvements or not is to examine whether the labour of fetching these things even from the places where they grow wild, or with less culture, be not less than that of the said improvements.

To express this in formal terms, we now simplify $t_r.d_{rL}$ and $t_s.d_{sL}$ to T_{rL} and T_{sL}, respectively (noting that the T parameter is here additive, not multiplicative – i.e. we still have Fournier's orange rather than Wat Waller's sturgeon), giving us the profitability condition for production in r rather than s, expressed in terms of prices, as follows:

$$(p_s + T_{sL}) \geq (p_r + T_{rL})$$

Now, Petty's category of rent is one from which, as has already been discussed, profit is as yet not differentiated,[211] and is, moreover – at any rate in the present context – entirely restricted to differential rent. From an absolute point of view, then, we are in a zero–profit, zero–rent situation,[212] and price of output (p_i) is identical with cost of production (l_i). We can thus express the above equation as

$$(l_o + T_{sL}) \geq (l_r + T_{rL})$$

Rearranging, and expressing $(T_{sL} - T_{rL})$ as T_{sr}, we have

$$T_{sr} \geq l_r - l_o$$

This is, then, Petty's 'touchstone' condition facing the producer in location r, who must balance the "cost of fetching" from s against the cost of introducing improvements in cultivation.

The differential nature of Petty's concept of rent in this context is shown in his reference to the further question of fetching products from "places where they grow wild". This may be expressed by positing a third area with K locations, where p_k go to zero at the limit. Then, to fetch such produce from location t in this further area, the producer in location s faces the profitability condition

$$p_t + T_{ts} \leq p_s$$

which, at the limit (i.e. as $p_t \rightarrow 0$), reduces to

$$T_{ts} \leq p_s$$

This train of thought of course brings to the fore the question of absolute rent. This issue is left hanging in the air, however; nor is this any great discredit to Petty's powers of analysis, considering that, even a century and a half later, the issue remained unresolved in the work of Ricardo, who was, moreover, to bequeath it not only to subsequent orthodox rent theory but profit theory also.[213]

We have now seen how Petty here concocts a kind of 'primordial soup', to which all subsequent theories concerned with rent and location can with justification trace at least some elements of their conceptual ancestry. Indeed, he here correlates a range of spatial and economic variables in a persuasive manner which, in purely formal terms, is probably better defined and more internally consistent than that other and more widely discussed 'soup': his value theory.[214]

4.2.2 Petty, von Thünen and beyond

In considering Petty's propositions on the effect upon agricultural rent of distance from a central town, we have arrived at the archetypal topic of spatial economics, for this same issue is precisely the starting point of von Thünen's seminal work of 1826, *The Isolated State*. The celebrated opening paragraph of that work posits an isolated town supplied by a surrounding agricultural area, with land rents reaching their maximum nearest the centre, where the most perishable crops, or those with the highest transport costs, are grown, and declining to zero at the outermost limit of cultivation. The outcome is that the agricultural landscape is configured in a pattern of concentric rings, each devoted to a particular crop or range of crops.[215]

The unrivalled profile enjoyed by von Thünen's 'model', in such few accounts as there are of the history of spatial economics, has resulted in the notion that the origins of the subdiscipline lie in a kind of primal bifurcation in economic theory: on the one hand, it is suggested, there developed an 'Anglo-Saxon' tradition of economics which, from Ricardo onwards, despatialised its analysis in favour of an exclusive focus on issues susceptible to definition in terms of time (interest, credit, and so on); on the other hand, there developed a 'Germanic' tradition, beginning with Von Thünen, which, conversely, detemporalised its analysis and focused on issues susceptible to definition in terms of physical space. This version of theoretical history originates in the work of Walter Isard,[216] the pioneer of the attempt to revive spatial-economic analysis in the 'Anglo-Saxon' world and founder of the discipline of 'regional studies', who famously criticised the marginalist tradition in its 'Anglo-Saxon' form for having created a "wonderland of no dimensions".[217] This perspective on the history of spatial economics remains current among the economic orthodoxy;[218] it is, for example, implicitly endorsed by Paul Krugman, though, as will be seen, he adds an extra leg to the narrative to give it his own characteristic spin, by claiming that the German theories were 'lost' until 'rescued' as a result of the 'increasing returns revolution'.[219]

By thus eliding the history of spatial-economic analysis before von Thünen, spatial economists are able to locate the theoretical origins of their subdiscipline entirely within the marginalist tradition. For von Thünen's theory may justly claim to be the first economic theory to be framed in marginalist terms, an assessment confirmed by no less an authority than Alfred Marshall, who states: "The term 'marginal' increment I borrowed from von Thünen" – in other words, not, as might have been expected, from Jevons or other early marginalist writers in the post-Ricardian 'Anglo-Saxon' tradition, but from the original 'Germanic' spatial economist.[220]

This seminal position of von Thünen's theory in the emergence of marginalist economics helps to explain the effortless manner in which it is commonly resolved into neoclassical terms by spatial economists, for this amounts to little more than marginalism reclaiming its own. His theory is, for example, readily credited with the neoclassical initial assumptions that "both producers and consumers have perfect knowledge and act perfectly rationally..., [and] behave in an optimal fashion", to assure "maximisation of profits" and "to minimise their outgoings in meeting their consumption needs".[221] In the same vein, other accounts credit the theory with illustrating "the simultaneous determination of goods and factor prices", "the ability of markets to achieve efficient outcomes",[222] interpolating further such anachronistic terms as "unplanned competition" and "perceived self-interest",[223] until, eventually, the theory is hailed as a classic example of how to model unintended outcomes in the economy based on convincing micro-foundations, or, to use Krugman's favoured expression, a model of 'micro-motives and macro-behaviour'.[224]

All this betrays an unquestioning assumption that the history of spatial-economic analysis lies solely within currents of thought which, like von Thünen's marginalist analysis, have contributed directly to the emergence of neoclassical economics, an assumption which is, of course, self-evidently in contradiction with the findings of the present study. Moreover, although the history of the subject prior to von Thünen is, admittedly, a sparsely populated field of research, there is, nevertheless, enough specialist literature to stand as a challenge to the casting of von Thünen in the role of unique founding father in the field. It has long been realised, for example, that explicit formulation of the idea of agricultural rent circles had already been 'in the air' for decades prior to von Thünen's work, the classic case being a passage in Sir James Steuart's 1769 *Principles of Political Economy*.[225] Nor is this passage unique; it was followed, some years later, by another such 'anticipation', evidently independent of Steuart's, in a paper by "an obscure surveyor and professor of mathematics at Buenos Aires" named Pedro Cerviño.[226] As for Petty, it is over a century since his editor noted that von Thünen was an economist "with whose aims Petty's thought exhibits much affinity",[227] while Goblet's extensive monograph of 1930, though it does not deal directly with parallels with von Thünen, at least draws attention to Petty's spatial-economic analysis in general.[228] Moreover, Cantillon has been described as "unquestionably a precursor of von Thünen",[229] and Isard's "conventional wisdom" concerning the "spaceless" character of the "Anglo-Saxon" tradition has also been explicitly challenged in connection with Smith's spatial-economic analysis, even provoking the comment that

> modern economists working in these areas [i.e. regional economics, etc.] remain cut off from the deepest traditions in their profession by the belief that their classical and neoclassical predecessors were little concerned with spatial matters.[230]

Far from responding to such challenges, however, the literature on the spatial-economy has in general been less ready than other branches of economic enquiry to take on board this earlier phase of the history of their predecessors' 'concern with spatial matters'.[231] For example, Petty's status as originator of the concept of locational rent, though widely acknowledged by historians of economic thought in general, has on the whole received little attention from spatial economists as such, and the few specialised studies concerning spatial aspects of classical political economy have hitherto received less attention than they deserve.[232] Indeed, there is a tendency to cut the history of their field even shorter than the post-von-Thünen period, to the extent that what remains is "often a total fixation on their own previous work", as has been acidly commented from within the field of economic geography.[233]

This retrospective incorporation of von Thünen into the theoretical heritage of the orthodoxy has the effect of obscuring what is actually new about his theory. For, as has now been seen, its innovative features do not lie in raising new questions, introducing new explanatory factors or drawing new conclusions, for, in all these respects, he had in fact long been anticipated by the 'Anglo-Saxon' William Petty; indeed, if there had been no von Thünen, it is possible to imagine that we might now be making do with Petty's 'circumjacent' counties round London as an alternative "brand name"[234] in the conceptual history of spatial economics. Rather, what is actually new in von Thünen's theory is that, even without the for-malistic makeover it receives in today's neoclassical expositions, it is already predicated upon an unprecedented degree of abstraction of both spatial and economic categories of analysis. This is clearly seen in the difference in the epistemological status of the concepts deployed by Petty and von Thünen in addressing the spatial component of rent. For Petty, despite the level of abstraction in his approach by comparison with other aspects of his own economic thought, there nevertheless remain numerous examples of how he embodies his propositions in immediate, or 'real', places and activities – London, Middlesex and other named counties, "digging instead of ploughing", and so on. This presents the strongest possible contrast to the world of von Thünen, who takes great pains to emphasise the abstraction of the logical relationships involved, with his featureless 'town' surrounded by an equally featureless 'plain', with constant fertility, constant transport costs, and so on. To describe such featurelessness, he chooses the term 'isotropic', which is, significantly, borrowed from physics (and chemistry), not from geography. Thus abstracted from any concrete historical, geographical or empirical reference, spatial economics, "as conceived by [von] Thünen, was deductive and abstract in its very foundations".[235]

Figures 4.2 to 4.7 neatly illustrate some of the steps involved in this long process of progressive abstraction. Petty's five-county area (Figure 4.2) is any-thing but geometrically regular, showing that our foregoing formal presen-tation, in terms of an 18-mile radius, was, to some extent, a caricature of the spirit of his discussion. Von Thünen's original diagram[236] (Figure 4.3), which, he says uninformatively, was "drawn by a friend of mine",[237] represents an enormous step forward towards abstraction of the issues involved, being, as it is, the first schematic diagram in the history of spatial-economic analysis.

Figure 4.2 The five counties "next circumjacent" to London

As listed in TTC: 51 §13 (showing today's boundaries, which have remained largely unchanged since Petty's time).

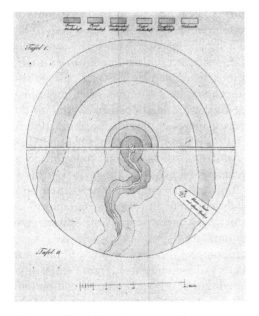

Figure 4.3 Von Thünen's original diagram

Source: Von Thünen 1826: bound in at end.

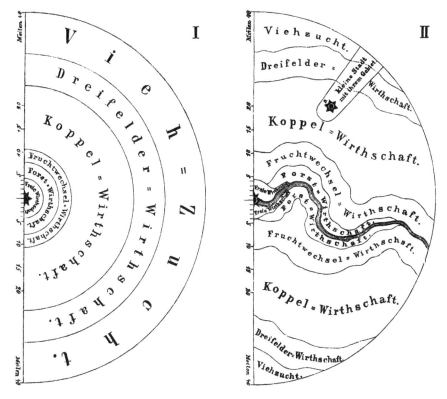

Figure 4.4 The diagram in the 1875 edition of von Thünen's work

Source: Von Thünen 1875: 390, 391. Reproduced from the 1966 reprint, by permission of the publishers, Wissenschaftliche Buchgesellschaft, Darmstadt.

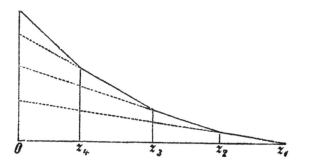

Figure 4.5 Launhardt's diagram, plotting distance against rent

Source: Launhardt 1885: 179, fig. 14.

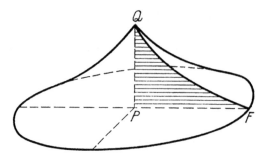

Figure 4.6 Lösch's three-dimensional 'demand cone' diagram
Source: Lösch 1954 [1940]: 106, fig. 21.

It is notable, however, that von Thünen's work was published by one of Germany's leading cartographic publishing houses,[238] the diagram being included as a fold-out sheet, bound in at the back, precisely in the manner of a map in a work of geography. It is therefore not surprising that the diagram still bears signs of its origin in the map, both in the provision of a scale, and also in the style of its depiction. This residual cartographic character is, in contrast, barely evident at all in the schematised version included in the post-humous edition of 1875, whose editor decisively transforms it from carto-graphic into diagrammatic form, as seen in Figure 4.4.[239] Ten years later, in an 1885 work by the pioneer mathematical economist Wilhelm Launhardt, the ultimate stage in abstraction is reached, whereby rent is placed on the vertical axis and distance on the horizontal, thus placing Cartesian space in graphical correlation with Euclidean, or physical, space (see Figure 4.5).[240] This form of representation was further elaborated by the 'location theorist' August Lösch in a discussion of the effect of location on demand, which he illustrated with a diagram of a 'demand cone', a three-dimensional figure with two horizontal (Euclidean) axes (see Figure 4.6).[241] This idea was sub-sequently adopted as a means of illustrating von Thünen's theory by a 'rent cone' (see Figure 4.7).[242]

This sequence of visual representations, combined with the foregoing dis-cussion of Petty's propositions on analogous issues, demonstrates that von Thünen's theory marked both the beginning of a new era in economic theory and also the culmination of a previous one. On the one hand, it has been seen that the fundamental categories of spatial-economic analysis upon which von Thünen draws were not generated within the marginalist tradition of eco-nomics pioneered by him, as hitherto widely assumed, but already had, on the contrary, a long and revealing pre-marginalist history. On the other hand, as has been illustrated graphically by the theory's progress from quasi-map to 'rent cones', it opened the door to yet further conceptual abstraction. This

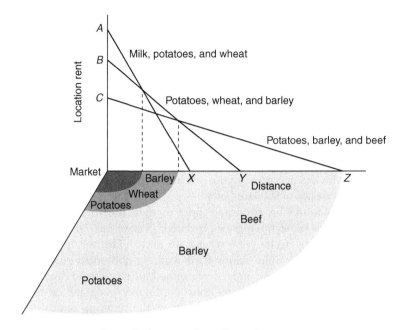

Figure 4.7 Von Thünen's theory in three dimensions

Source: Dicken and Lloyd 1990: 58, fig. 1.27. © 1990. Reprinted by permission of Pearson Education, Inc., New York, New York.

latter development will now be followed to its conclusion, by entering a world in which abstract geometrical landscapes do not, like von Thünen's concentric circles, merely represent spatial-economic relationships, but are actually generated by them.

4.3 Krugman's 'new economic geography' outlined

4.3.0 Introduction

The past 30 years or so have witnessed a (re)discovery of geography by economists. The 'new economic geography' advanced by Krugman and his associates is not the only initiative resulting from this development; it has been, however, "perhaps the best-known example".[243] An most elaborate exposition of this initiative was set out in a 1999 volume by Masahisa Fujita, Paul Krugman and Anthony Venables, entitled *The Spatial Economy: Cities, Regions, and International Trade*.[244] This work declares itself to be an addition to a succession of volumes emanating from a series of new developments in economics, described as "judiciously-timed monographs that endeavoured to synthesise each field into a coherent whole",[245] the fields in question having been industrial organisation, international trade and economic growth.[246] In adding spatial economics to this list, the 1999 volume claimed to have placed this field, for the first time, on solid micro-foundations, thus rendering it 'respectable' for the economic 'mainstream', and thereby initiating the 'fourth wave' of an 'increasing returns revolution'.[247] Whatever the success or otherwise of these aspirations, the profile of the initiative was certainly raised to a high level with the award to Krugman in 2008 of the 'Nobel Prize in Economics'.[248]

At any rate, the authors of the 1999 volume are justified – on their own terms, at least – in claiming that it "develops a common 'grammar'"[249] for much of the relevant neoclassical literature, and, in what follows, it provides a convenient framework for the discussion of the relation of that literature to equivalent aspects of the writings of William Petty.

The term Krugman and his associates apply to their initiative is controversial. In launching his project, Krugman declared: "I have chosen to appropriate the term 'geography' to describe what I am up to." This was in the full knowledge that his choice would "annoy hard-working traditional economic geographers".[250] These latter have indeed responded, often with undisguised irritation, by suggesting alternative names, most commonly 'geographical economics'.[251] Identification with particular currents in the resulting critical literature will, in what follows, be avoided by coining the pedantic, but neutral, acronym 'MCSE' – 'monopolistic competition spatial economics'; this follows a suggestion by a geographer who declares: "I will rename it the monopolistic competition approach to distinguish it from other conceptualisations of increasing returns."[252] The term thus has the added advantage of differentiating this particular initiative from other neoclassical forays into economic geography, such as those modelling regional growth and convergence.[253]

It will already be evident, from the high-flown language of the above-quoted claims of its proponents, that, in assessing MCSE's standing among economists and economic geographers, it is necessary to take account of the fact that "good marketing is certainly part of the story".[254] Although it would be perverse to suggest that good marketing necessarily entails bad economics, the salesmanlike manner in which the claims are advanced begs the question of whether the initiative's high standing is an imaginative figment of its own vigorous self-promotion rather than an indication that it has actually shown itself capable of passing the "test of the intellectual market place".[255] A review of the reception which MCSE has received from economists and economic geographers will be postponed to the next chapter of the present study, however; meanwhile, its main features will be presented in outline, to prepare for a comparative assessment of spatial-economic analysis as it exists in the neoclassical tradition and in the writings of Petty.

4.3.1 From Marshall to model

The declared aim of MCSE is "to explain concentrations of population and of economic activity", such as "the distinction between manufacturing belt and farm belt, the existence of cities, [and] the role of industry clusters", by means of models which capture the effects of the "three-way interaction" which has already become familiar in primitive form in the foregoing study of Petty's spatial-economic analysis, namely the interaction "among increasing returns, transportation costs, and the movement of productive factors".[256]

The forces at work in this spatial configuration of the economy can be categorised as centripetal and centrifugal. The classic reference for the centripetal category is a passage in later editions of Marshall's *Principles of Economics*, which foreshadows what were subsequently referred to collectively as 'positive locational externalities'; these, in turn, fall into the three subcategories of market size effects, knowledge spillovers and thick labour markets for specialist skills.[257] The countervailing centrifugal forces lack such a standard subcategorisation, but clearly include, on the supply side, the immobility of some factors of production (such as agricultural land, or labour in cases when there are barriers to migration) and, on the demand side, the advantages of access to dispersed markets, particularly in the presence of high transport costs; furthermore, high urban land rents or house prices may encourage dispersion, as also may negative externalities such as congestion and pollution.

MCSE does not aim to model this entire catalogue of centripetal and centrifugal forces but, rather, just singles out one of each. From the full, or Marshallian, range of centripetal forces, it singles out market size effects, in the form in which they were elaborated in the field of development studies in the 1950s and 1960s by Albert Hirschman and Gunnar Myrdal: the more economic activity becomes concentrated in a given location, the greater the market to which firms have immediate access (backward linkages) and the greater their access to local advantages in costs of production, such as cheaper intermediate goods (forward linkages).[258] From the possible range of centrifugal forces, MCSE singles out the (im)mobility of factors of production.[259] These two forces selected for modelling by MCSE – which are, together, termed 'pecuniary'[260] – thus represent only a selection from the wider range of centripetal and centrifugal forces, the reason for singling out these particular two being, first, that they can both be expressed formally in terms of the same parameters, and consequently equated in a way that captures the "tension", or "tug-of-war", between them, and, second, that both "are naturally tied to distance" (as "mediated by transportation costs") and are, hence, more immediately tractable to expression in spatial terms than the other items listed above.[261]

There is thus nothing conceptually new in the basic formulation of the centripetal and centrifugal effects incorporated in the MCSE models; nor, for that matter, do they constitute the first attempt to use these concepts as a 'hook' for the modelling of cumulative causation in the spatial configuration of the economy, as is freely acknowledged by Krugman.[262] Where MCSE does claim innovative status, however, is in modelling such cumulative causation on the basis of the standard assumptions of microeconomic theory. This has, so it is claimed, enabled MCSE to challenge orthodox neoclassical 'factor endowment' theory (as exemplified in the Heckscher–Ohlin model) more effectively than development theory had been able to do, since it challenges it on its own terms. Krugman acknowledges that development theory had, long since, anticipated MCSE in representing the presence of factors of production, along with the associated economic activity, as an outcome generated endogenously by their models, rather than being a result of 'natural' endowment. Nevertheless, so runs Krugman's argument, it is only MCSE which has rendered this insight acceptable within 'mainstream' economics, by finding a solution to what was formerly regarded as the intractability of cumulative causation to incorporation within the neoclassical framework. The breakthrough in this respect was made possible by advances in the modelling of monopolistic competition, as will now be explained.

4.3.2 The spatially adapted Dixit–Stiglitz (SADS) model of monopolistic competition[263]

The assumption of constant returns to scale in the presence of transport costs has the logical implication that it is in the interest of firms to disperse their production among an unlimited number of small local plants, to gain better access to raw materials and markets, a scenario that has been termed 'backyard capitalism'.[264] The fact that, on the contrary, firms normally concentrate their production in only one location, or a small number of locations, is evidently motivated by the advantages of scale economy. Modelling such scale economy is, in traditional microeconomics, almost synonymous with modelling monopolistic behaviour, yet at the same time a requirement of a model of spatial concentration is, clearly, that there should be free entry and exit of firms in response to locational market advantages, and these latter features are, in contrast, inseparable from the perfect competition model.[265] The resulting problem of how to reconcile the monopolistic and freely competitive elements of this situation was long regarded as technically insuperable. Eventually, however, a way of getting round the problem was developed in a model of monopolistic competition advanced by Avinash Dixit and Joseph Stiglitz in 1977,[266] and this model, in a spatially adapted version, is a "crucial ingredient"[267] of the MCSE modelling strategy.

The spatially adapted Dixit–Stiglitz (SADS) model considers, in its basic form, an economy with two sectors, agriculture and manufacture.[268] The agricultural sector is perfectly competitive and produces a single, homogeneous good; the manufacturing sector produces a large variety of differentiated goods. The 'action' takes place in the manufacturing sector, which consists of a large number of firms – so large, in fact, that they can be modelled as a continuum.[269] Each manufacturing firm produces a single good, individually differentiated from all others; they all have an identical production function, with equal fixed costs and a constant mark-up over marginal costs, and thus all benefit to an identical degree from scale economies in production.

Each good enters perfectly symmetrically into consumption, every consumer having an identical demand function, in which there is constant elasticity of substitution (CES) between all the manufactured goods; in formal terms, the utility function is $U = M^\mu A^{1-\mu}$, where M and A are manufactured and agricultural goods, respectively, and μ is the proportion of manufacturing in the economy as a whole. The demand for (the composite of) manufactures is represented by the CES function $M = [\Sigma m_i^\rho]^{1/\rho}$, where m_i are the individual manufactured goods, $\rho = {}^{(\sigma - 1)}/_\sigma$, and σ expresses the "intensity of preference for variety".[270] So central is the CES functional form to the modelling strategy that its proponents admit that their work "sometimes looks as if it should be entitled 'Games you can play with CES functions'".[271] Crucial, likewise, is the associated behavioural assumption that consumers value variety as well as quantity – or, in other words, that "a unit of a product that is not yet consumed is always preferred to an additional unit of a product that is already consumed".[272]

Deft choice of units enables increasing returns to be "hidden" in the number of firms, so that scale economies can be modelled entirely at the level of variety.[273] The process of cumulative causation leading to locational concentration thus takes the form of the movement of firms into a given location to benefit from economies of scale in production, which consequently increases the number of goods produced there, with resulting forward and backward linkages which, in turn, attract yet more firms. In this way, the model achieves the purpose of reconciling economies of scale and monopolistic behaviour at the level of the firm with the free entry and exit of firms in a given market along the lines of models of perfect competition and general equilibrium.[274]

Transport costs are modelled in 'iceberg' form: a proportion of each item transported simply melts away en route at a certain rate per distance; this is expressed by the parameter T, which represents the amount of a good dispatched per unit received.[275] This obviates the need for modelling a separate transport industry, and preserves the CES structure of the model.

The model thus allows its users to have their cake and eat it in a number of respects: firms have free entry to (and exit from) markets (i.e. locations), and yet benefit from increasing returns to scale when they get there; firm behaviour is monopolistic and yet not strategic or collusive; there are individual firms yet in such large numbers as to escape integer constraints; and there are transport costs, yet at the same time constant elasticity of substitution between all goods. The drawback is, of course, that the model is unrealistic in the extreme, and that to move from such a restrictive particular case to the extraction of generally valid results requires "at least some degree of faith".[276] Nevertheless, from the point of view of addressing the spatial economy in the framework of an integrated equilibrium analysis, its versatility certainly substantially exceeds that of former spatial-economic modelling strategies.

4.3.3 The core–periphery model

The application of the SADS model may be illustrated in the case of the simple core–periphery (CP) model, a "minimal model that shows how a two-region economy can become differentiated between an industrialised core and an agricultural periphery".[277]

In this model, there are two sector-specific factors: manufacturing workers and agricultural workers. Concentration of manufacture takes place through manufacturing workers moving between locations in response to locational real wage differences; agricultural workers are evenly spread and immobile. A CP pattern exists when all the manufacturing is concentrated exclusively in either one of the two locations; 'symmetrical equilibrium' exists when it is divided exactly evenly between them. The model considers the effects of changes in the parameters T, σ (or, alternatively, its transform ρ[278]) and μ on the sustainability or otherwise of the CP and symmetrical patterns.

The formal structure of the model consists of four pairs of equations, giving expressions for aggregate incomes, price indexes, wages and real wages in each of the two locations; this allows market size effects to be expressed in terms of a general equilibrium framework.[279] The 'price index effect' states that a location with a large manufacturing sector will have a lower price index for manufactured goods because a smaller proportion of its inputs bears transport costs.[280] The 'home market effect' states that locations in which there is a higher demand for manufactures will a more than one-to-one increase in manu-facturing output and will consequently also 'export' manufactured goods.[281]

It is variation in T which focuses much of the interest of the model, as may be seen in the 'tomahawk' bifurcation diagram[282] (Figure 4.8). This shows the effect of changes in T on the parameter λ, which denotes the share of manufacturing in one of the two locations, so that, for example, $\lambda = 1$ ($\lambda = 0$) indicates that location 1 (location 2) is a core, and $\lambda = \frac{1}{2}$ indicates symmetrical

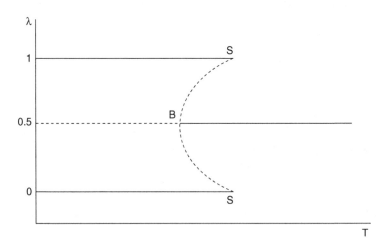

Figure 4.8 The 'tomahawk' diagram

Note: The effect of changes in transport costs (T) on the parameter λ, with sustain and break points shown as S and B, respectively.

Source: Adapted from Fujita, Krugman and Venables 1999: 68, fig. 5.4. © 1999 Massachusetts Institute of Technology, by permission of the MIT Press.

equilibrium. The parameter T not only functions as a proxy, or 'metaphor', for all transaction costs over space[283] but also doubles up as a reverse expression for time (T ~ -τ), on the assumption that there is a long-term tendency of transport costs to fall – or, from a historical point of view, modes of conveyance consist of "first caravels, then steamships and railroads, then air freight...".[284]

Transport costs are initially so high that no significant trade is possible between the two locations; firms located in one cannot compete with firms located in the other. In such a situation, the benefits of dispersion outweigh those of concentration; manufacturing is distributed symmetrically between the two locations, and this constitutes a stable equilibrium. As transport costs begin to fall, however, trade gradually becomes more feasible. Forward and backward linkages develop in whichever location gains an initial advantage, and a process of cumulative causation sets in: more firms move into the advantaged location to benefit from economies of scale in production there, leading to further intensification of the effect of the forward and backward linkages, which, in turn, attracts yet more firms. Eventually a new equilibrium emerges, in which manufacturing becomes concentrated exclusively in the advantaged location, which is termed, accordingly, the 'core', reducing the other location – the 'periphery' – to agricultural production only.

When transport costs are in the intermediate range, a complex system of stable and unstable equilibria exists, in which there are two critical points: a 'sustain' point (the point S in Figure 4.8), at which, as T falls, a CP equilibrium becomes sustainable; and a 'break' point (the point B in Figure 4.8), at which, as T falls even further, symmetrical equilibrium becomes no longer stable. In other words, these are, respectively, the points "at which a core–periphery geography *can* arise and under which it *must* arise".[285] Thus, with T taken to represent the reverse of τ, the 'tomahawk' diagram may be interpreted as displaying (from right to left) the 'history' of the sustainability of the CP pattern as transport costs fall over time.

All this illustrates that, in MCSE, as in other component elements of the 'increasing returns revolution', the equilibria considered are, characteristically, not unique, and, in many cases, are unstable and involve discontinuities. This differs from the situation in traditional general equilibrium analysis, in which such features are, in general, regarded as a 'nuisance', or at any rate confined to exceptional cases. For MCSE, on the contrary, it is precisely in the resulting 'structure of equilibria' that the 'action' in the models takes place.[286]

Turning from the effects of changes in T to changes in the parameters σ and μ, the results are less graphically distinctive, but no less essential to the logic of the model.[287] For this purpose, the expression for ω_1, or real wages in location 1, is normalised to 1. The expression for ω_2 is then differentiated with respect to T. Figure 4.9 shows how, when T = 1 (i.e. when transport costs are zero), $\omega_2 = 1$. At low values of T, $d\omega_2/dT < 0$, so that $\omega_2 < \omega_1$; there is, consequently, no motivation for workers to migrate from location 1 to location 2, so that concentration in the former is sustainable and the CP pattern is robust. As T increases further, an inflection occurs in the ω_2 curve as the benefits

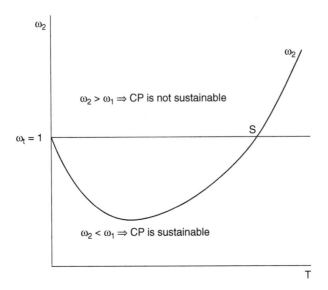

Figure 4.9 Locational real wage and core–periphery equilibrium

Source: Adapted from Fujita, Krugman and Venables 1999: 71, fig. 5.5. © 1999 Massachusetts Institute of Technology, by permission of the MIT Press.

of dispersion catch up on those of concentration; the point of intersection $\omega_2 = 1 = \omega_1$ represents the sustain point; beyond this, $\omega_2 > \omega_1$, so that workers in location 1 have an incentive to migrate to location 2, and the CP pattern is no longer sustainable.

The results of variation in the parameters μ and σ can be represented in terms of their effect upon the ω_2 curve. As μ increases, the forces for concentration increase and the ω_2 curve is stretched outwards; in other words, the range of values of T for which CP is sustainable increases. Conversely, as σ increases, the forces for concentration weaken, since consumers are less flexible in accepting a lower level of variety of manufactured goods; consequently, the ω_2 curve swings inwards, and the range of values of T for which CP is sustainable decreases.

A necessary condition for the existence of an inflection in the ω_2 curve is that the centrifugal forces can potentially outweigh the centripetal. This is not necessarily the case. Figure 4.10 shows a situation that can arise when the values of μ and σ are, respectively, sufficiently high and low that the forces for concentration outweigh those for dispersion for any value of T. In other words, producers may never have any motivation to move to location 2; there is no point of inflection in the ω_2 curve, the model collapses and all manufacturing becomes inevitably stuck in a 'black hole', with CP being the only possible configuration. To get round this problem, it is necessary to impose the "No-Black-Hole" condition that $\rho > \mu$.[288]

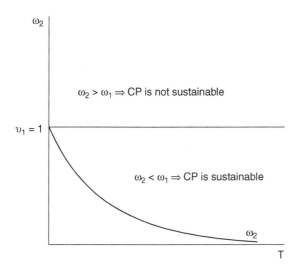

Figure 4.10 Violation of the "No-Black-Hole" condition

Notes: Centripetal forces always outweigh centrifugal effects, there is no point of inflection in the ω_2 curve, and core–periphery is the only possible pattern.

Source: Modified from Fujita, Krugman and Venables 1999: 71, fig. 5.5. © 1999 Massachusetts Institute of Technology, by permission of the MIT Press.

This diagrammatic analysis relates to the sustain point; analysis of the break point is more complex, and less susceptible to informal presentation.[289] One thing they have in common, however, is that, in both cases, the concept of symmetrical equilibrium plays an essential technical role in the underlying algebraic operations. This feature epitomises the lack of realism inherent in the MCSE modelling strategy, since an unstable equilibrium of this kind can be upset by the slightest perturbation – or, in other words, by even the most infinitesimal movement of production from one location to the other. In anticipation of subsequent critical analysis of MCSE, it may here be pointed out that the allotment of such a crucial role to such a fictitious concept illustrates the adverse effects of "trying to force increasing returns ideas into equilibrium models" in this way.[290] In fact, for all the claims to represent something 'new', "the ghosts of…equilibrium solutions still haunt much of his [Krugman's] analysis".[291] Certainly, in this case, "equilibrium conditions are smuggled in",[292] and the model remains as technically dependent upon notional equilibrium as the perfect competition models it purports to supersede.

4.3.4 Extending and elaborating the modelling procedure

The CP model has illustrated how transport costs affect the relations between locations in MCSE. This is only one among the family of MCSE models, however, which are differentiated from each other by the imposition of different initial

assumptions regarding the locational and inter-sectoral mobility of factors of production. For example, in the basic SADS and CP models, we had immobility of
agricultural workers and mobility of manufacturing workers between locations,
with each category of worker unable to transfer to the other sector; other models
may have different patterns, such as immobility of all workers between locations
but inter-sectoral transferability of workers within each location, and so on.

Besides models extending and elaborating the bifurcation structure exemplified in the CP model, a further family of MCSE models is based on mathematical
techniques developed by the biologist Alan Turing. Here, the economy takes the
form of a continuum of locations arrayed around the circumference of a circle
(hence, it is sometimes termed a 'racetrack economy'), with economic activity initially spread evenly among them (a situation referred to, in the international context, as a 'flat earth'). The key algebraic expressions are reformulated in dynamic
terms, which generate fluctuations; these perturb the initially even spread of economic activity and thus generate agglomerations. While this formal structure is, of
course, utterly distinct from that of the SADS model, it is used with great ingenuity
to explore some equivalent issues in a multi-location context,[293] enabling Krugman
to claim that MCSE has escaped the limitation of being, "like much of traditional
trade theory, stuck with 'two-ness' and all the limitations that implies".[294]

4.3.5 Urban models

The formal structure of the MCSE models has now been outlined. Their application takes place at three different levels of scale – the regional, the urban and
the international. It is the regional scale to which the above-outlined CP model
is, in the first instance, applicable, and, though its fundamental logic recurs in the
urban and international models, it has most immediate relevance to issues such
as the emergence of industrial and agricultural belts in the nineteenth-century
United States or Italy.[295] An outline will now be presented of the MCSE models
at the other two levels of scale – the urban and international.

MCSE urban models take up a number of issues that have long preoccupied urban economists: the formation of 'cusps' in the market, and how these
become 'locked in' to the spatial structure of the economy; the conditions under
which new cities can emerge, whether on the basis of such cusps in the market
or as a result of growth in a surrounding agricultural population; the formation
of an 'urban hierarchy' of towns of different sizes and types; the role of natural
advantages such as transport 'hubs'; and so on.[296]

The starting point of MCSE urban models is von Thünen's theory of agricultural rent,[297] whose exemplary synthesis of 'micro-motives and macro-
behaviour' makes it, in the eyes of the proponents of MCSE, quite simply "a
thing of beauty".[298] At the same time, however, it is, from their point of view,
only half a theory, and "arguably the less interesting half";[299] it shows how dispersion of economic activity takes place around a pre-existing centre, but not
how that centre came to be there in the first place. In the new economic geography, in contrast, cities are not "primitive concepts" but are generated endogenously by the models, unlike the situation in von Thünen's theory, which "simply

assumes the thing you want to understand: the existence of a central urban market".[300] It is claimed, in fact, that the new economic geography has supplied the missing half-theory that completes, or closes, that of von Thünen.

In addressing this issue of how centripetal forces can be modelled to explain the emergence of cities, MCSE applies an adaptation of the same analytical apparatus as has been illustrated in the case of the CP model. One illustration of its approach concerns a long-standing topic of spatial-economic analysis, which is a scenario in which, beginning from a monocentric ('von Thünen') situation, growth in the surrounding agricultural population results in some manufacturers 'defecting' to outlying areas, leading to the emergence of new cities;[301] in a two-dimensional model, these may be represented as two identical 'flanking cities', as shown in Figure 4.11. MCSE models this in terms of the sustainability of the monocentric pattern, allowing formal expression of, first, the critical level

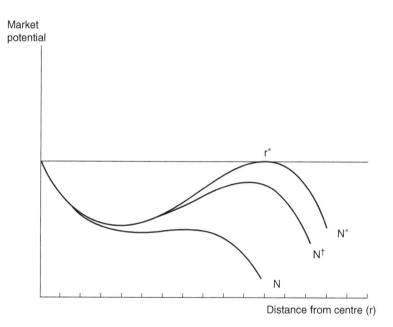

Figure 4.11 The emergence of flanking cities

Notes: The vertical axis represents 'market potential' as a function of σ, μ and transport costs (of both manufactures and agricultural goods). The horizontal axis represents distance from the centre (r). The market potential function is shown for ascending values of the population of the surrounding agricultural area (successively N, N' and N⋆). The point r⋆ shows the 'critical distance' at which firms 'defect' from the centre and a 'flanking' city emerges; this is equivalent to the break/sustain point analysis shown in the tomahawk diagram – i.e. it is the point at which monocentricity becomes no longer sustainable. Only locations to the right of the initial city are shown; the process is symmetrical to the left, where another 'flanking city' emerges.

Source: Adapted from Fujita, Krugman and Venables 1999: 142, fig. 9.4. © 1999 Massachusetts Institute of Technology, by permission of the MIT Press.

of population beyond which monocentricity becomes no longer sustainable and, second, the 'critical distance' at which new (or 'flanking') cities emerge. The claim of MCSE to innovative status, in this case as in the case of the CP model, lies in the fact that these long-standing elements of spatial economics are, for the first time, generated as the outcome of processes incorporated within a fully specified model of market structure.

The urban models go on to explore further possibilities for providing such micro-foundations for concepts previously existing in spatial economics. The Turing model is applied to a multi-centre (multi-city) situation, with the claim that this can provide micro-foundations for concepts pioneered in that field by the German location theorist August Lösch.[302] It is also shown how the emergence of a hierarchy of cities of different types and sizes, along the lines of the 'central place' theory advanced by another German writer, Walter Christaller, can be modelled by representing manufacturing as a number of separate industries, each with different transport costs and/or economies of scale.[303]

4.3.6 International models

Having now considered MCSE's regional and urban models, we turn, finally, to the international level. Here, countries are defined as locations between which labour is immobile; workers now 'migrate' not between locations but between the agricultural and manufacturing sectors,[304] so that "vertical linkages between upstream and downstream industries...play a role equivalent to that of labour migration" in the regional CP model.[305] Firms use each other's outputs as intermediate inputs, and it is now through the 'migration' of production between locations (i.e. countries), rather than the migration of labour, that forward and backward linkages develop. The resulting concentration of manufacture is modelled in terms of the same concepts of sustainability and symmetry breaking as in the CP model, with inputs modelled along the same CES lines as consumer demand, so that all firms use all goods as inputs and benefit from their variety. Now, however, a crucial direction of causation is reversed: in the CP model it is locational wage differences that 'drive' regional outcomes (i.e. the sustaining of concentration and the breaking of symmetry), whereas, at the international level, it is the behaviour of the firm which leads to the concentration of manufacture, and this outcome, in turn, 'drives' global inequalities in wages.

The resulting international models illustrate both the advantages and the limitations of the MCSE approach. The advantages are immediately evident in the new vistas that open up for formal modelling once the restrictions of the factor endowment (Heckscher–Ohlin) approach are lifted; in particular, the new approach provides a solution to the problem faced by factor endowment theory in the fact that a large proportion of international trade takes place between countries whose initial endowments are broadly similar.[306]

Furthermore, the models are applied with great virtuosity to capture effects observed in today's international economy which had previously been assumed to be impossible to model in formal terms; the claim is, in fact, nothing less than that MCSE provides a way of modelling 'globalisation'. To explain this claimed achievement, it is necessary to return to the basic CP model, which, it will be recalled, portrays the emergence of a core–periphery pattern as an inevitable historical outcome, as T falls over time. The inexorable and unidirectional nature of this movement is predicated, however, on the assumption of zero transport costs for the 'agricultural' good (i.e. the output of the periphery). If this assumption is lifted, there is not only an obvious gain in realism but also a fundamental change in the nature of the model, for it gives rise to new centrifugal forces which have the important result that the tendency towards concentration is no longer monotonic but is, on the contrary, liable to be reversed at sufficiently low levels of T,[307] as shown in Figure 4.12. This additional effect of continually diminishing transport costs occurs when T falls to a level at which firms which had previously been concentrated in the core location find it advantageous to 'defect' to the periphery and thus benefit from the lower wages there. In graphical terms, the tomahawk diagram of Figure 4.8 becomes the double tomahawk of Figure 4.12, and new break and sustain points emerge.

At the international level, this effect is held to underlie the "globalisation phase" of the recent era – in other words, the "reverse flow"[308] of manufacturing

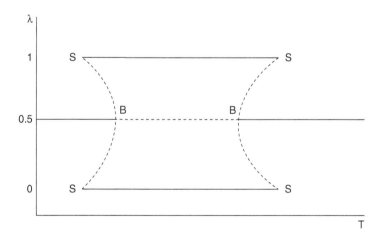

Figure 4.12 The 'double tomahawk'

Note: The progression towards a CP pattern is no longer monotonic, and may be reversed (by firms 'defecting' back to the periphery) at sufficiently low levels of T.

Source: Adapted from Fujita, Krugman and Venables 1999: 109, fig. 7.6. © 1999 Massachusetts Institute of Technology, by permission of the MIT Press.

activity from core countries to the global periphery. Since, in these international models, the concentration of manufacturing drives national wage differentials, this effect brings us to the heart of the approach of MCSE to the issue of global inequality.[309] The conclusion of the models is that the issue can be represented as an "inverted-U relationship", in which "declining trade costs first produce, then dissolve, the global inequality of nations".[310] In face of the continuing reality, and in many cases the exacerbation, of such inequality, it is admitted that the path towards ultimate 'factor price equalisation' does not benefit all peripheral countries synchronously; accordingly, further ingenious modelling is undertaken to suggest reasons why the catching-up process takes a "sequential and rapid" form, affecting individual countries in series, rather than being a gradual process spread evenly across the global periphery as a whole.[311]

4.3.7 MCSE and the liberalisation of international trade

MCSE has, then, opened up an expanded frame of reference in the formal modelling of the global economy, enabling it to address issues which were intractable to analysis in terms of traditional international trade theory. The limitations of the approach, on the other hand, may be illustrated in the case of the final model of the series presented in the 1999 volume. This model incorporates and extends conclusions drawn from a number of the other regional, urban and international models in the series, to explore the question of how international trade affects a country's internal economic geography;[312] it is, in fact, MCSE's showcase model, hailed by its proponents as "the most rigorous and complete assessment of the locational forces identified by the [MCSE] models".[313]

Unlike all the other models in the volume, this particular one explores the effect of lifting the "No-Black-Hole" condition; instead of this condition, a new parameter (δ) is introduced to indicate 'congestion diseconomy'.[314] A further feature which is unique to this model is that it is closely related to a particular empirical issue: that of changes in the location of manufacture in Mexico following alterations in that country's trade regime during the 1980s.[315] The previous era is depicted as one of an inward-looking economy, pursuing a strategy of state-driven import substitution; as a result, there is a high concentration of manufacture around Mexico City, which consequently suffers from a resulting high δ. Then, as trade liberalisation proceeds, culminating in the establishment of the North American Free Trade Agreement (NAFTA), the relative importance to firms of proximity to domestic customers and suppliers declines,[316] and Mexican industry begins to decentralise, with a trend towards relocation in regions bordering the United States. Thus, the growth of the openness of the Mexican economy is seen as eroding the formerly unchallenged dominance of the forward and backward linkages associated with access to domestic markets and domestically produced inputs. The model further suggests that there is more to this development than a simple matter of physical proximity to Mexico's main export market and source of imported inputs. For the lower δ of the regions to which firms relocate is an added factor that further helps to outweigh the advantages formerly enjoyed by location at the heart of the previously highly centralised (and consequently high-δ) economy; furthermore, such relocation opens up the advantages of the 'clustering' of particular industries in the new locations.[317]

Besides its δ parameter and its explicitly empirical reference, there is yet another, and third, element of this model that is unique to the series, which is that it explicitly raises the issue of 'welfare gains', which, in turn, inevitably gives it a prescriptive note. This runs counter to the general tenor of the models as a whole, whose proponents admit to "a certain reticence" about welfare implications. This reticence is justified by the argument that a premature move in this direction might encourage a repetition of the undesirable precedent experienced in the case of the new trade theory, when "outsiders" motivated by "crude neo-mercantilism" attempted "to hijack the new theories on behalf of interventionist policies".[318] This standpoint invites the riposte that what is offered as an alternative amounts to little more than 'crude neoliberalism', in that, when eventually the 'welfare', normative or prescriptive dimension is hesitantly raised, the result is merely to reiterate the exhortation to Mexico to concede further liberalisation of its trade with the United States.[319] This is all the more disappointing given the intellectually demanding task of following through the highly technical series of models, to which this familiar message is the limp conclusion.

In many other contexts, Krugman, the leading proponent of MCSE, has adopted a penetratingly critical standpoint towards simplistic market solutions to economic problems. Yet his retreat from the neoliberal extremism that prevailed in the economic orthodoxy in the 1980s is, in this case, shown to be so partial and reversible that his theorising amounts to little more than the provision of a new brand of formalistic underpinning for an old and discredited message. This ambiguous standpoint has prompted the comment that Krugman appears to hold "two opposing convictions" on such matters, portraying free trade as "not an absolute ideal" while, at the same time, believing "that it is still the best general policy or rule of thumb".[320]

In what follows, MCSE's categories of analysis will be placed in a new light by confronting them directly with their equivalents as they appear in primitive form in Petty's writings, to see what this can reveal about the fault lines in its conceptual structure which have resulted in such a disappointing outcome.

4.4 From Petty to neoclassical economics

4.4.1 Equivalence and affinity

A wide epistemological gap yawns between Petty's concrete and immediate mode of spatial-economic analysis and the abstract and deductive theoretical structure of MCSE. Nevertheless, there are fundamental points of equivalence between these two bodies of thought, concerning not only the issues they address but also the analytical apparatus with which they address them. It is worth pausing to establish some particularly notable instances of this equivalence, before proceeding to the more substantial task of assessing what lessons can be learnt regarding the analytical capacity of MCSE to perform the tasks it sets itself.

The outstanding point of analogy is the core–periphery relationship, which, as has been seen, is explored by Petty primarily in relation to the polarity between compactness and dispersion of population. While this focus on population places a limit on the parallels with MCSE, the analogy is sufficiently close to merit further exploration, particularly in the case of his population transfer scheme. For, in this latter case, Petty not only distinguishes between the two fundamental subsectors of the agrarian economy (i.e. the agrarian and the pastoral) but also goes on to use this distinction in the explicitly spatial-economic analysis on which he bases his policy proposal and the associated cost–benefit assessment. Furthermore, he elsewhere discusses other inter-sectoral distinctions apart from the agricultural–pastoral; it has been seen, for example, that he comments with approval on the advantages to Holland of its practice of importing agricultural produce from its inland (upriver) neighbouring regions, allowing an international division of labour, in which Holland is free to specialise in commerce and manufacture.[321] Such discussions suggest that there would be ample opportunity for the formal modelling of Petty's spatial-economic propositions in the MCSE manner, if that was the course which the present study intended to follow.

Three further specific elements of Petty's writings may be cited as particularly striking examples of analogy with MCSE. The first such element directly concerns the formulation of the core–periphery relationship. This is Petty's practice of associating the compactness–dispersion polarity with a further polarity, between homogeneous consumption in the periphery and variety in the metropolitan core. This brings the range of analogy – and contrast – into the very heart of the MCSE's modelling strategy, the SADS model.[322]

Secondly, there is an equally conspicuous point of equivalence between Wat Waller's sturgeon and Samuelson's iceberg.[323] For the rate at which the latter melts away can just as well be restated as the rate at which sturgeons die off en route from Archangel. In fact, the advantage of obviating the need to model a separate transport sector is more convincing in the latter case than the former; in 'reality' someone would have to tow the iceberg, whereas fish are self-propelling, with the last one swimming, so to speak, right into the kitchen. This notion corresponds with Petty's explicit contention that the cost of droving terrestrial livestock is zero,[324] and may be compared with von Thünen's answer to the same problem, in which the horses used to transport the corn eat a given proportion of it en route.[325]

A third close equivalence may be identified in the case of the δ parameter used in the 'Mexico' model to represent negative externalities, such as congestion and pollution. For Petty, the equivalent role is played by the danger of plague. For, he argues, the "touchstone" to determine the ideal size of London is to make a "just balance…between the disadvantages from the plague with the advantages accruing from the other particulars above-mentioned",[326] the latter being a reference to a preceding exposition of the advantages of compactness.

Besides such neat analogies as these, there are many further instances in which Petty's writings display a more general, but nonetheless unmistakable, affinity with the MCSE approach. For example, the Marshallian 'trinity' of external economies, though only partially incorporated into MCSE, is never-theless an important element of its intellectual ancestry, and Marshall's seminal exposition might, in turn, equally well trace its ancestry back to Petty's descrip-tion of London's watch-making quarter; in this connection, Petty observes, for example, that "in towns and in the streets of a great town, where all the inhabitants are almost of one trade, the commodity peculiar to these places is made better and cheaper than elsewhere".[327]

Likewise, Petty's comments on the situation of London form a convenient baseline for the history of the analysis of city location. He states, for example:

> The Thames, being the most commodious river of this island, and the seat of London the most commodious part of the Thames; so much doth the means of facilitating carriage greaten a city…[328]

It is observations such as these which Smith places at the heart of his analysis of the advantages of the extension of the market;[329] they also prefigure, though admittedly somewhat tenuously, the concept of the 'transportation hub' as it appears in MCSE.[330]

The search for further analogies and affinities could be greatly extended; one commentator has even pointed to Petty's use, in connection with parish boundary reform, of the term "central place", and finds, not only in the use of that term but in Petty's discussion as a whole, "a crude central place system" of the kind subsequently elaborated under that name by Walter Christaller, one of the seminal figures in German location theory.[331] That same commentator concludes, more generally, and surely incontestably, that, just as Petty has been called 'the founder of [classical] political economy', so also "it seems as if Petty might also be given credit for at least mentioning very important aspects of what has become known as location theory".[332] In arguing that MCSE brings back into currency analytical concepts first formulated by Petty, we are, then, doing no more than adding historical depth to MCSE's own claim that it has 'rediscovered' location theory.

4.4.2 Analytical strength: the balance of gain and loss

An equivalence – or, at least an affinity – has now been established between MCSE and Petty's spatial-economic analysis, across a range of both formal and informal issues; furthermore, it has been shown, in a number of cases, that, for all the difference in epistemological basis, the equivalence lies not only in the subject matter but also in the conceptual apparatus used to analyse it.

Yet, in juxtaposing Petty's spatial-economic analysis and MCSE, the point of greatest correspondence – the spatial specification of economic categories – is, at one and the same time, the point of most conspicuous contrast. For Petty commonly applies spatial specification literally; for him, it is, in the first instance, a matter of recording units of distance and area ('measure') in the manner of a land surveyor, as seen in the trade circles of Tables 4.1 and 4.2. For MCSE, conversely, spatial specification takes the form of the essentially 'scale-independent' terms and parameters out of which it subsequently proceeds to construct its geometrical landscapes.

Petty's explicit spatial specification is only one example of the concrete and immediate character of his thought, which has now been noted in a number of contexts: for example, it has been seen how grids of spatial-economic activity are portrayed not just as areas of different radii but, rather, as representative of different categories of economic transaction in the agrarian economy (transactions at subsistence level, cash sale, town–country trade, etc.); compactness, dispersion and the intermediate range are embodied in the characteristics of particular European countries; efficiency in state and Church administration (through economy of scale) is addressed in terms of topical legislative issues; efficiency in production (through division of labour and the diffusion of technical knowledge) is addressed in terms of the 'commanding heights' of the economy (notably ship building, cloth and precision instruments); transport costs are embodied in particular types of vessel, vehicle and route; core and periphery are presented in terms of London and its agrarian and colonial hinterland; and so on.

It is not adequate for the purposes of the present enquiry, however, merely to highlight the epistemological divide which separates this mode of analysis from that of MCSE; rather, the task must be to identify which particular issues provide the best opportunity to assess the balance of what has been gained and lost in analytical strength in the passage from one to the other.

Most of the issues to be considered in this connection have already been touched upon, but they will now be revisited, with explicit reference to this task, under five headings, as follows: the conflictual reference that pervades Petty's thought; the inseparability of his economic analysis from policy application; his frank articulation of his own social and political orientation; his endorsement of social stratification in consumption; and, finally, his colonialist orientation.

(i) The most conspicuous such substantial issue which is lost from view, in consequence of crossing the epistemological divide into the world of Petty, is the conflictual reference which is such a prominent characteristic of his thought. It is true that this feature is not always as inescapably manifest in the field of spatial-economic analysis as in other fields of economic enquiry, since in this case Petty's approach brings out the more abstract and deductive aspects of his thought, as has been seen in his discussion of locational rent. To return to the consideration of his political economy from a more all-round point of view, however, is to be sharply reminded how fundamentally it contrasts with the conflict-free fantasy world of MCSE and orthodox economics generally.

Take, for instance, Petty's discussion of rates of "exchange or local usury":

> As for the natural measures of exchange, I say that in times of peace the greatest exchange can be but the labour of carrying the money in specie, but where are hazards [and] emergent uses for money more in one place than another, etc., or opinions of these true or false, the exchange will be governed by them.[333]

In this passage, Petty relates exchange rates directly not only to the costs of conflict but also to expectations of it ("opinions...true or false"). Here, any calculations regarding transport costs as such ("the labour of carrying the money in specie") are explicitly stated to be conditional on occurring "in times of peace". In other words, by raising the issue of 'the angry part', he makes explicit the no-conflict assumption ($\kappa = 1$) which is present only by implication in his discussion of locational rent. It is true that this latter discussion is more elaborate in formal terms, but it is, by the same token, devoid of what is, more commonly, such an outstanding characteristic – and strength – of Petty's economic thought, which is his attention to the "correlation between economic perspectives and policies on the one hand and military perspectives, policies and technology on the other".[334] It is on the basis of this latter aspect of his thought that he achieved such impressive accuracy in his forecasts of the state's future military budget requirements;[335] in contrast, it is hard to imagine how his schematic statements on the relative prices of corn in the various counties around London could have had any empirical or predictive value, whatever their significance for the conceptual history of locational rent. Such is the loss in analytical and predictive power incurred even by these first few steps taken by Petty on the road that was eventually to lead to the dominance of deductive logic in economic analysis, a dominance exemplified in such neo-classical initiatives as MCSE.[336]

(ii) Petty's concern with conflictual issues of course reaches its most explicit expression in the case of his policy proposals directed towards military, naval and fiscal-military ends. This brings us to the next outstanding contrast with MCSE, namely the inseparability of Petty's spatial-economic analysis from policy issues. For, just as Petty's economic concepts are commonly embodied in immediate, concrete form, so also is his motivation always immediately and undisguisedly concrete and practical, however peculiar or eccentric his ideas of practicality in particular instances. Given this motivation, it is not surprising that his most elaborate and 'advanced' (in the sense of anticipatory) economic analysis was formulated in the context of specific policy proposals, from those contained in his *Treatise of Taxes* and *Verbum Sapienti* in the 1660s to his final scheme of 1687. This is the reverse of the principle proclaimed by the proponents of MCSE, which is that the field should be put on "a solid theoretical and empirical footing before it begins speculating about [policy] interventions", a principle that accords with their "reticence" about welfare implications.[337] It need hardly be pointed out that Petty's writings display no such hesitancy in proposing policy interventions, let alone reticence. There is more in common between the two standpoints, however, than this apparently stark antithesis at first suggests. This common element becomes clear once the issue of policy formulation is placed in the wider context of the underlying motivation in each case.

(iii) Along with Petty's practicality of intent goes a disingenuous transparency and frankness in acknowledging – indeed, advertising – the motivation of his innumerable policy proposals. The nature of this motivation reflects, in turn, the outstanding feature of his social position, which is its transitional nature; on the one hand, there stands the influence of his background in military-bureaucratic officialdom and his defence of a neo-feudal land settlement in colonial Ireland, both of which give his writing the air of a defence of feudal privilege; on the other hand, there stands his incipient, though theoretically significant, response to elements of the nascent ideology of capitalism. His declarations of commitment to particular social or economic ideals are, in consequence, as complex and contradictory as they are frank. It will be recalled, for example, that in his fiscal proposals he calls for more taxation of wages, and yet, at the same time, he does not take account of the uneven spread of the wage system, let alone of the accumulation of capital which was only gradually leading to that system's consolidation. His price theory displays a similarly contradictory character; he assumes some form of 'natural' regulation of prices in the economic sphere, and yet has barely even the most rudimentary idea of the equilibration of supply and demand, and is explicitly derogatory with respect to market forces. Again, his perspective on the labouring population moves from that of the neo-feudal freebooter, as anxious for tied labour as for land, to the advocacy of labour mobility, or, rather, labour transfer.[338] All these themes illustrate the fact that the difficulties of elucidating his standpoint in any given instance arise either from the essential complexity and contradictory nature of the issues involved or from his own incomplete conceptualisation of them; they do not, in other words, arise from a lack of frankness on his part, let alone from conscious or systematic obfuscation of his own motives.

The motivation of MCSE is, in contrast, painstakingly buried under thick layers of elaborately contrived mathematical abstraction. Indeed, it is hardly necessary to add that MCSE's own position, based as it is on the positivistic concept of mathematical 'neutrality', is to deny that its models are 'motivated' at all, in the sense of favouring particular historically contingent social and economic interests. Despite any such disclaimer, however, the MCSE approach is clearly based on hidden assumptions which impel its analysis towards conclusions that favour interests of precisely such a kind; a prime example is the supposed imperative for Mexico to liberalise its trade with the United States – an 'imperative' which is, transparently, no less indissolubly linked to an endorsement of particular, historically contingent socio-economic interests than the pioneering economic proposals advanced by Petty. The advantage of placing the two modes of analysis in apposition is that it helps to penetrate behind MCSE's mathematical abstraction and identify those features of its logical structure which are most influential in ensuring that its models reach conclusions which are in accord with the interests it in fact serves.

(iv) One element of MCSE modelling strategy which needs to be questioned in this connection is its specification of the parameter σ, representing "intensity of preference for variety" in differentiated goods.[339] It is impossible to exaggerate the significance to MCSE of this parameter; it enters into the optimising decisions of all agents, and, by the same token, permeates the mathematical structure of the entire set of MCSE models,[340] with the result that variations in its value can determine the geographical distribution of economic activity across regions, countries and whole continents; take it away and there would be no 'action' in the monopolistic–competitive sector, no cumulative causation, no mathematically tractable outcomes to market transactions – in short, no 'new economic geography'.[341] Yet, despite these demanding tasks imposed upon it, σ is a Cinderella parameter: unlike, say, transport costs (T), it is endowed with no 'history', of whatever description, let alone a theoretical profile as a behavioural principle with resonance outside the field of economics.[342] Even within economics itself, all that is provided by way of its conceptual justification is the fact that "the desirability of variety" is already embodied in "the convexity of indifference surfaces of a conventional utility function",[343] a statement which does no more than shift the question backwards to a previous phase of the orthodoxy's own theoretical history.

There is, in contrast, no equivocation or embarrassment for Petty in his approach to the desirability of variety; for him, "great variety of commodities"[344] is an analytical category whose application is, quite simply, restricted exclusively to the luxury consumption of the rich. This is as true of his earlier and more austere writings, in which such luxury is mentioned with disapproval,[345] as it is of his later writings, when he has settled wholeheartedly into the self-indulgence of the wealthy elite of Restoration society. An intermediate stage is discernible, in which he calls for the development of "arts of pleasure and ornament" to be conditional on first substituting for imports,[346] but in his final years all such caution is thrown aside.[347] His examples of specific 'differentiated goods' are, accordingly, entirely within the luxury sphere: coaches,[348] valuable household furniture,[349] jewellery,[350] fine clothing,[351] elaborate cuisine,[352] choice wines and spirits,[353] and so on. Coaches, which he more than once cites as an indicator of the level of national wealth,[354] are at the same time most indicative of the narrow social range of his discussions of such luxury goods, for their users are unlikely to have comprised as much as 2 per cent of the population in England, and considerably less than 1 per cent in Ireland.[355]

Turning from the consumption of the rich to that of the poor, we find that here the issue of variety quite simply does not arise, and, significantly, he makes it clear that the very term 'consumption' is not applicable to the labouring population at all; for example, he states that "where the consumption of a commodity is, viz. among the gentry, the vendors of the same must seat themselves".[356] In the case of the labouring population, then, there is no place at all for a theory of 'consumption', as Petty sees it; rather, in this connection it has, more appropriately, been suggested that he be credited with "some primitive conceptualisations of input–output systems".[357] This perspective, in which consumption is replaced by 'input', has already been illustrated in the case of Petty's vision of a 'new model Ireland', with its 'uniform' clothes, its undifferentiated housing and, of course, a diet often explicitly homogenised in his value theory as the single commodity 'corn'. This last element can also, of course, occur in the yet more abstract form of a subsistence consumption bundle, a category which receives its archetypal formulation in Petty's memorable definition: "[C]orn, which we will suppose to contain all necessaries for life, as in the Lord's Prayer we suppose the word 'bread' doth."[358]

The restriction of the labouring population to homogeneity in 'consumption' is, for Petty, not a merely descriptive feature but, rather, a necessary element of the struggle to keep wages "certain" (i.e. constant), and thus to prevent any 'backward bending' in the labour supply curve.[359] Furthermore, "equal spreading of wealth", he holds, "would destroy all splendour and ornament",[360] "there being a great difference between a raw sheepskin and a piece of Spanish cloth embroidered, and between a cottage of wattles and a cabinet-work closet".[361] Even more generally still, Petty's endorsement of social inequality embodies an all-embracing commitment to social stratification in principle: spread wealth equally and it would "leave the face of beggary upon the whole nation, and withal such parity would beget anarchy and confusion".[362]

In MCSE, in contrast, this crucial social dimension of the polarity between variety and homogeneity in 'consumption' is swept out of sight and buried under a supposedly 'neutral' methodological formalism. In the core–periphery model, for example, the sole element identified as an economic agent is the category 'workers'. The movement of these 'workers' is determined by the concentration, in each location, of the differentiated goods sector, and the level of this concentration is, in turn, subject to determination by variations in the value of the σ (variety preference) parameter. Petty's writings reveal, however, that the formulation of the concept of a polarity between variety and homogeneity is, in its primitive form, inseparable from the assumption that 'workers' do not 'consume' the differentiated goods in any case, but only the composite homogeneous one. Nor is this assumption confined to Petty's writings; it is a commonplace in the economic history of the period that the goods on which the early growth of manufacturing were based did not reach the vast majority of the population.[363] Thus, the SADS model, while it certainly provides MCSE with a logically watertight modelling strategy, performs this task at a high cost, which is no less than the suppression from view of the realities involved in its core concept of the polarity between variety and homogeneity. Once this polarity is subjected to even the most cursory empirical examination, its capacity to function as a socially neutral category of analysis is shown to be illusory, with all that means for the analytical capacity of MCSE as a whole.

(v) There remains, finally, the theme which, from the point of view of the present study, underlies all the others which have here been reviewed: Petty's colonialist outlook, which leads him constantly to extend his endorsement of social stratification in general to endorsement of national stratification in particular. The lack of attention hitherto paid to this issue by historians of economic thought reflects the dominance, within the field of economics as a whole, of what has been described as "an impoverished notion of what constitutes the nation and the nation-state".[364]

This analytical impoverishment is taken to extremes in MCSE, which inherits the perspective of Bertil Ohlin, who, in his seminal work of 1933, represents international trade theory as no more than "an application of the theory of interregional trade to a special case, where the regions are different countries".[365] Thus, for MCSE, the distinction between nations and regions is glossed over, and it has rightly been pointed out that in MCSE 'regions' are presented indiscriminately as any territorial units that are "roughly at the scale of US states or European nation-states".[366] From this point of view, "international trade theory is simply international location theory",[367] albeit raised to a higher scale.

By adopting such a standpoint, MCSE is able to define nations simply by means of assumptions regarding factor mobility, normally the assumption that they are "geographical units that can trade, but among which labour does not move". From such a perspective, national borders, also referred to as "arbitrary lines called borders", are no more than barriers to labour movement, and "do not introduce qualitatively new issues" over and above those existing at the regional and urban levels.[368] Accordingly, MCSE questions the "inherent importance in drawing a line on the ground and calling the land on either side two different countries'.[369] Equivalently, in the multi-locational or "seamless world" of the Turing model, labour is fully mobile everywhere, resulting in "a world in which borders are irrelevant".[370]

The claim of MCSE to address 'international' issues consequently rests on a misnomer. Its aim is, on the contrary, totally to separate economic analysis from any consideration of the political sphere, which is, precisely, the sphere in which nations and their mutual relations are constituted.

It is in such a world, reduced to an amorphous, or 'isotropic', arena for the operation of spatial-economic forces, without any specifically national impediment to their operation, that MCSE addresses the issue of international inequality. Such is the context of its assertion that a non-monotonic movement takes place in which "declining trade costs first produce, then dissolve, the global inequality of nations".[371] Thus, declining trade costs are all that MCSE has to offer by way of 'history', this indeed being the grandiose term used in the working title of the paper in which the concept was initially launched – "History of the world, part 1".[372] The reduction of history to this drastically depleted form opens the door for the reintroduction of the effectively neo-liberal message that a country which concedes free entry to US-dominated world trade is thereby setting out on the road to 'factor price equalisation' with the global 'core'; for such a message can be formulated only on the basis of a 'history' from which all record of colonialism has been expunged and all understanding of its heritage thus rendered impossible.

4.5 Conclusions

The issue of international inequality has, in the recent period, been addressed by a range of social sciences in terms of the process of 'globalisation'. While this term has been subject to widely differing definitions, there is, surely, none so simplistic as that of MCSE, which sees the 'historical' process involved as nothing more complex than the secular fall in transaction costs, or, more nar-rowly still, transport costs as a proxy, or 'metaphor', for transaction costs as a whole. That MCSE responds to the vast and expanding literature on globalisa-tion in such a theoretically limited manner is further testimony to the isolation of economics from the other social sciences. Even within the constricted terms of MCSE itself, however, it has been possible to identify aspects of its mod-elling strategy which irrevocably tie it to assumptions which, by their nature, undermine its capacity to provide a real alternative to the crude neoliberalism it claims to supersede.

The present study is far from the first to question the analytical capacity of MCSE to achieve its stated objectives; on the contrary, there exists a long-standing and continuing critique of neoclassical economics, including specifically MCSE, conducted from within the field of economic geog-raphy.[373] For geographers face Krugman's 'new economic geography' across a yawning epistemological gap. For them, the subject matter of geography is comprised of 'real places' – that is, spatial units with empirically observable characteristics which are specific to different levels of scale. In Krugman's initiative, in contrast, abstract and scale-independent geometrical landscapes are constructed out of a priori theoretical concepts, an approach which thus represents the very opposite of the geographical project as perceived by geographers. Krugman has swept aside such criticisms as nothing but an "anti-model, anti-quantitative backlash", making it clear that, in his eyes, this is effectively synonymous with a wilful rejection of scientific method.[374] Geographers have shown that they can give as good as they get, describing his initiative, variously, as "highly simplistic", "patronising" and "not recommended",[375] "dated, historically and intellectually", based on the "flimsiest of empirical support",[376] "simply building formal models of old and familiar ideas",[377] a return to the methodology of "theory-enslaved idealised facts",[378] a "bad case of intellectual isolation",[379] guilty of "outrageous claims of priority" and "selective myopia",[380] and so on. Economic geographers have accordingly declared themselves "aghast" at the suggestion that they could even contemplate abandoning the "hard-won work of the past twenty years aimed at integrating spatial hetero-geneity into the theoretical core of economic geography", in favour of an approach whose rejection was the precondition of all they have since achieved.[381]

The particular contribution which the present study aims to make to this geographical critique is to draw attention to the range of insights that emerge once the search for the roots of spatial economics is extended back from its conventional starting point of von Thünen's theory to embrace Petty's writings as well. For the consequences of extending the theoretical history back in this way are indeed nothing short of spectacular: the cosy world of microeconomic dogma quite simply falls apart, and the analytical apparatus of MCSE appears, in primitive form, as a direct descendant of early efforts to formulate predatory and colonialist fiscal-military policies; gone is the veil of formalistic neutrality, and, in its place, we find a theoretical apparatus derived on the basis of an acceptance of the most extreme social and national stratification – an endorsement not only undisguised but even advertised in the most unabashed manner.

With an analytical apparatus of such an intellectual pedigree, it is not sur-prising that MCSE underpins arguments for countries such as Mexico to liber-alise their trade with the United States, and to help persuade the less developed countries of the world to entrust their future to the mirage of 'factor price equalisation', by meekly joining the queue until such time as 'sequential and rapid' development comes their way. Above all, the task of MCSE is to reinforce the message that any aspiration by a country of the periphery to develop an economy and society that is independent of the United States and other dom-inant powers must be renounced, not only at the policy level but also in intel-lectual life, at all levels, from day-to-day political discourse and popular culture to the academic sphere, including the theory of economics and, where possible, other social sciences as well.

Notes

1 Fujita, Krugman and Venables 1999: xi.
2 Throughout the discussion that follows, it will be assumed that this would inevit-ably mean a drastic reduction in Ireland's population; indeed, this is the explicitly stated intention in some of Petty's earlier discussions of such population transfer. There is a complicating issue here, however: in his later writings he focused on population exchanges rather than a one-way movement out of Ireland, and moreover in some writings his growing 'populationism' led him also to discuss

the potential benefits of that population increasing. On the apparent contradiction between these two currents of thought, see the discussion on Fox 2009 in Chapter 5.1.

3 Mirowski 1989: 153.

4 PA: 244. For early modern usage of the phrase 'number, weight and measure', which is derived from the Bible (*Wisdom*, 11, 17), see Debus 1968: 3f., 13, etc.; and Webster 1975: 351.

5 Letwin 1963: 130.

6 Rothbard 1995: 302, who borrows this terminology from Sorokin 1956: 102–173 (where the precise terms used are, in fact, 'quantophrenia' and 'metrophrenia'). Dockès 2013 writes, equivalently, of Petty's "arithmetical mania".

7 Aspromourgos 1996: 55.

8 This yearbook was subsequently taken over by Chamberlayne's son, and continued to be published until 1755.

9 See PA: 284, 308, for explicit references.

10 See PAI: 122f (Hull's introductory comment).

11 Published under the title *England's guide to industry*, the text is described by Keynes 1971: 21–22 as "pirated and corrupt".

12 Petty cites Fortrey at PA: 309; see also the editorial notes to PA: 252, 297.

13 See, for example, Hull 1899: lxxii; McNally 1988: 46–48; Poovey 1994: 20–32; 1998; and Wood 2002: 161 (on which see Chapter 2.2).

14 *Reflections*: 12.

15 BA: xvii.

16 Commemorative inscription drafted by Petty, in Fitzmaurice 1895: 314.

17 PP1: 104.

18 TI: 614f.

19 Strauss 1954: 151. Also discussed by Andrews 1985: 80, 69 (note 67).

20 See Everitt 1967: 496–502; and Goodacre 1994: 21–34.

21 Compare, for example, PAI: 180f. and 192.

22 PP1: 32 §6.

23 For a description of this method, the 'surround survey', see Andrews 1997: 118f.

24 BA: xiii–xiv, xvii.

25 DS: 143, referring to the "accounts" tabulated on pp. 137–153.

26 This point is made by Hull 1899: lxxi.

27 See Chapters 1.1 and 3.2.2.

28 Andrews 1985: 95.

29 As McNally 1988: 43 points out, Petty appears to have borrowed this term from a 1659 work by James Harrington (on whom see also Chapter 3.2.2). See Harrington 1977 [1659]: 656.

30 Aspromourgos 2001: 15, 22 (note 12). This theme is the subject of a steadily expanding literature within the field of economic geography today.

31 Jones 1994: 77f. There is a long-standing literature on this topic, much of it centring on some oft-cited passages in Petty's writings in which he flamboyantly displays his command of medical terminology. See, for example, Sharp 1975: 348f.; Webster 1975: 421, 423f., 430, 434; Roncaglia 1985 [1977]: 25–28; McNally 1988: 43; Christensen 1989: 704f., etc.; Olson 1993: 68f.; Keller 1993: 87f.; Mykkänen 1994: 80f.; Poovey 1994: 31; Coleman 1995: 37f.; Finkelstein 2000: 111; and Aspromourgos 2001; and, for more general discussion of the issues involved, Kern 1983: 224–228; Harvey 2000: 230; Groenewegen 2001; Clément 2003; and

Desmedt 2005. Only quite recently, however, has the literature engaged sufficiently closely with advances in the history of early modern medicine to draw convincing conclusions about the actual nature of this influence, rather than its use in Petty's self-promotion. Sivado 2017 provides a good example of the insights that can be gained from such engagement (see Chapter 5.2); he also counters a tendency among former commentators to jump to simplistic assumptions on the matter, regarding, for example, the supposed influence of Harveyan circulation theory on Petty's monetary theory. Jordan 2007a and 2007b, compilations of wide-ranging biographical information, reflect the author's medical background and his consequent eye for medical issues.

32 For further discussion of possible influences from the natural philosophy of his day, see Chapter 5.2.

33 Lynam 1932: 418.

34 See Goblet 1930: I, vi; and II, 344, 356f. See also *ibid.*: I, vi, where Petty is described as "the discoverer and first explorer of the field where geography, economics and sociology meet". See also Goblet 1955: 5–8. For some current trends in the literature on Petty's spatial economic thought, see Chapter 5.2, discussing Dockès 2013 and Dimou and Pecqueur 2012.

35 Appleby 1978: 73.

36 For citation of examples, see Hull 1899: lxxii; editorial notes to TTC: 26 and PA: 250–257; and Riley 1985: 50f., 161 (note 57); and, for more extensive discussion, Appleby 1978: 73–98,

37 In a list of his own writings (PP2: 261), he records the title as *A collection of the frugalities of Holland*. The note on Holland at PP2: 185f. evidently dates from much later (see Harris 2000: 13f.), and has no connection with any such early work, *pace* Lansdowne's editorial note on p. 185, and, evidently following him, Goblet 1930: I, 188f.; and II, 351; and Strauss 1954: 26f.

38 PA: 249 (heading of chap. 1).

39 See Chapter 3.2.2. Although Petty cites the example of Holland only in one of his various proposals for a land registry (PA: 264f.), his editors assume that the Dutch example also informs his other proposals as well; see editorial notes at PP1: 75 and TTC: 26 §27.

40 See TTC: 26 §27; and PA: 265f. For general discussion of the issues involved, see Dickson 1993: chap. 3 (particularly pp. 54–56); and also O'Brien and Hunt 1999b: 219.

41 See, in particular, TTC: 95 §13; and, for further discussion of relevant issues, Kennedy 1913: 61; Veenendaal 1994: 96; Aspromourgos 1996: 31 (discussing PA: 269); and Chapter 3.1.4.

42 PA: 266–268 (compare PA: 281f., where he displays a different attitude to mercenaries at sea).

43 *Ibid.*: 262–264.

44 Strauss 1954: 28.

45 PA: 267f.

46 *Bills*: 354, assuming these to be the words of Petty rather than Graunt, as seems likely in this particular instance. For discussion of this passage, see Buck 1977: 72.

47 Greenleaf 1964: 257f., summarising PA: 255–258. For other summaries, and further discussion, see Bevan 1894: 53f.; Goblet 1930: I, 317–319 (with table); and Dockès 1969: 151–155.

48 PA: 255.

49 *Ibid.*: 254f.
50 Hull 1899: lxi.
51 O'Brien and Hunt 1999a: 60.
52 O'Brien 2002: 249.
53 Strauss 1954: 142f.
54 PA: 300 §8.
55 Aspromourgos 1996: 189 (note 2.3).
56 PA: 286.
57 *Ibid.*: 287.
58 Yang 2003: 1, as already noted in Chapter 2.1.
59 Clark 2003: ('rural–urban continuum').
60 Defoe 1724–27: III, 97–100. See also pp. 256f. of the 1991 edition (with illustration); and, for discussion, Daunton 1995: 148f.
61 PA: 255 §1.
62 PAL: 471, though, in the second edition of this work, he revised his estimate of the built-up area to "less than 2500 acres". See Table 4.2.
63 See Goblet 1930: II, 337–342, discussing, in particular, *Bills*: 423; PAL: 457; and EW: 526. See also Dockès 1969: 133–141.
64 TTC: 48 §5.
65 See Anderson 1998: 28f.
66 See Prendergast 1870: 70, 226–235.
67 Spiegel 1983: 130.
68 Roncaglia 1985 [1977]: 59.
69 Strauss 1954: 202. For further discussion, see Poovey 1994: 27f. A line of argument resembling that of Petty is pursued to its conclusion by North, Anderson and Hill 1983: 16, who suggest that economy of scale in the enforcement of property rights constitutes "one of the basic reasons for the existence of the state". Such an approach is greatly elaborated by Barzel 2002; see chapters 3 and 8, on scale economies in 'enforcement' and 'protection', respectively, and, in particular, the comment (p. 25) that population density is among the factors increasing scale economies in 'enforcement'.
70 TTC: 34 §12.8.
71 PA: 255. See also PP1: 36 §4; TTC: 46f §27.5; PAI: 168f.; and TI: 568 §4; and compare Barzel 2002: chap. 9 (on scale economies in the emergence of legal institutions).
72 PAL: 472 §2. See also PP1: 36 §5.
73 "I say, easily, because they speak an hour, or more together." This statement is in fact from *Bills*: 382, but it seems reasonable on stylistic grounds to suggest that it is likely to have one of Petty's interpolations in Graunt's generally far more pedestrian text.
74 TTC: 79 §9.
75 Marx 1963–71 [1862–63]: I, 354, commenting on TTC: 25 §22.
76 PAL: 472f §3. See also TTC: 73 §27–28; and, for further references, the index entries "Parishes, inequality of" in both EW and PP2. Petty clearly uses the term 'uniformity' with reference to the Act of Uniformity, whose passage through parliament was proceeding at precisely the same time as TTC was being published, and of which his tongue-in-cheek quantitative calculations are effectively a parody.
77 TTC: 11 (sub-heading to chap. 2).

78 *Ibid.*: 24 §16.

79 Compare also VS: 116 and Table 4.1, where the example of rationalisation of parish boundaries might perhaps have suggested to him the idea of a grid of 450 tax collection areas.

80 PA: 255f.

81 PAL: 473f §6. Noted by Whittaker 1960: 141f.

82 TI: 568 §3–5.

83 *Ibid.*: 568 §6. See also *ibid.*: 559 §13, 567f.

84 *Ibid.*: 568 §2.

85 Roll 1973: 104. For similarly exaggerated assessments, see Bevan 1894: 100; Schumpeter 1955: 214; and Finkelstein 2000: 304f (note 109).

86 Goodacre 2010c.

87 This distinction was pointed out by Stewart [1855]: 312; and further elaborated by Marx 1970 [1867]: 364–367. See also Lowry 1987: 68–73, whose index includes (on p. 360) the entry: "Petty, Sir William, use of Xenophon's writings"; such a suggestion is not actually made in the body of the work, however (nor, for that matter, has any evidence yet been adduced that Petty was aware of Xenophon's work).

88 PAL: 473 §6, the reference being to watch making, as discussed further below.

89 See Meek 1973a: 39–41; Foley 1984 [1974]: 341–343; and Berg 1983: 35–37.

90 This issue was to remain imprecisely formulated even in Smith's account, as discussed by Marx 1970 [1867]: 354–359.

91 BA: xiv.

92 The best-known such list is at PA: 260 §5, but the most extensive is at PP1: 190. See also the index entries for 'cloth' in both EW and PP2.

93 PAL: 473 §6.

94 Feld 1977: 191, 194.

95 PP1: 190.

96 His paper, delivered to the Royal Society in 1662, is entitled "An apparatus to the history of the common practices of dyeing". He also wrote a paper on wool (Birch 1756–57: I, 55–65), on which see Ochs 1985: 136.

97 Strauss 1954: 17.

98 His paper on dyeing gives no indication that he envisages an urban environment in any one of the innumerable processes he describes.

99 PAL: 473 §6. Dockès 1969: 138 comments that watch making was, in this period, more familiar in small cities (as, for example, in Switzerland) than in large towns; but London already had a watch makers' quarter in Clerkenwell in Petty's time which would most likely have fitted Petty's description.

100 PAL: 471 §10. See Chapter 1.2.

101 *Advice*: 8f., 12f. Keller 1993: 87 suggests that Petty has in mind a 'zoo', thus spontaneously, and unjustifiably, providing his proposal with urban connotations.

102 See Chapter 1.1. Jesuit and Baconian influences are evident in Petty's *Advice* in roughly equal measure. Keller 1993: 87 is typical of commentators on the work in ignoring the former in favour of an exclusive emphasis on the latter.

103 Neveux 1981: 120.

104 PP2: 171–179.

105 It was, indeed, in this lecture that, for the first (and possibly the only) time, he referred to London as a 'metropolis'; see PP2: 172 ("our Methropolise London").

106 PP1: 40–42 §3, 6, 7, 10, 11. This note is in Petty's own handwriting, and appears to date from the 1680s; see Harris 2000: 21 (who queries the semi-legible 'endorsement' in which Petty appears to date it to 1687).

107 PAL: 475, §10.

108 Indeed, Smith's celebrated calculations of the output of pins may perhaps – consciously or unconsciously – have constituted a parody of political arithmetic, a mode of analysis in which he famously declared that he had "no great faith". Smith 1976 [1776]: 534.

109 See Stull 1994 [1986].

110 As Finkelstein 2000: 122 observes, Petty knew that division of labour would increase with rising productivity and wealth, but "the market was the last agent he would trust to maximise this wealth".

111 DB: 48.

112 On Petty's naval philosophy', see note in Chapter 3.2.1.

113 Hall 1970: 339. On the 'double bottom', see DB, which includes extensive and characteristically informative editorial comment by Lansdowne; see also Sharp 1977: 245–248, 302–304, 326–329; and, for brief narrative accounts, Fitzmaurice 1895: 109–114, 255–257; Hull 1899: xxii–xxiii; and Strauss 1954: 115–119. For further references, see the index entry 'Double-Bottom' in PP2 and PSC; Finkelstein 2000: 300 (note 33); Lynch 2001: 229 (note 141); and McCormick 2009: 150–156. See also Chapter 1.2.

114 *What a Compleat Treatise of Navigation Should Contain*: 658 §18.

115 PP1: 238.

116 DB: 5.

117 *Ibid.*: 5f., 44, 103.

118 Petty does not himself claim that the 'double bottom' is suitable for inland as well as maritime navigation, though this view is ascribed to him in a reported interview. DB: 45.

119 PA: 312.

120 DB: 87.

121 *Ibid.*: 64. See also Strauss 1954: 114–117; and PSC: 283.

122 Smith 1976 [1776]: 408–410.

123 *Pace* Lansdowne PP1: xxxvii. For a fifteenth-century example, see Tarr 1969 [1968]: 181f. (with illustration). The idea was also taken up by Leonardo da Vinci in his mechanical drawings at the end of that century, by which time it already "falls into an earlier tradition" (Zöllner 2003: 616; see also plate 579 on pp. 632–633).

124 PP2: 71–76.

125 *Experiments to be Made Relating to Land Carriage*: 666.

126 See the reports on the society's meetings between late 1663 and early 1668 in Birch 1756–57: I, 30, to II, 236. For a technical discussion, see Terrier 1981.

127 PP2: 147–151.

128 PP1: 171 §7, 173 §7.

129 *Ibid.*: 88, 171 §7, 173 §7, 179 §11.

130 *Ibid.*: 86 § 2; see also 81.

131 *Ibid.*: 179.

132 *Ibid.*: 173 §10.

133 *Ibid.*: 209 §11, on which see Lansdowne's editorial comment (203f.); and Harris 2000: 13f.

134 PA: 256 §4.

135 Southwell 1757 [1675]: 207f. For discussion, see Willan 1936: 119.

136 Smith 1976 [1776]: 32f.

137 *Experiments to be Made Relating to Land Carriage*: 666.

138 Southwell 1757 [1675]: 208.

139 PA: 249f. Southwell, in contrast, considers that the cost ratio of "horse-carriage" to "wheel carriage" is only "three to two".

140 Petty's editor, in a comment on this passage (see editorial note to PA: 259f.), considers that his proposed experiments on the mechanics of transport, "if performed, would yield data concerning traction similar to those which Petty here assumes"; he cites no technical references for this statement, however, and the continuing absence, over a century later, of technical assessment of this, and nearly every other, aspect of Petty's scientific and technological involvements is highly frustrating, in turn, for the assessment of the influence of these aspects of his work for his economic thought, as also discussed in Chapter 1.2.

141 See Chapters 2.2 and 3.1.4.

142 See Chapters 3.1.3 and 3.1.4.

143 TTC: 68.

144 For discussion of the origins of this concept, see Christensen 1989: 704f., citing, among other precedents, Hobbes 1651: 295. See also Hueckel 1986: 42, 59f. (notes 15–17).

145 For discussion, see Aspromourgos 1996: 89–95; and Finkelstein 2000: 116–118.

146 Schumpeter 1955: 214; and, evidently following him, Deane 1968: 67.

147 See the discussion by Marx 1956 [1885]: 366–393 on Smith's perception of the constant part of capital.

148 This is, for example, standard procedure in today's microeconomic trade theory. See Krugman and Obstfeld 2003: chap. 2 ("Labour productivity and comparative advantage: the Ricardian model").

149 TI: 583 §4.

150 See Aspromourgos 1996: 40f., etc.

151 Quite apart from the 'cattle ranch' project of his final scheme, Petty had long been a campaigner against the imposition of restrictions on the import of Irish cattle. See PAI: 160f. (with editorial note); PA: 299; and Chapters 2.5 and 4.2.1.

152 TI: 559 §12; see also 555; and PP1: 65 §4. This case is not noted in Aspromourgos 1996: 40f. As with all elements of Petty's approach to such issues, there are counter-currents, and one such may briefly be noted. This is that, paradoxically, the pamphlet literature with which Petty was associated in the Cromwellian period indicates that, at that time, he was likely to have been concerned with the amount of 'stock' or capital required by prospective colonists in Ireland (see Gookin 1655: 18). The fact that he did not return to this issue in his final scheme may be explained by the fact that the scheme was precisely a manifestation of his disillusionment with the idea that any such body of well-capitalised settlers would ever materialise.

153 See Chapter 3.2.1.

154 TI: 572, 557 §3, 567 ("a stock of six millions for the year of war").

155 For discussion, see Goodacre 2010b.

156 Pasquier 1903: 157f. See also Tribe 1978: 103 ("limited conception of capital").

157 Aspromourgos 1996: 49–51, 124f.; 1998: 196f.; 2001: 18f.

158 Aspromourgos 1998: 197.

159 Aspromourgos 2001: 19.

160 See Aspromourgos 2000: 62.

161 *Ibid.*: 59. On Petty's relation to subsequent corn–corn 'input–output' analysis, see note in Chapter 4.4.2 (iv). See also Roncaglia 1988: 158, 178; and Kurz and Salvadori 2003 [2000]: 41f., as discussed in Chapters 2.1 and 4.4.2 (iv).

162 McNally 1988: 54.

163 Walsh and Gram 1980: 17.

164 Marx 1963–71 [1862–63]: I, 357. See also Rubin 1979 [1929]: 368; and Meek 1973a: 25–27 (profit appears "under the heading of rent"), 36, 61f.

165 There is also, in early modern economic thought, commonly a conflation of profit with wages, the assumption being that trades were, as a rule, practised by independent tradesmen labouring alongside their employees. See Meek 1984 [1954]: 60; Meek 1973a: 26; and Walsh and Gram 1980: 17.

166 Robinson 1649: 3f. The author goes on to point out that "such cities should be situated near unto navigable rivers". For discussion, see Appleby 1978: 77.

167 Robinson 1652: 8, 9 ("to make all rivers navigable", etc.).

168 PP2: 34.

169 TTC: 31 §41.

170 See, for example, PA: 249f., as discussed in Chapter 4.1.4.

171 TTC: 42 §11; see also p. 20, where the list also includes aqueducts and havens.

172 TTC: 7 §6, 31 §41. On his concern with this trade, see PAI: 160f., with editorial note; PA: 299; and discussion in Chapters 2.5 and 4.1.5.

173 See Willan 1936: 28–51 (on the lobby in general) and, in particular, 39f. (on Petty).

174 He once mentions the related field of drainage works, but only in a derogatory comment on Ireland; see PA: 286.

175 TTC: 83 §9.

176 Smith 1976 [1776]: 724–731.

177 PP2: 186, where he also notes its 'grafts' (mistranscribed by the editor as "grasses"), or paved canal-side routes, which served as tow paths.

178 Willan 1936: 5.

179 PA: 256 §4. Southwell 1757 [1675]: 208 contracts this 'estimate' even further, stating that "no part is one quarter of a mile from some navigable water".

180 PA: 293.

181 See Southwell 1757 [1675]: 208. Southwell's calculations concurred with those of Petty in the case of England, but, in the case of France, he finds δ_C to be 85 miles (he also gives a figure of 15 miles for Ireland).

182 Willan 1936: 5, who makes this attribution, evidently mistakes the date of the first publication of PA – i.e. 1690 – with that of its composition in the early 1670s, thus coming to the conclusion that Petty conducted the calculation only "fifteen years later" than Southwell's paper (by which time, of course, Petty was in fact dead).

183 For further discussion of this calculation, see Goblet 1930: II, 318–322; and Willan 1936: 5.

184 PA: 278f. Moreover, although Petty does not mention the fact, France has the further disadvantage of a high δ_W.

185 PA: 247, 278, 298 (headings to chaps. 3 and 5).

186 Willan 1936: 5.

187 Goblet 1930: II, 344.

188 Gyorgy 1944.

189 See Goblet: 1955, a rather esoteric work.

190 See Harvey 1990: 147 (a definition), 207–209 (on Nazi Geopolitik), 275 (on Ratzel); and, similarly, Harvey 2000: 230. For further discussion of the space-time compression concept, in relation to current issues, see Sadler 2000: 327f., 337f.; Schoenberger 2000: 383–388; and (with particular reference to finance) Leyshon 2000: 440, 337. See also Ó Tuathail, Dalby and Routledge 1998

191 See, for example, PP2: 47–58. For further discussion of the widespread advocacy of population increase in this period, see Furniss 1920 (seen by Finkelstein 2000: 305 (note 113) as still "the most detailed treatment"); and the discussion by Riley 1985: chap. 3 on 'populationism', a concept he defines as "a preference for a larger than existing population joined sometimes with proposals about how to induce growth". See also Finkelstein 2000: 122–124, 305 (notes 113–125).

192 See Chapter 2.2.

193 See Chapter 2.3. The idea of a specifically pastoral sector is clearly implied in his discussion of the relations of Holland with its inland neighbouring regions, which specialise, he says, in "the old patriarchal trade of being cow-keepers" (PA: 267), but such an idea is not drawn out in his descriptive writings on Ireland, even when, as at PAI: 201f., he writes of the influence on Irish traditions of the way of life of "the patriarchs of old".

194 Although Petty wrote a number of papers relating to Ireland during 1686 (for examples, see PP1: 49–64), it appears that no mention is made of the 'ranch' scheme until 1687, in PP1: 65 §2.

195 Goblet 1930: II, 344f.

196 PP1: 46 (editorial note). On the historical background, see Chapters 1.2 and 1.3.

197 Olson 1993: 65.

198 TI: 597 §4. This proposition is omitted from the important discussion of Petty's views on the "limits to rational quantification" in Aspromourgos 2000: 66f. In PAI: 154, Petty begins a discussion of the causes of the wars in Ireland in quantitative mode (for example, the Catholics aimed at recovering the Church revenue of £110,000, and so on), but not as a prelude to a political-arithmetical calculation; on the contrary, all that follows is the limp and self-serving conclusion that the winners have a "gamester's right at least to their estates", and that "God knows" who occasioned the bloodshed.

199 *Experiments to be Made Relating to Land Carriage*: 666, as discussed in Chapter 4.1.4.

200 In contrast to his discussion of the effect of the civil wars on rates of "exchange or local usury" in TTC: 47f §2, as discussed in Chapters 3.2.1, 4.1.5 and 4.4.2 (ii).

201 Fournier 1643: 202f (154f in the second (1668) edition); also cited (with a summary) by Dainville 1940: 259. Fournier was the principal object of Petty's critique of French claims to potential maritime predominance; see TTC: 278–284. Interestingly, Petty notes geography as a subject on the curriculum at the Jesuit college at the University of Caen, where he claims to have studied in the late 1630s, and, though Fournier was not teaching there at the time, he had connections with that college, and Petty's teachers would have been his close associates. See PP2: 245f.; Sharp 1977: 4–18; and Romano 1999: 576.

202 PSC: 164. Wat Waller was Petty's brother-in-law, and son of the regicide Hardress Waller, on whom see Chapter 1.2.

203 This multiplicative expression will be encountered again in the 'iceberg' model of transport costs, as discussed in Chapters 4.3.2 and 4.4.1.

204 Smith 1976 [1776]: 163.

205 See, for example, Routh 1975: 36; Hueckel 1986: 62 (note 33); Kurz and Salvadori 2003 [2000]: 36; and Dockès 1969: 141 ("rente de situation"). More generally, Petty is credited with anticipating the overlapping concept of differential rent, as in Beer 1938: 171; Desai 1967: 61; Roll 1973: 106f.; and Aspromourgos 1996: 161f.; or the concept of the extensive margin, as in Whittaker 1960: 59f.; or a combination of these, as in Aspromourgos 1996: 192 (note 29) ("a localisation of differential rents").

206 TTC: 51f §13–16. This passage is discussed by, among others, Marx 1963–71 [1862–63]: I, 361; Brewer 1992a: 716; Parel 1997: 120; and Pinto 1997. On this five-county area, see also Figure 2 and further discussion in Chapter 4.2.2.

207 See discussion in Chapter 4.4.2 (iv).

208 Marx 1963–71 [1862–63]: I, 361, comments that Petty "means here the price or wages of labour".

209 Brewer 1992a: 716 finds Petty's views on returns to scale in agriculture to be ambiguous. He interprets the present passage to indicate that land is "(perhaps) subject to decreasing returns", but that land round London is a special case. Elsewhere, he finds Petty to imply (as, for example, at PA: 286) constant, and even (as at PA: 289f.) increasing, returns. McNally 1988 comments only in general terms on Petty's recognition of "the differential productivity of land in the case of equal inputs of labour".

210 Petty "had little or nothing to say...about the determination of wages" (Brewer 1992a: 716; as also Brewer 1992b: 130). Rather, as has been seen, he merely assumed that they must be held constant ("certain"), implicitly by state enforcement. See Chapter 3.1.4.

211 See Chapter 4.1.5.

212 As Brewer 1992a: 718 points out, Petty is far from consistent in adopting a surplus approach.

213 As Fine 1982: 93–98 relates, Ricardo's theory of agricultural rent was generalised by the early marginalists to industry as well as agriculture, a move which might well appear to be a theoretical 'victory' for rent theory but which in fact led, on the contrary, to the dissolution of rent as a specific category of revenue.

214 In fact, the range of variables in Petty's full formulation of his 'touchstone' concept is wider still, since he also goes on to make a comparison with "a like scope of other land" in which there were fewer consumers ("consumptioners"), thus including the further variable of population density.

215 Von Thünen 1966 [1826]: 1. This is, of course, a highly simplified (though very standard) account of von Thünen's theory; for a fuller outline, see Blaug 1985: 614–617.

216 See, in particular, Isard 1956: 24–27.

217 Isard 1990 [1949]: 28.

218 It survives intact in Ohta and Thisse 1993, and is broadly consistent with the more nuanced account given in Blaug 1979 and Blaug 1985: 614–631.

219 Krugman 1995: 34, as also Fujita, Krugman and Venables 1999: 25f., in both of which the terms 'Germanic' and 'Anglo-Saxon' are replaced by references to Germany and the 'English-speaking world'. See further in Chapters 4.3.5 and 5.1.2.

220 Marshall 1920: x (note), as noted by Hall in his editorial introduction to Von Thünen 1966 [1826]: xi.

221 Dicken and Lloyd 1990: 17f; see also 61–67 ('bid rent curves', etc.).

222 Krugman 1995: 53.
223 Fujita, Krugman and Venables 1999: 16; see also 15–18 and 133f.
224 This expression is borrowed from the title of a 1978 book by Schelling. See Krugman 1995: 77; 1998: 7; and 1996: 10–12.
225 Steuart 1966 [1767]: I, 134f. For discussion, see Beckmann 1981: 4–6. See also Dockès 1969: 356f (with diagram); and Perelman 2000: 157f.
226 Fernández López 2002, who takes Cerviño's paper, which was written in 1801 (though not published till 1955), as a case study in unacknowledged theoretical anticipation, but, ironically, ignores the previous formulation by Steuart.
227 Hull 1899: lxv.
228 Dockès 1969: 132–157 also covers much of the relevant ground.
229 Dockès 1969: 249, commenting on Cantillon [2015]: 252–261. See also Hébert 1981. Aspromourgos 1996: 202 (note 12), noting that "economic aspects of location are a major theme" of Cantillon's work, suggests that this might point to his exposure to Petty's TTC.
230 Stull 1994 [1986]: 80, the mention of 'neoclassical' predecessors presumably being a reference to Marshall, on whose spatial-economic views see Chapter 4.3.1.
231 For notable exceptions, see Dimou and Pecqueur 2012 and Dockès 2013, as discussed in Chapter 5.2.
232 For example, the above-mentioned specialist study by Stull 1994 [1986] is not mentioned in Mellinger, Sachs and Gallup 2000: 170, 177, though both of them discuss the same comments on the advantages of coastal proximity in Smith 1976 [1776]: 32–36. On issues of urban location, see further in Dimou and Pecqueur 2012, as discussed in Chapter 5.2.
233 Peet 2002: 391. It may be added, however, that the elision of the pre-von Thünen period has remained largely unchallenged within the field of economic geography as well.
234 This term is used in connection with von Thünen's theory by Krugman 1995: 37, discussing Blaug 1985²: 618–623.
235 Blaug 1979: 23, who is in fact here referring specifically to location theory; see also *ibid.* 28f., where Blaug attributes to the location theorist Alfred Weber and his successors "a highly abstract character associated traditionally with the writing of Ricardo and Walras but deriving in this case from the writings of [von] Thünen".
236 Von Thünen 1826: bound in at end.
237 Von Thünen 1966 [1826]: 215.
238 Corsten *et al.* 1990: V, 601f. (Perthes).
239 Von Thünen 1875: 390f. A similar schematised version is included in the 1966 translation, at von Thünen 1966 [1826]: 216. Blaug 1985: 615 also discusses a further version in part II of von Thünen's work, published in 1842.
240 Launhardt 1885: 179, fig. 14, as discussed by Blaug 1985: 619f.
241 Lösch 1954 [1940]: 106, fig. 21.
242 The example in the figure is from Dicken and Lloyd 1990: 58, who also reproduce (on p. 64) a similar figure from a 1967 article by Sinclair. A kind of hybrid version, or flattened cone, is included in Fujita, Krugman and Venables 1999: 16.
243 Barnes and Sheppard 2000: 3. The publication of Krugman 1991 may be taken to mark the 'launch' of the initiative as such, though Dymski 1996: 440 traces its first enunciation back to a paper which Krugman delivered in 1989 and published in 1990.
244 Referenced, in the remainder of the present chapter, by the abbreviation FKV.

245 FKV: 4.
246 *Ibid.*: 3; Krugman 1998: 10.
247 A "peaceful revolution" (Krugman 2000: 49).
248 More properly, the "Prize in Economic Sciences in Memory of Alfred Nobel" which is awarded by National Bank of Sweden. Members of the Nobel family have contested the use of the term "Nobel Prize in Economics".
249 FKV: xi.
250 Krugman 1991: xi; Krugman 2000: 50.
251 See Chapter 5.1.2.
252 Sheppard 2000a: 101.
253 For a critical review of this literature (which includes Barro and Sala-i-Martin 1995), see Martin 1999: 71–74.
254 Schmutzler 1999: 358.
255 Krugman 1995: 41.
256 FKV: 4, xi.
257 Marshall 1920: book 4, chap. 10 ("The concentration of specialised industries in particular localities"), particularly 271f.; see also part IV, chap. 12, particularly 296 (on cutlery manufacture in Sheffield). Krugman 1991: 36–38 conveniently quotes some of the relevant passages. See also FKV: 4f., 18; Krugman 1995: 49–52; 1998: 8f. (which includes a tabular presentation); and 1999: 143–145.
258 This terminology was introduced by Hirschman; Myrdal used broadly similar concepts, which he termed 'backwash' and 'spread' linkages, respectively. See Krugman 1995: 19–23; and Schmutzler 1999: 357f.
259 FKV: 5; Krugman 2000: 59.
260 See, for example, Krugman 1995: 50. On the history of this term, see Martin and Sunley 1996: 266.
261 FKV: 4–5; Krugman 1998: 8f. ("tug-of-war"); and also Krugman 1999: 143–145.
262 He explains, for example, that this was precisely the basis of Vernon Henderson's 'urban system' models. Krugman 1995: 51, 90; FKV: 19–22.
263 This section can be skimmed over by the non-technical reader, who will, hopefully, be able to pick up the thread of the main arguments in the following section.
264 Krugman 1995: 35f. "Each consumer becomes a Robinson Crusoe producing for his own consumption" (Ottaviano and Puga 1997: 3).
265 For a critical account of the competition issue as it is represented within spatial economics, see Sheppard 2000b: 171f., *passim*.
266 Dixit and Stiglitz 1977.
267 FKV: 45.
268 Besides the extended exposition of the SADS model in FKV: chap. 4, see the briefer discussions in Krugman 1995: 60f., 93f. and 97f., as well as the alternative, largely informal, exposition in Schmutzler 1999: 360f.
269 Krugman 1998: 10; FKV: 7.
270 FKV: 46.
271 *Ibid.*: 6.
272 Schmutzler 1999: 360.
273 Krugman 1995: 98, where this is described as "'quantisation' of production". For a simplified account of the principles involved, see Krugman and Obstfeld 2003: 119–124.
274 Schmutzler 1999: 361 usefully summarises these modelling advantages in informal terms.

275 FKV: 49, as also Krugman 1998: 10f. The 'iceberg' concept derives from a 1952 article by Samuelson, whose iceberg is, of course, prefigured in Wat Waller's sturgeon, as discussed in Chapters 4.2.1 and 4.4.1.
276 Schmutzler 1999: 373f.
277 FKV: 11. For a highly condensed exposition, see Krugman 2000: 53–55, where the model is described as "a basic introductory framework" for MCSE: "[I]n this sense it is like the two-by-two models of textbook trade theory." Other thumbnail versions are provided by Boddy 1999; Lanaspa, Pueyo and Sanz 2001; and Meardon 2002: 229–232.
278 Since $\sigma > 1$ and $\rho = {}^{(\sigma - 1)}/_{\sigma}$, we have $0 < \rho < 1$.
279 FKV: 55–58.
280 *Ibid.*: 55f. This concept has an affinity with that of 'market potential', pioneered in the 1950s by Chauncey Harris; see FKV: 32f.; Krugman 1995: 99; 2000: 57f.
281 Krugman 1998: 15; FKV: 57.
282 See Krugman 1998: 11f.; and FKV: 65–68. For a formal introduction to bifurcation diagrams, see FKV: 34–41.
283 FKV: 98.
284 *Ibid.*: 253.
285 Krugman 2000: 54 (emphasis in original).
286 Krugman 1995: 47; 1998: 12. See also Chapter 5.1.5; and, for examples of such use of multiple equilibria in other fields of economics, Schmutzler 1999: 377 (note 31).
287 See Krugman 1995: 104; FKV: 71, etc.; and, in less formal terms, Schmutzler 1999: 362.
288 On the "No-Black-Hole" condition, see FKV: 58f.; and Krugman 1995: 100–105.
289 For a full algebraic workout in the case of the CP model, see FKV: 71–75, and the appendix on pp. 76f.
290 Sunley 2000: 191.
291 Martin and Sunley 1996: 287.
292 Sheppard 2000a: 113.
293 FKV: chaps. 6, 10, 17. See also Krugman 1995: 105–108; and (even more briefly), Krugman 1998: 13f. Schmutzler 1999: 366 remarks that these models 'lack transparency', though this assessment pre-dates the intensive effort in FKV to relate their results to those of the bifurcation models. Krugman 1996 consists of a wider exploration of the underlying theory; for critical comment, see Dymski 1996: 442f.; and Martin 1999: 69.
294 Krugman 2000: 57.
295 Krugman 1998: 13.
296 FKV: 119–132.
297 *Ibid.*: 15–18, 133f.; Krugman 1995: 52–55.
298 Krugman 1995: 65, as also at p. 53.
299 Krugman 1996: 13.
300 Krugman 1995: 53. So also Krugman 2000: 50.
301 FKV: 140–143. This concept was derived from within the theory of 'market potential'.
302 Meardon 2002: 223–227 finds this claim exaggerated, no substantial progress having been made in endogenising the determination of boundaries between the spatial units in question.

303 See FKV, chaps. 9–11.

304 *Ibid.*: 239–241, 259, etc.

305 Ottaviano and Puga 1997: 7, citing a seminal 1996 paper by Venables. See also Krugman 1998: 14; 2000: 55f.; and Schmutzler 1999: 371–373.

306 Krugman and Obstfeld 2003: 131–134; and Sunley 2000: 189. See also Meardon 2002: 219–223 for a more critical, though generally favourable, assessment of MCSE's achievements in this respect.

307 FKV: 110f.

308 Venables 1998: 3.

309 FKV: 251–256 (a section entitled "Agglomeration and national inequality"), 258f. See also Schmutzler 1999: 372.

310 FKV: 259f. So also Krugman and Venables 1995: *passim.*

311 FKV: chap. 15, particularly 254 ("factor price equalisation"), 263f., 277 ("dramatic developmental spurts"). So also Venables 1998: 2, 5 ("sequential and rapid").

312 FKV: chap. 18. See also Schmutzler 1999: 367–369 for a review of some critical reactions to the initial formulation of this model.

313 Ottaviano and Puga 1997: 23.

314 Wages are deflated according to the expression $w_i (1 - \lambda)^\delta$, where $0 < \delta < 1$. On other attempts to model such additional centrifugal forces, see Schmutzler 1999: 364f.

315 The empirical reference is largely drawn from the work of Gordon Hanson, for a summary account of which see Hanson 1998.

316 "A reduction in trade barriers facilitates the separation of production from consumption" (Venables 1998: 3).

317 FKV: 335–337. Thus, Krugman 1999: 156 comments that the case of Brazil "would be a cleaner example of our story than the case of Mexico because proximity to the border is not an issue".

318 FKV: 348f. Similarly, Krugman 1999: 159 deplores the "frantic efforts of interested parties to recruit reputable economists to endorse questionable interventionist policies".

319 It is ironic that these arguments hinge on the effects of state policy, an element which the model itself excludes; accordingly, as Isserman 1996: 42 tellingly observes, even if the conclusions regarding these effects are accepted, this "does not qualify as a new insight *provided by the model*".

320 Martin and Sunley 1996: 275. A less restrained comment has been that, though "[he] himself [was] something of a liberal", his views on international trade may be summed up in the phrase "God bless the multinationals!" (*Monthly Review*: 2002: editorial). For further discussion of Krugman's commitment to the market, see Chapter 5.1.5.

321 PA: 267, where the agricultural-pastoral distinction is still very explicit, though in this instance clearly perceived as secondary to the distinction between both, on the one hand, and commerce and manufacture, on the other. On this passage, see also Chapter 4.1.6.

322 This practice also reflects his spontaneous assumption of social stratification in consumption, as discussed further in Chapter 4.4.2 (iv).

323 Though the sturgeon proposition is, of course, not Petty's own but, rather, his correspondent Southwell's. See Chapter 4.2.1.

324 See, for example, TTC: 31 §41, as discussed in Chapter 4.1.4.

325 Von Thünen 1966 [1826]: chap. 4. "Hence the von Thünen model may be considered as the predecessor of the 'iceberg transport technology'" (FKV: 59 (note 2)).

326 PAL: 476 §12. Dockès 1969: 140 comments that "Petty's ideal is a small economic circuit where all the activities will be localised in one point... Such a circuit needs, so to speak, no space." Petty's countervailing point about plague is noted by Goblet 1930: II, 342.

327 PAL: 473 §6. Hutchison 1997 [1988]: 23 uses the term 'external economies' to describe Petty's intentions in this passage; the term 'positive locational economies', normally used in connection with Marshallian theory, would be even more apt. See Chapter 4.3.1.

328 TTC: 41f §9, where he also adds interesting observations on the influence of prevailing winds on the direction of London's 'urban sprawl'. For discussion, see Goblet 1930: II, 337–342; and Dockès 1969: 133–135.

329 Smith 1976 [1776]: 32–36. See also Mellinger, Sachs and Gallup 2000: 170, 177.

330 MCSE portrays such 'hubs' as a 'catalyst' – critical in the early stages of a city's formation, but, having once set in motion a process of cumulative causation, potentially dwindling into insignificance. See FKV: 236, and chap. 13 generally. This idea is discussed further in Goodacre 2005a, where it is contrasted with the different approach of Sachs to such geographical issues. See also Dimou and Pecqueur 2012 on these issues, as discussed in Chapter 5.2.

331 Pinto 1997, discussing TTC: 24 §18. On Christaller, see also Chapter 4.3.4.

332 Pinto 1997.

333 TTC: 48 §4. See also Chapters 3.2.1, 4.1.5 and 4.2.1.

334 Lowry 1991: 7, as also discussed in Chapter 3.2.1.

335 Brewer 2003: 84, as discussed Chapter 3.2.1.

336 Goblet regards it as "the tragedy of his [i.e. Petty's] life" that he made the "fatal passage" from inductive to deductive logic, by abandoning the approach adopted in his early surveying and information-gathering work in favour of the political arithmetic of his later years. See Goblet 1930: I, 352; and 1955: 7. For discussion of the contested issue of Petty's relation to the various currents in the philosophy of scientific enquiry, see Aspromourgos 1996: 55–72; and, for a different view, Brewer 1992b: 126. For a more positive and comprehensive assessment of Petty's contribution to the "information gathering" which Goblet complains Petty abandoned, see Reungoat 2004, as discussed in Chapter 5.2.

337 FKV: 348f.

338 On these contradictions within Petty's thought, see Chapters 2.2 and 3.3.

339 FKV: 46. See Chapter 4.3.2.

340 This is even more the case than at first appears, since it is, in many cases, spirited out of the picture by deft choice of units. See equations 4.24, 4.31 and 4.32, in FKV: 52–54.

341 Compare the more general comment that "the whole edifice of the orthodoxy would collapse if preferences were endogenised" (Fine and Leopold 1993: 46).

342 It is, of course, not alone in microeconomic consumption theory in being unjustifiably "sealed off from other social sciences" in this way; see Fine and Leopold 1993: 46–54.

343 Dixit and Stiglitz 1977: 297.

344 PP1: 214.

345　See, for example, PP1: 213; and also *Bills:* 397.

346　PA: 270f.

347　See, for example, PAL: 474 §7; and PP1: 40–42 ("The uses of London").

348　PA: 243, 305; PAI: 143; *Bills:* 381; PP1: 197 §21; PP2: 149–151; PSC: 12–14, 40–42, 51. See also Petty's 1684 paper *Experiments to be Made Relating to Land Carriage,* as discussed in Chapter 4.1.4.

349　TTC: 34 §14; VS: 106f §11; PA: 269, 305; PP1: 214; PP2: 236 §126.

350　VS: 107 §3; PA: 259f §4, 285.

351　VS: 107 §3; PA: 269, 290; PP1: 42 §13, 214; PP2: 187 §6, 188 §1. See also Ochs 1985: 136.

352　VS: 107 §3; PP1: 42 §13, 206, 213f.

353　VS: 107 §3; PP1: 42 §15; PP2: 230 §70. See also index to EW ("Wine, importation of").

354　PA: 243, 305. The coach retained an equivalent symbolic significance for Smith; see, for example, Smith 1976 [1776]: 73, 93.

355　These percentages are suggested by rough-and-ready calculations on information provided in PAI: 143; PAL: 470; EW: 399, 534; and Mountfield 1976: 3.

356　*Bills:* 381.

357　Kurz and Salvadori 2003 [2000]: 42, as discussed in Chapters 2.1 and 4.1.5.

358　TTC: 89 §17. "The labouring class, in particular, is strongly identified with the consumption of corn" (Fine and Leopold 1993: 258). See also PAI, 181, where "day's food" plays a central part in establishing the 'par' between labour and land. Petty's citation of the Lord's Prayer in this connection is by no means original; it had been a familiar feature of doctrinal discussion since the time of the early Christian fathers.

359　See discussion in Chapter 3.1.4.

360　PAI, 193f §3.

361　PP1: 214.

362　PAI, 193f §3. Spurr 2000: 144f. cites a similar comment by Petty's contemporary Houghton.

363　See, for example, Weatherill 1996: 191f., citing works of Spufford and Thirsk; and, for a critique of the neoclassical approach to this issue, Perrotta 1997: 306, etc.

364　Fine 2001: 40 (note 47).

365　Ohlin 1933: 68.

366　Boddy 1999: 821; so also 827. So also Krugman 1991: 8, who singles out Europe as the prime example of the fact that "the lines between international economics and regional economics are becoming blurred in some important cases".

367　FKV: 239.

368　*Ibid.:* 259, 309, 240, 239f.

369　Krugman 1991: 71f.

370　Krugman 1998: 14.

371　FKV: 259f. See Chapter 4.3.6.

372　FKV: 253, referring to Krugman and Venables 1995.

373　For a review of some of this literature, see Goodacre 2005a.

374　Krugman 1991: xi; 1995: chap. 3; 2000:50. See, in particular, Krugman 1995: 85, where he shows that he regards the theories in question as not worthy of even the most cursory investigation; this passage is accordingly excoriated by Martin 1999: 82; Boddy 1999: 817; Oberhauser 2000: 63; and Peet 2002: 388.

375　Johnston 1992.

376 Hoare 1992: 679.
377 Sunley 2000: 190.
378 *Ibid.*: 197, citing Clark 1998: 83, *passim*.
379 Peet 2002: 389.
380 Berry 2002: 359.
381 Clark 1998: 74f.

5 William Petty and colonialism
A selective review of some current debates

5.0 Introduction: an "alternative genealogy of the history of political economy"?

Even as the research for this book has been proceeding, it has been increasingly widely recognised in the steadily expanding secondary literature on William Petty that the colonialist roots of his thinking can no longer be neglected in any assessment of his economic thought. Indeed, Cronin 2014 has called for nothing less than an "alternative genealogy of the history of political economy" that traces it back to its colonialist origins, which are revealed so graphically in Petty's maps and writings. The following brief and very selective survey reviews some of the current lines of research and debate which may be expected to impinge more or less directly on progress in establishing precisely such an "alternative genealogy".

It is not surprising that such a forceful demand for attention to the colonial context as Cronin's should be found in a study closely relating to Petty's spatial-economic approach, considering the flourishing state of critical literature in the field of economic geography. Such a perspective is seen not only among Irish authors such as Cronin but, historically, more especially in the French-language literature, where the interlinked question of Petty's contribution to the history of demography and its relation to his colonialist projects has also received authoritative attention, in Reungoat's 2004 monograph *William Petty, observateur de la population des îles britanniques*. Another flourishing area of research concerns the influence on Petty's thought of his engagement in natural philosophy – that is, early modern science – which has been encouraged not least by McCormick's 2009 monograph, *William Petty and the ambitions of political arithmetic*, and the colonial context has figured prominently in such studies. The literature on the history of economic thought, in contrast, while continuing to open up significant new lines of enquiry, for example in Aspromourgos 2005, only occasionally engages directly in discussions of the colonial context, a feature of that literature which the present study aims to remedy.[1]

In what follows, then, some current research and discussion will be surveyed, first, regarding Petty's spatial-economic thought and, secondly, regarding the influence on his thinking of the natural philosophy of his time. Next, current research in more well-trodden fields in the history of economic thought will be considered, notably Petty's contribution to the emergence of classical political economy, and the relation of his ideas to those of today's economic analysis. Finally, this current situation in the secondary literature on Petty will be placed in the context of wider debates on the capacity of concepts and methods forged in a specifically colonial context to address in an acceptable manner the major issues confronting the world economy today.

5.1 Petty's spatial-economic thought: a French–English zigzag

Dockès 2013 writes aptly of the relation between the English and French literatures on political economy in early modern times as a 'zigzag'. Discussion of the spatial-economic aspect of Petty's thought in its colonial context is an instance when that zigzag course remained, for a prolonged period, since the publication of Goblet 1930, almost entirely on the French side of the Channel. Dockès continues in that tradition in this follow-up to the account of Petty's spatial-economic thought in his 1969 monograph, though he now extends his discussion into Petty's political economy as whole, setting it firmly in its colonial context.

Dockès provides extensive detail on the historical, intellectual and political context of Petty's political economy, discussing his standpoint on all manner of colonial issues, along with associated matters relating to trade policy, his comments on race and slavery, and the place of colonies in his constitutional thought. He also provides a valuable assessment of Petty's 'cost–benefit' analysis of his population transfer scheme, a scheme of "social engineering on a massive scale" in which, he comments, populationism and authoritarianism are interlinked, the aim being "integration in submission". He draws attention to Petty's oft-repeated refrain that the colonised peoples are better off under colonial rule than if left under the domination of their former native rulers, for example in his rhetorical question: "What should they have gotten if the late Rebellion [of 1641] had succeeded, but a more absolute servitude?"[2] Dockès points out the enduring resonance of this "classic argument of colonialists", describing it as "worthy of the colonialist propagandists of the late nineteenth and the twentieth centuries".[3]

Of particular value in this study is that Dockès not only surveys such aspects of Petty's thought as these, which most obviously reflect the colonial context, but also places in that context a number of his pioneering political-economic concepts which have commonly been discussed without reference to it. He points out, for example, that Petty's formulation of his views on devaluation, interest rates, exchange rates and exports, banking and other matters were in a number of cases prompted with specific reference to the colonies, most often Ireland, which Dockès describes as "the colony *par excellence*" of the time.[4] Such examples illustrate how English political economy emerged in inseparable connection with the forging of colonialist ideology. As Dockès comments,

> The colonies are not a secondary question for Petty; colonisation is not studied in a last, marginal chapter. It is a central question and the problem of colonial development is the lifeblood of his work [*irrigue son oeuvre*].

In contrast, Dimou and Pecqueur 2012, in their study of Petty's contribution to the history of urban economics, make no reference at all to the colonial context, despite directly addressing many of the very same aspects of the matter as those discussed by Dockès, as well as in Part III of the present work.[5] Their article nevertheless constitutes a valuable contribution to the literature on Petty's spatial-economic analysis. They usefully review themes familiar from Hull 1899 onwards, such as the parallels with von Thünen's model and the cost-saving effect of economies of scale on public expenditure. They also compare and contrast the dominance of the benefits of compactness in Petty's discussions of efficiency with the market-based approach of Smith, a theme I have explored in detail in Goodacre 2010c. They comment that Petty's statistical indicators are remarkably closely equivalent to those used in town-planning decisions even today, and they contrast his consistent advocacy of concentration of population with the more balanced approach required by today's regional development policy. They note his attention to the continuing influence of physical geography on urban growth, in contrast to some of today's urban economic modelling, which has incorporated this influence with respect to towns' initial location only.[6] They even claim that Petty may be regarded as having anticipated the concept of an urban hierarchy.[7]

The overall assessment reached by this article is that Petty was ultimately incapable of building an actual model of urban development due to the absence in his time of the necessary mathematical apparatus. While this endorsement of the credo of writers such as Krugman regarding pre-marginalist economic thought shows that their theoretical approach is quite the contrary of that of the present study, their wide-ranging, well-targeted and authoritative references to current spatial-economic theory, and even in some cases to public policy issues of today, provide a valuable example of how the assessment of economic ideas of the past can contribute powerfully to the task of assessing those of the present, not only in theory but in practice.

It is not only in the case of spatial-economic analysis that French authors have dominated a particular aspect of Petty's writings; to that field must now be added the closely interlinked subject of his contribution to the history of demography, to which Reungoat 2004 has contributed by far the most comprehensive treatment to date. If, as the book's conclusion assumes, the systematic study of demography was definitively set on course by Thomas Malthus and his focus on the relation of population to means of subsistence, then Reungoat is justified in claiming that she has firmly established Petty as the discipline's outstanding precursor.[8] Moreover, though anchored in its chosen discipline of demography, Reungoat's monograph provides an example of how, no matter what entry point is taken in terms of today's disciplinary boundaries, any study that breaks new ground in its own field inevitably brings with it new insights than cannot be ignored from within any field of research on Petty's thought, activities and outlook.[9]

Reungoat's book reflects the relation between demography and spatial-economic analysis to which Cronin 2014 refers, in her observation that Petty wrote at a time when the Peace of Westphalia which concluded the Thirty Years War of 1618–48 had, for the time being at least, achieved a settlement among the European powers regarding their respective areas of territorial control. As Cronin points out, it was now the population within those territories which became their central concern. Indeed, the problems faced by the various powers in this respect even prompt Dockès 2013 to quote Bertolt Brecht's celebrated poem in which it is suggested that some governments might well wish to "dissolve the people and elect another". Petty's concept of population 'transmutation' responded to precisely such a governmental fantasy (without the election, of course!), and Reungoat accordingly places Petty's population transfer scheme firmly in the context of this central preoccupation of the states of his time.

Reungoat usefully places Petty's oft-mentioned 'populationism' in the context of a review of other relevant literature in his period.[10] Such aspects of the book inevitably extend into a number of different aspects of economic thought, including different attitudes to unemployment, to take only one example.[11] As for the relation of Petty's thought to colonialist thought in general, she makes a telling link between his advocacy of restraint in England's territorial ambitions and his concept of the 'value of people', commenting that that this amounts to a theory of colonialism in terms of the 'market value' of the colonised people rather than the extent of territorial control. Such was the power of Petty's political arithmetic to portray the aspirations of the post-Westphalian states in the crudest possible monetary terms.[12]

All this ground-breaking French-language literature, from Goblet to Dockès and Reungoat, has yet to be adequately assimilated into the English-language literature. One example where this would be beneficial concerns an apparent contradiction in Petty's standpoint on Ireland's population. In the final years of his life he wrote of his vision of an increase in that population, while he was also, of course, at the very same time further elaborating his more long-standing discussions of his population transfer scheme in which he had discussed the benefits of drastically reducing it.

For writers in the French-language literature, this apparent contradiction is discussed and explored. As Dockès 2013 points out, Petty's population transfer scheme reflected his priorities regarding the peopling of the territories under England's control: first to be fully peopled was England, the metropolitan core, while Ireland and the rest of its colonial empire were to stand ready as a kind of "reservoir" to be filled up once that core territory was fully peopled. Dockès sees this as the colonial dimension of a 'general law' in Petty's thinking, which is that the advantages of population density are such that the transfer of populations from more sparsely to more densely populated locations always takes priority, a 'law' also reflected in his writings on the advantages of urbanisation. Seen in this light, the two different strands in Petty's writings on the Irish population, whatever their conflicting implications for immediate colonial policy, are not ultimately contradictory. Indeed, Reungoat 2004 aptly argues that Petty's standpoint was not in the long term incompatible with even the most megalomanic (*megalomane*) ambitions for England to rule the world, if it could take a lead in the 'multiplication of mankind' and thus progressively extend the territory of its colonial empire in step with its capacity to people it fully.[13]

The consequences of a lack of interaction with such discussions in the French-language literature are seen in Fox 2009, an article which usefully outlines the contents of some unpublished manuscripts on Ireland written by Petty in his final years, in which he advocates measures for the expansion of Ireland's population. As Dockès points out, populationist ideas "grew" on Petty as time passed. Fox's article is very useful in its close examination of these manuscripts, which show how, in the later years of his life, populationism dominated his perspective to the extent that in these cases it crowded out any mention, let alone approbation, of any effects his schemes might have in depopulating Ireland. Fox's article, by restricting its focus entirely to these particular manuscripts advocating an expansion of that country's population, without reference to the other writings in which his standpoint involved drastically reducing it, leaves the contradiction hanging in the air and its implications unexplored. This unresolved conundrum could have been avoided had the article taken account of the French-language literature; as Dockès 2013 points out, ideas in Petty's writings which at first sight appear contradictory may often be found to follow a certain underlying logic once they are placed in their colonial context.

The present study, as well as Goodacre 2009 and 2010c, have aimed to reduce the amplitude of this zigzag course between the French and English literatures on Petty's spatial-economic analysis and its relation to his colonialist thought. Far more significant is a new movement of the zigzag towards Ireland itself. As Cronin 2014 illustrates, from the perspective of that country it can readily and immediately be appreciated that Petty's ideas were not originated to deal with populations in general but specifically with colonial populations. His goal for the populations of the territories under England's control was, observes Cronin, to transmute them into "a mobile, transnational labor force", and the central pillar of this policy was to establish "a form of colonial government aiming to secure and regulate the Irish colony through the management of the mobility and behaviour of the Irish population" through the implementation of his "highly gendered" intermarriage scheme.

In Petty's words, Ireland was "as a White Paper", on which the English were to "pass into Positive Laws whatsoever is right reason and the Law of Nature", while in his maps, notes Cronin, all such "political and cultural assumptions... were obscured". Such abstraction of social reality from his maps – his initial point of analytical reference – prefigures the deductive approach of neoclassical economic models, whose initial point of analytical reference – Cartesian space – takes abstraction to its extreme. Indeed, even more strikingly, Petty's call for a "new geography of Ireland"[14] cannot fail to bring to mind the connecting thread between his thought with that of the neoclassical 'new economic geography" in particular.

5.2 Petty's natural philosophy in its colonial context

The study of influences upon Petty's political-economic thinking from within the various fields of natural philosophy and experimentation in which he participated has received increasing attention in recent years, in line with the increasing interest in general in the identity of early modern natural-philosophic, social, political and economic thought. McCormick 2009 and other works by that author have been giving a powerful impulse to this field of enquiry, and much of the resulting literature focuses on Petty's schemes for Ireland, and, by extension, his contribution to colonialist ideas in general. Indeed, Attis 2014 situates Petty's mathematical method on an "intersection" between, on the one hand, the "scientific story" (seen as one of progress towards the truth of nature, the quest to find correct methods of investigation, and so on) and, on the other hand, the "Irish story", which is one of "sectarian hatred and unabashed colonialism".[15]

Other relevant studies include Carroll 2006, a monograph which devotes a substantial proportion of its text – two whole chapters – to a discussion of Petty's main writings on Ireland, arguing that he applied a mode of thought pioneered by Robert Boyle in his scientific work on "meters, scopes, graphs and chambers". Petty's schemes for Ireland, argues Carroll, are an application of this "engine science", an argument he pursues in great detail. Another study, Sivado 2017 argues that Petty's revival of Anne Green functioned in his thinking as an example of a life-and-death case in which, in contrast to the general trend towards minimal intervention in the medical thought of his time, drastic intervention was needed. This, argues Sivado, influenced Petty's thinking on Ireland, which he saw as a nation in a mortal state, and thus substantiating his drastic proposals for the country.[16] Both Carroll and Sivado perform the useful function of taking forward long-standing discussions within the secondary literature on Petty by relating them to relevant current literature on the history of early modern experimental science and medicine respectively. Unlike Attis 2014, however, they both distance their discussions from the kind of post-colonial standpoint generally present in discussions of Petty's schemes for Ireland, explicitly so in the case of Sivado, who comments that it would be "uncharitable" to see Petty's scheme as "equated with the logic of colonialism and disenfranchisement".

Petty's oft-cited comments on non-European "species of men" clearly began to generate the terminology of racism as we know it today, and they certainly lack nothing in nastiness, especially considering his endorsement of the African slave trade. Lewis 2011 confronts this subject directly, exploring the distinctive features of Petty's comments that reflect the intellectual life of his time. In particular, Petty's standpoint on what was perceived to be the diversity of mankind reflects the continuing influence of classical 'geo-humoral' ideas – that is, a standpoint based on environmental, rather than physical, factors.[17] These environmental factors, though initially climatic, extend also into the social and cultural environment as well, and were consequently, Petty considered, open to improvement. This, in turn, rendered all peoples capable of improvement as well – that is, improvement to the level of Europeans.[18] One 'practical' advantage of this standpoint, Lewis points out, is that it rendered his ideas acceptable in political-religious terms, since the idea of different lineages of mankind in addition to the 'Adamite' line was at the time repudiated by the Church as a heresy;[19] Petty's use of the term 'species' is thus distinct from its usage in subsequent biology. Another advantage of this standpoint for Petty, of course, is that it is consistent with the idea that his colonialist and demographic schemes were in the interests of the advancement of the colonised peoples themselves.[20]

The formidable erudition displayed in Lewis's study provides a sobering example of the range of issues to which any branch of the history of ideas potentially leads, as indeed do the studies of other writers such as McCormick, Attis, Carroll and Sivado. Whether or not such studies directly engage with economic issues as such, and whether or not their standpoint is in accord with that of the present study, they all exemplify the kind of open-ended interdisciplinarity whose insights into the history of economic thought are all too often missed in the literature of the economics subdiscipline concerned with that subject.

5.3 Petty, colonialism and historians of economic thought

It is evident, then, that commentators on Petty's writings from within a range of fields of enquiry now emphasise, or in some cases even centralise, the colonial context in which his thinking was rooted, thus bringing to the fore his ideological motivation to justify and impel forward England's colonial ambitions. In contrast, there are, even now, few historians of economic thought who take account of this aspect of Petty's thought, the general preference being to remain on more well-trodden ground, notably the status of Petty in relation to classical political economy, and other issues concerning the relation of his thought to various features of economic analysis today.

Writers broadly classified as adhering to the 'surplus school' associated with Piero Sraffa have continued to dominate much of this output. Aspromourgos 2005 has broken new ground in a pioneering study of Petty's participation in the activities of the Hartlib circle, exploring the possible influence of this period in the intellectual trajectory followed by him in his path towards formulating the celebrated discussions of surplus and distribution in his 1662 *Treatise*. The article shows how archival research can inject new momentum into discussions which have long remained static. The article leapfrogs Petty's ensuing seven years' service in the Cromwellian colonial administration in Ireland, however, leaving the impression that those years were an unproductive interruption in the development of his economic ideas rather than a formative period. Nor does Roncaglia, the other author long identified with the promotion of Petty's standing as a pioneer of classical political economy, make substantial reference to the colonial context in his monographs of 2005 and 2017.[21]

In a rejoinder to Aspromourgos 2005, Brewer 2011 contests the views of such adherents of 'surplus' schools. Placing the points at issue in the context of the preoccupations of the time, he argues that Petty's contribution to the emergence of classical political economy has been overestimated, as also has his status as a forerunner of today's economic ideas such as those of macroeconomics.[22] Murphy 2009, in contrast, argues that Petty's writings embrace "many of the foundation stones for macroeconomics", and that, in particular, *Verbum Sapienti* "put in place the template for macroeconomic analysis".[23] Ullmer 2004 likewise finds anticipations of subsequent macroeconomic ideas in passages from Petty's writings, while Ullmer 2011 analyses Petty's methodology on the basis of the mainstream's favoured – and widely criticised – assumption that there exists a sharp distinction between positive and normative statements. Goodchild 2017, in a sensitive study of the concept of trust, traces what he sees as a movement from a "concern for credit" to a "concern for self-interest", with the financial revolution that followed Petty's death marking a major turning point.

In any event, both within the mainstream and heterodox literature on the pre-Smithian period, the received view that Petty is a pioneer – or even the outstanding pioneer – of modern economic thought remains, on the whole, as firmly entrenched as ever. A further feature shared by all too many contributors to this literature is that Petty's economic thought is discussed within the framework of a 'closed economy'. This can preclude insights into the origination of ideas which have unjustifiably become regarded as lacking a connection with international affairs. For example, as Dockès 2013 points out, even one of the most central concepts discussed by the surplus schools – the surplus product itself – was formulated by Petty in connection with the international context, as a matter concerning the comparative gross surplus produced by, respectively, England and France.[24] Such international aspects of Petty's perspective on economic concepts remain poorly explored in the existing literature, lack of attention to the issue of colonialism being the outstanding example.[25]

In the case of some aspects of Petty's economic thought, then, it may require effort to break with long-standing and ingrained decontextualised perspectives that abstract it from its international and colonialist context. But it might at least have been expected that more attention could have been paid to those elements of his writings which so directly and self-evidently connect with the issues addressed by development economics, that branch of the discipline concerned with those "cheap and common animals" of today – the countries still suffering from the legacy, or even in some cases the present reality, of colonialism and neo-colonialism. As I have argued, for example in Goodacre 2005b[26] (much of the text of which is substantially the same as Part I of the present study), the connection here is so obvious that it is disappointing that Petty still receives little more mention in connection with the history of that economics subdiscipline than the occasional use of the term 'Petty's law' (as, for example, in Murata 2008 and Vélez Tamayo 2017) or other passing references.

Like Dockès 2013, Wendt 2014 stands out as a welcome exception to the evasion of the international and colonial context of Petty's thinking as a whole. He comments that Petty's colonialist activities in Ireland "left their mark on the formulation of his scientific work, which cannot be sensibly detached from them", and, like Dockès, he notes that the justification of colonialism as a policy serving the interests of the colonised population and social progress in their country "was an early formulation of a figure of argumentation that has survived until the present time in colonialist and neo-colonialist discourses".[27] It is indeed gratifying to find, in the work of writers such as Dockès and Wendt, that such endorsement of the general trend of commentary from outside the literature on the history of economic thought is now becoming voiced from within it as well.

5.4 Petty, Whig history and colonialism

The "Whig interpretation of history" is a term popularised by the historian Herbert Butterfield to characterise a standpoint that praises intellectual 'revolutions' provided they have been successful and sees intellectual history as a progress towards a present which is represented as a triumphant culmination of all that is valuable in what has gone before. The term has accordingly proved attractive to critics of the currently dominant orthodoxy in the economics discipline, established as it was by that most successful of revolutions in economic thought, the 'marginalist revolution' of the 1870s. Yet, despite the fairly wide currency of the term among the economics heterodoxy, the aspect of Butterfield's formulation of the concept which is most directly relevant to the present study has not received the attention it deserves. This is that Butterfield links the concept inseparably to a tendency "to write on the side of Protestants and Whigs", in such a way as to produce "a scheme of general history…demonstrating throughout the ages the workings of an obvious principle of progress, of which the Protestants and Whigs have been the perennial allies while Catholics and Tories have perpetually formed obstruction".[28]

In the context of Irish history, to "write on the side of Protestants" is, of course, inevitably associated with arguments in favour of Ireland's union with Britain, a euphemism for English colonial domination, or "integration in submission", as Dockès aptly describes it. As Reungoat 2015 points out, Petty was a major player in the formulation of an ideology to justify this form of submission, which involved underpinning the identity of the dominant Protestant community, an identity in which the early modern science movement played a substantial role.[29] Petty's political arithmetic is an extreme example of the claim to ideological neutrality by supporters of England's colonial empire that its domination was in the interests of the colonised country's 'improvement', and thus in the interests of the colonised population as well as well as those of the colonising power. This aspect of the colonialist thought of the time,

Reungoat points out, was in striking contrast with, yet coexisted with, the inherited stereotypes and prejudices regarding the largely Catholic population, which were to be further rationalised and reinforced under the 'Protestant Ascendancy' of succeeding centuries.

It is now widely accepted that English colonial domination of Ireland was an archetype of the colonial relationship which was subsequently globalised. As the schemes by Petty to manipulate the country's religious demography illustrate, part of that archetypal process was to pioneer the divide-and-rule policies, all too often exploiting religious differences, whose consequences still bring devastation to so much of the world scene today. Such was Petty's close engagement in both the practice and, to an even greater extent, the ideological legitimation of the formative stages in the emerging colonial world order.

One debate which has in recent years been generating a number of studies of Petty's contribution to colonialist thought, much of it from within the field of historical geography, has centred on the question of the applicability to his writings on Ireland of Michel Foucault's concept of governmentality. As has been seen, this concept is discussed by Mykkänen 1994 in relation to Petty's writings on London, in which, Mykkänen argues, the various elements of control which Foucault groups together under this term are already identifiable. More recently, Henry 2014 has questioned this, on the basis of an exhaustive juxtaposition of Petty's account of the Down Survey with aspects of the governmentality concept relating to the question of territorial control. His conclusion is that the context confronted by Petty was so different from that of the eighteenth-century countries around which Foucault framed the concept that it is not, in fact, applicable in Petty's case.

Morrissey 2012, in contrast, makes a detailed defence of the application of the governmentality concept to colonial Ireland, arguing that the issues Foucault discusses under that heading have not been adequately assessed in the case of control of colonial populations, and in particular Ireland, and he is critical of Foucault for focusing his discussions on the metropolitan countries of eighteenth-century Europe.[30] Cronin 2014 takes up this point with specific reference to Petty, arguing that his perspective on the matters in question originated within the colonial context and thus specifically with respect to the control of colonial populations. She accordingly writes:

> This may have merit in the context of the European Metropole but in the context of a colonial geography I would argue that forms of governmentality as outlined by Foucault can be traced much earlier to the work of Petty and his experiences in seventeenth-century Ireland.

One result of the historically truncated perspective criticised by Cronin is that it serves to reinforce what she describes as "the received Enlightenment narrative of political economy through the figure of Adam Smith". Significantly, then, her critique parallels some of the critical points made in relation to neoclassical economics in the present study.

Whatever the outcome of this particular debate – a debate within a current of thought of which the economics discipline has never taken any account[31] – there is surely at any rate less and less justification for turning a blind eye to the colonialist context in any assessment of Petty's legacy to economic thought, or to allow to pass unchallenged the assumption that his plans for Ireland offered the most favourable future for the Irish people as well as for the colonising power – that "classic argument of colonialists", to borrow the phrase of Dockès. This is not to decry the service to scholarship of past writers who have shared such an assumption; on the contrary, to name only the most prominent example, Petty's own descendants Fitzmaurice and Lansdowne – in the long view beneficiaries in terms of social position and even materially of his colonialist activities – have earned the deserved gratitude of generations of students of his life and writings for their valuable research and publication work.[32] But for such assumptions to continue to exist in the secondary literature today indicates a drastic disjuncture from what has now become the main motivation for post-colonial studies, and indeed a disjuncture from the generally accepted standpoint of liberal opinion. Such outmoded survivals from standpoints and attitudes embedded in the intellectual culture of the colonial countries of previous generations now constitute a barrier to the assessment of ideas and methods inherited from that source.

5.5 Conclusions

"The difficulty lies not so much in developing new ideas as in escaping from old ones," as Keynes famously remarked with reference to the grip of an inflexible orthodoxy on the economists of his day. This difficulty has now been further illustrated in the case of the uneven success with which the various different currents of thought within the current literature on the history of economic thought, even those critical of that orthodoxy, are succeeding in escaping from the intellectual legacy of colonialism. In any event, discussion and debate on issues arising in connection with Petty's life and writings are clearly flourishing, and arguments for and against the standpoint advanced in the present study are becoming more widespread, transcending differences of the discipline or school of thought of the various commentators.[33] In every case the associated research and discussion have enriched the debates in question and demonstrated that they have a long way to go and a valuable task ahead in assessing ideas that remain current in the economics discipline today.

Notes

1 See also Goodacre 2005b, 2009, 2010a, 2010b and 2014.
2 See PAI: 202–203, where Petty also discusses the fate of those Irish forced to leave their native land, commenting that this is "manifestly" in their own "interest", a comment that has a particular resonance in the case of Ireland's history, considering that country's experience in the mid-nineteenth century.

3 Translations from Dockès and other items in French are here, as elsewhere in this study, my own.

4 He cites, for example, PAI 193, 219, 222.

5 Apart from one passing reference to Petty's population transfer scheme, in which Ireland is referred to as his "native land".

6 Commenting on TTC: 41 §9, on the effects of wind direction on urban spread.

7 Commenting on the conclusion to the last of Petty's 1687 *Five essays in political arithmetic* (EW: 544).

8 Reungoat 2004: 167–173.

9 On Reungoat's discussion of Petty's contribution to the history of statistics, see Chapter 3.2.2.

10 Reungoat 2004: 231–249.

11 *Ibid.*: 163–173.

12 *Ibid.*: 198.

13 *Ibid.*: 249.

14 TTC: 5–6.

15 Attis 2014: 14, 29, 49, in a study of mathematics in Ireland. Sy and Tinker 2014, who describe Petty as "the first general comptroller of England", extend the discussion of Petty's influence into the field of accounting.

16 For further discussion of Sivado 2017 and other studies of the influence on Petty of his medical background, see Chapter 4.1.1.

17 Some of the same issues are also discussed in McCormick 2013a.

18 Or more specifically to the level of the English, their value being, by Petty's calculations, somewhat higher than that the French, let alone the Irish. See Chapter 3.1.4.

19 For another discussion of the Pre-Adamite heresy and other religious connotations of the discussions in which Petty was engaging, see McCormick 2013b.

20 It is hard to imagine a more extreme example of the point made by Dockès 2013 that ideas in Petty's writings which at first sight appear contradictory may often be found to follow a certain underlying logic once they are placed in their colonial context. It also illustrates the consequences of detaching abstract logic from all ethical considerations.

21 For a review of Roncaglia 2005 [2001], see Goodacre 2008.

22 For a brief critical assessment of this interchange, see Goodacre 2014.

23 Murphy 2009: 36.

24 Dockès 2013: 13 (note 40, discussing DPA).

25 Among the exceptions are Brewer 2011; Murphy 2009; and also Mendoza Herrejon 2017, who places Petty's writings on England's overseas empire in the context of its trade rivalries with its competitors.

26 The volume in which this study is contained has been published in two editions in India, as well as in translation in Vietnamese.

27 This monograph usefully summarises the biographical context of Petty's economic writings and provides thought-provoking outlines of aspects of the writings of Thomas More, Bacon, Hobbes and the Hartlib circle that have relevance to economic issues.

28 Butterfield, 1931, v, 12. In Goodacre 2014 I have discussed the residual 'Whiggism' in Butterfield's own standpoint, not least his sponsorship of the 'value-free' historiography for Ireland that was the object of the criticism by Bradshaw 1994 [1989].

29 Similarly, Attis 2014: 31 says that, in early modern Ireland, science was a "practical tool for the extension of Protestant rule and English commerce". Barnard 2008 includes authoritative accounts of Petty's activities in Ireland, placing them in historical context in great detail. Valeri 2010 discusses the reception of political economy in the American colonies in the context of the religious debates of the time, largely in relation to Puritan teachings.

30 McCormick 2014, in a review of the debate on the applicability to political arithmetic of the governmentality concept, takes a kind of middle view, arguing that its seventeenth-century pioneers played only an 'anticipatory role' in a process which did not come to fruition till shortly before 1789.

31 Krugman 1995: 85 dismisses all such discussion with the exclamation "Deconstructionist geography!", lumping together under that heading a number of distinct currents of thought in this term in an ignorant manner that earned him the excoriation of Martin 1999: 82; Boddy 1999: 817; Oberhauser 2000: 63; and Peet 2002: 388. On the 'real' deconstructionist geography, see Gibson-Graham 2000: 97 (Derrida), *passim*.

32 Not least the present study, including as it does 37 references to Fitzmaurice and 87 to the editions by Lansdowne.

33 Published material includes not only commentary but the publication of more Petty texts, such as those already discussed in Reungoat 2004 and Lewis 2012a, as well as other texts of various kinds, such as those in Love 2007 and Jordan 2010. The Down Survey maps are now available on the website of the L Brown Collection at www.lbrowncollection.com/ireland-counties-sir-william-petty-1655-bro-09, and the 1659 census of Ireland, in which it is assumed that Petty took a role, has also been placed online at http://clanmaclochlainn.com/1659cen.htm. Translations include the important Reungoat 2017, a translation of TTC, VS and PA, with an informative introduction that situates these writings in the context of the current literature on Petty's writings, and also includes an account of the reception of his writings in translation in France. Other useful material includes the masterly summary biography by Barnard 2004, and Lewis 2012b.

Postscript

William Petty and the colonialist roots of economics

Some decades after Petty's death, Jonathan Swift, best known as author of *Gulliver's Travels*, drew attention to the appalling reality behind the clinical terms of Petty's 'political arithmetic' in his celebrated 1729 parody entitled *A modest proposal for preventing the children of poor people from becoming a burthen to their parents or country, and for making them beneficial to the publick*. In terms which imitate Petty's mode of expression with icy accuracy, this pamphlet puts forward a gruesome proposal for the breeding of Irish children as livestock. They would, he suggests, make "excellent nutritious meat" – "whether stewed, roasted, baked or boiled" – for sale to "persons of quality and fortune". The proposal is advanced complete with Petty's characteristic panoply of statistical justification, covering the demographic aspects, the average weight of each carcass, the numbers to be "reserved for breed", the costs of rearing ("about two shillings per annum, rags included"), potential uses for the hides ("gloves for ladies, and summer boots for fine gentlemen"), the export potential, the implications for the revenue of the Church, and so on.[1]

Swift's satire would retain less of its bite had not the subsequent history of colonialism in Ireland made a reality of what, for Petty, had been a mere "dream or reverie" – his discussions of the advantages of the mass removal of Irish people from their native land. For, as the geographer Goblet, writing in 1930, tellingly observed, Petty's scheme was grimly prophetic of what was actually to transpire in the two centuries that followed, when Ireland was indeed emptied of the majority of its inhabitants, its language and traditional way of life had to fight for survival and much of its territory (at any rate in the southern, 26-county, state) served, as it largely did in Goblet's time, as one vast cattle ranch. This prompted Goblet to ask:

> What politician has ever put forward a plan, be it never so formal and official, which has been realized so comprehensively, point by point, as the "reverie" of Sir William Petty?[2]

A reviewer of Goblet's work commented, similarly, that Petty's schemes for Ireland "would be ludicrous if the next two centuries had not proved them to be in many ways prophetic".[3]

Petty's writings not only point forward to such effects of the colonialism of the centuries that were to come but also endorse the Atlantic slave trade that was gaining momentum in his lifetime. Indeed, as has been seen, slavery plays a central part in his economic thought in connection with his concept of the 'value of people'.[4] Moreover, this helped to anchor the use of the concept of slavery in the literature of classical political economy and beyond, to the disgust of the philosopher Jean-Jacques Rousseau, who, almost certainly with Petty in mind, expressed his disapproval of those who hold that "a man is worth the price he would fetch in Algiers".[5] Rousseau bracketed this standpoint with that of others who "evaluate men like herds of cattle", this apparently being a reference to a passage in Cantillon's *Essai*, in which the advantage of slaves over free peasants is stated to be that their proprietor "can sell the surplus slaves as he does his cattle",[6] a remark which, according to one commentator, might, in turn, have been suggested to Cantillon by his reading of Petty.[7] Nor did such statements in the literature of classical political economy end there,[8] for Adam Smith continued to bracket together "the wages or maintenance of the labourers and labouring cattle",[9] and suggested that agriculture is the most productive sector, since, for the farmer, "not only his labouring servants, but his labouring cattle are productive labourers".[10] Even Smith's celebrated critique of slavery, while undoubtedly of practical use to anti-slavery campaigners of the time, centred on its inefficiency as much as on its inhumanity.[11]

But the unconcealed predatory intent and the reality of colonialist devastation and the slave trade that lie behind Petty's economic thought have been as clear as day to writers as diverse as the satirist Swift, the philosopher Rousseau, the Irish nationalist Mitchel and the French geographer Goblet, and is now increasingly brought to the fore by commentators and researchers in various fields of enquiry, as has been illustrated in the survey of current literature on Petty in the last chapter of this book.

Given the centrality of the history of Ireland throughout the present study, it is fitting to conclude by turning to a body of historical writing which, under the banner of the 'reappraisal of Irish history', confronted the intellectual legacy of a period in which much of Ireland's own historiography had been dominated by a 'revisionist' current, which had adopted a dismissive attitude to its own country's anti-colonial and nationalist traditions. In a seminal article calling for such a reappraisal, it was pointed out that "austerely clinical terms" had come to be seen as an essential prerequisite for an "academic" approach to Irish history. Such an approach had resulted in the elision of the "catastrophic dimension" of that history, "thereby de-sensitising the trauma" of the country's colonial experience.[12] It was further pointed out that Ireland's traumatic experience has not been unique; it was shared in early modern times by those other countries and nations of Europe that were also engulfed by the so-called 'wars of religion' in the aftermath of the Reformation; and, of course, as the great divergence in the fortunes of the world's peoples grew ever wider, the same experience came to be shared by the majority of humankind.

The tasks faced in the course of the 'reappraisal of Irish history' are not of Irish interest alone but are, clearly, of significance for the reassessment of the intellectual legacy of the colonial period of world history as a whole. The aim of the present study has been to extend this reappraisal into the field of the history of economics, and to show that the built-in bias concealed beneath the yet more 'austerely clinical terms' of today's formalistic economic models cannot be brought to light without bringing back into view the 'catastrophic dimension' of the context in which the roots of economics lie. In a world still suffering from the legacy of the colonial era, such a reappraisal is not confined in significance to the past so long as ideas forged to justify the trauma of colonial domination are still allowed to pass unchallenged in the present.

Notes

1 Swift 1729. Some of the literature on this pamphlet makes little or no reference to Petty, focusing instead on literary aspects, such as its use of the symbolism of cannibalism. Briggs 2005 suggests that Graunt was uppermost in Swift's mind, though Reungoat 2004: 289–290, Goodacre 2010a and Dockès 2013 all assume that, to the extent that any individual was intended as the target, it was Petty, who was acknowledged by Swift's contemporaries to be the originator of the political arithmetic he was satirising. For a thorough discussion of Swift's intentions in their historical context, with relevant references to Petty's writings, see Welch 2013. Sussman 2004 takes this pamphlet as a reference point for a discussion of the reception of political arithmetic in the American colonies, usefully relating Petty's schemes on Ireland with subsequent discussion of 'mobile populations'.
2 Goblet 1930: II, 305.
3 Lynam 1932: 418.
4 See Chapter 3.1.4.
5 Rousseau 1986 [1750]: 16 §41. Rousseau does not cite Petty by name, but the context makes it more than likely that his remark was provoked by a passage in a pamphlet by Petty, *Two Essays in Political Arithmetick*. This pamphlet, on the relative populations of London and Paris, was evidently aimed as much at a French as an English readership; it was, in fact, first published in French, as *Deux Essays d'Arithmétique Politique*. See Aspromourgos 1996: 200 (note 16, discussing EW: 512); EW: 502 (editorial comment), 642f §18a, 18b; and Keynes 1971: 25–28.
6 Cantillon 1931 [*c*. 1730]: 35. As already noted in Chapter 3.0, Cantillon uses the term *esclave* indiscriminately to apply to slave and wage labourer alike.
7 Aspromourgos 1996: 200 (note 16).
8 On Marx's origination of the term 'classical political economy', and the place of Petty within the first, preliminary or formative phase of its history, see Aspromourgos 1996: 2f.; and, for discussion, Goodacre 2012.
9 Smith 1976 [1776]: 68.
10 *Ibid.*: 363. "Fine compliment for the labouring servants!" observed Marx 1956 [1885]: 365.
11 For discussion of Smith's comments on slavery, see Goodacre 2010b. 'Cattle feed' still enters into discussion of wage theory in Sraffa 1960: 9, as discussed by Aspromourgos 1996: 200 (note 16).
12 Bradshaw 1994 [1989]: 201–204.

Bibliography

Works of William Petty

There are two very detailed bibliographies of Petty's published works, which both contain full information on their publishing history. The first is by Hull in EW: 633–660; and the second, even fuller, is Keynes 1971. The following is merely a selective list, including only those items referred to in the present study, roughly in the order in which Petty wrote them.

Page references to the major economic works are to the pages in EW, which has established itself as definitive; this edition in most cases includes the pagination of the early editions in the margin.

EW retains Petty's orthography and punctuation throughout; these have largely been modernised in quotations in the present study, however.

Compilations

EW   *The economic writings of Sir William Petty, together with the Observations upon the Bills of Mortality, more probably by Captain John Graunt.* Edited by Charles H. Hull. 2 volumes. Cambridge: Cambridge University Press. 1899.

PP1, PP2   *The Petty papers: some unpublished writings of Sir William Petty.* Edited from the Bowood Papers by the Marquis of Lansdowne. 2 volumes. London: Constable. 1927.

PSC   *The Petty–Southwell correspondence, 1676–1687.* Edited from the Bowood Papers by the Marquis of Lansdowne. London: Constable. 1928.

DB   *The double-bottom or twin-hulled ship of Sir William Petty.* Documents introduced and edited by the Marquis of Lansdowne. Oxford: printed for presentation to the members of the Roxburghe Club. 1931.

            Tracts, chiefly relating to Ireland, containing: I. A treatise of taxes and contributions. II. Essays in political arithmetic. The political anatomy of Ireland. By the late Sir William Petty. To which is prefixed his Last Will. Dublin: Boulter Grierson. 1769.

Individual works

Advice   *The advice of W. P. to Mr. Samuel Hartlib for the advancement of some particular parts of learning.* London. 1648. Subsequently included in *Harleian Miscellany*, volume VI (1744): 1–14.

BA   "A brief account of the most material passages relating to the survey managed by Doctor Petty in Ireland, anno 1655 and 1656". Apparently written around 1656. Included by Larcom in DS: xiii–xvii.

DS   *The history of the survey of Ireland commonly called the Down Survey, by Doctor William Petty, A.D. 1665–6.* Edited by Thomas A. Larcom. 1851. Apparently written in 1659–60.

Reflections *Reflections upon some persons and things in Ireland, by letters to and from Dr. Petty, with Sir Hierome Sankey's speech in Parliament.* London: John Martin, etc. 1660.

Bills   *Natural and political observations mentioned in a following index, and made upon the Bills of Mortality. By John Graunt, citizen of London* [evidently with some collaboration by Petty]. *With reference to the government, religion, trade, growth, ayre, diseases, and the several changes of the said City.* London: John Martin, etc. 1662.

TTC   *A treatise of taxes and contributions. Showing the nature and measures of Crown-lands, assessments, customs, poll-moneys, lotteries, benevolence, penalties, monop-olies, offices, tythes, raising of coins, harth-money, excize, &c. With several intersperst discourses and digressions concerning warrs, the Church, universities, rents and purchases, usury and exchange, banks and Lombards, registries for conveyance, beggars, ensurance, exportation of money [and of] wool, free ports, coins, housing, liberty of conscience, &c. The same being frequently applied to the state and affairs of Ireland.* London: printed for N. Brooke. 1662. In EW: 1–97.

            "An apparatus to the history of the common practices of dyeing". Paper delivered to the Royal Society. 7 May 1662. In Sprat 1667: 284–306.

VS   *Verbum sapienti.* Written 1665. First published 1691. In EW: 99–120.

DPA   A dialogue on political arithmetic. [Original is untitled.] In Matsukawa 1977. Reprinted in Hutchison 1997: 113–143.

PAI   *The political anatomy of Ireland.* [Apparently written in 1671, but first published in 1691.] In EW: 121–231.

PA   *Political arithmetic, or a discourse concerning the extent and value of land, people, buildings; husbandry, manufacture, commerce, fishery, artizans, seamen, soldiers; publick revenues, interest, taxes, superlucration, registries, banks; valuation of men, increasing of seamen, of militia's, harbours, situation, shipping, power at sea, &c. As the same relates to every country in general, but more particularly to the territories of His Majesty of Great Britain, and his neighbours of Holland, Zealand, and France.* [Written in around 1671–2, but first published in 1690.] In EW: 233–313.

A discourse of duplicate proportion. The discourse made before the Royal Society, the 26 of November 1674, concerning the use of duplicate proportion in sundry important particulars, together with a new hypothesis of springing or elastique motions. London: John Martyn, printer to the Royal Society. 1674.

PAL   *Another essay in political arithmetic, concerning the growth of the City of London, with the measures, periods, causes, and consequences thereof.* London: H. H. for Mark Pardoe. 1682. In EW2: 451–478.

Sir William Petty's Quantulumcunque concerning money. To the Lord Marquess of Halyfax, 1682. [First printed in 1695.]

"Experiments to be made relating to land carriage proposed by the learned Sir William Petty Kt." *Philosophical Transactions* 1684, 14 (161): 666–667.

A treatise of naval philosophy in three parts. I: A phisico-mathematical discourse of ships and sailing. II: Of naval policy. III: Of naval œconomy or husbandry. Published as an appendix to a work [by Thomas Hale?] entitled *An account of several new inventions and improvements now necessary for England, in a discourse by way of letter to the Earl of Marlbourgh, relating to building of our English shipping, etc...* London: James Astwood. 1691.

Two essays in political arithmetick, concerning the people, housing, hospitals, &c. of London and Paris. London: printed for J. Lloyd. 1686. In EW: 502–513. Already published earlier in the same year as *Deux essays d'arithmétique politique, touchant les villes et hospitaux de Londres et Paris. Dédiés au Roy, par le Chevalier Petty, de la Société Royale.* Londres: Chés B. G. 1686.

TI   *A treatise of Ireland.* Written in 1687. First published in 1899 in EW: 545–621.

Other early works to 1890 (including subsequent editions)

Aubrey, John [1813] *Lives of eminent men. Published as an Appendix to a compilation entitled Letters written by eminent persons in the seventeenth and eighteenth centuries,* 2 volumes. London: Longman. [The life of Petty is at volume II: 481–491.]

Aubrey, John [1949] *Aubrey's brief lives,* edited by Oliver L. Dick. London: Secker & Warburg.

Aubrey, John [1971] "Sir William Petty" [verbatim transcript of the original manuscript], in Keynes, Geoffrey, ed., *A bibliography of Sir William Petty FRS and of Observations on the bills of mortality by John Graunt FRS.* Oxford: Clarendon Press: 85–92.

Biographia Britannica (1747–66) *Biographia Britannica, or the lives of the most eminent persons who have flourished in Great Britain and Ireland from the earliest ages down to the present times...* London: W. Innys, etc.

Birch, Thomas (1756–57) *The history of the Royal Society of London for Improving of Natural Knowledge, from its first rise, in which the most considerable of those papers communicated to the Society which have hitherto not been published are inserted in their proper order...*, 4 volumes. London: printed for A. Millar.

Bodin, Jean (1962 [1576]) *The six bookes of a commonweale [Les six livres de la République]*, facsimile reprint of the English translation of 1606, edited by Kenneth D. McRae. Cambridge, MA: Harvard University Press.

Cantillon, Richard (1931 [*c.* 1730]) *Essai sur la nature du commerce en général*, edited and translated by Henry Higgs. London: Macmillan.

Chamberlayne, Edward (1669, etc.) *Angliæ notitia, or the Present state of England, together with divers reflections upon the antient state thereof.* London: in the Savoy.

Cossa, Luigi (1880 [1876]) [*Guida allo studio dell' economia politica.*] *Guide to the study of political economy*, translated from the second [1878] edition by W. Stanley Jevons. London: Macmillan.

Davenant, Charles [1771] *The political and commercial works of that celebrated writer Charles D'Avenant...*, edited by Charles Whitworth. London: Horsfield.

Defoe, Daniel (1724–27) *A tour through the whole island of Great Britain, 1724–6*, 3 volumes. London: G. Strahan.

Evelyn, John [1971] Diary, 22 March 1675, in Keynes, Geoffrey, ed., *A bibliography of Sir William Petty FRS and of Observations on the bills of mortality by John Graunt FRS.* Oxford: Clarendon Press: 93–95 [reprinted from the de Beer edition of 1951: 4, 56–61].

Fortrey, Samuel (1663) *England's interest and improvement, consisting in the increase of the store and trade of this kingdom.* Cambridge.

Fournier, George (1643) *Hydrographie, contenant la théorie et la practique de toutes les parties de la navigation.* Paris: Michel Soly [second edition: 1668, Paris: Jean du Puis].

Gadbury, John (1691) *Nauticum astrologicum, or, The astrological seaman: directing merchants, mariners...how...they may escape divers dangers...* London: Matthew Street.

Gookin, Vincent (1655) *The great case of transplantation in Ireland discussed; or, certain considerations, wherein the many great inconveniences in the transplanting the natives of Ireland generally out of the three provinces of Leinster, Ulster, and Munster, into the province of Connaught, are shewn. Humbly tendered to every individual Member of Parliament, by a well-wisher to the good of the Common-wealth of England.* London: printed for I. C.

Hardinge, William H. (1865) "On an unpublished essay on Ireland, by Sir William Petty, A.D. 1687". *Transactions of the Royal Irish Academy* 24, Third Series (Antiquities): 371–377.

Harleian Miscellany (1744–46) *The Harleian Miscellany, or, a collection of scarce, curious, and entertaining pamphlets and tracts, as well in manuscript as in print, found in the late Earl of Oxford's library*, 8 volumes London. [Petty's *Advice* is at volume VI (1745): 1–13].

Harrington, James (1659) *The art of law-giving in III books: the first, shewing the foundations and superstructures of all the kinds of Government; the second, shewing the frames of the Commonwealths of Israel and of the Jewes; the third, shewing a model fitted unto the present state or balance of this nation. To which is added an appendix concerning an House of Peers.* London: H. Fletcher. [Also in Harrington [1977]: 599–704].

Harrington, James [1977] *The political works of James Harrington*, edited by John G. A. Pocock. Cambridge: Cambridge University Press.

Hobbes, Thomas (1651) *Leviathan, or the matter, forme, and power of a common-wealth, ecclesiasticall and civill*. London: Andrew Crooke.

Hume, David (1955 [1752]) "Of taxes", in Hume, David, *Writings on economics*, edited by Eugene Rotwein. Edinburgh: Nelson: 83–89.

Larcom, Thomas A. (1851) Introduction and editorial material to DS.

Launhardt, Wilhelm (1885) *Mathematische Begründung der Volkswirthschaftslehre*. Leipzig: Verlag von Wilhelm Engelmann.

Locke, John (1689) Two treatises of government. London: Awnsham Churchill.

Locke, John (1692) *Some considerations of the consequences of the lowering of interest and raising the value of money*. London: Awnsham and John Churchill.

Macaulay, Thomas B. (1848–1862) *History of England from the accession of James II*, 5 volumes. London: Longman.

Marx, Karl (1956 [1885]) *Capital: a critique of political economy [Das Kapital: Kritik der politischen Ökonomie]*, volume II, edited by Friedrich Engels, translated from the second German edition by I. Lasker. Moscow: Progress Publishers.

Marx, Karl (1963–71 [1862–63]) *Theories of surplus value [Theorien über den Mehrwert]*, translated by Emile Burns, 3 volumes. Moscow: Progress Publishers.

Marx, Karl (1970 [1859]) *A contribution to the critique of political economy [Zur Kritik der politischen Ökonomie]*, edited by Maurice Dobb, translated by Salomea W. Ryazanskaya. New York: International Publishers.

Marx, Karl (1970 [1867]) *Capital: a critique of political economy [Das Kapital: Kritik der politischen Ökonomie]*, volume I, edited by Friedrich Engels, translated from the third German edition by Samuel Moore and Edward Aveling, new edition. London: Lawrence & Wishart.

McCulloch, John R. (1845) *The literature of political economy: a classified catalogue of select publications in different departments of that science, with historical, critical and biographical notices*. London: Longman.

Mitchel, John (1873) *The crusade of the period; and Last conquest of Ireland (perhaps)*. New York: Lynch, Cole and Meehan.

Montesquieu, Baron de (1989 [1748]) *The spirit of the laws [L'ésprit des lois]*, edited and translated by Anne M. Cohler, Basia C. Miller and Harold S. Stone. Cambridge: Cambridge University Press.

Mun, Thomas (1664) *England's treasure by forraign trade, or, The ballance of our forraign trade is the rule of our treasure*. London: John Mun.

Munk, William (1861) *The Roll of the Royal College of Physicians of London, compiled from the annals of the College*, 2 volumes. London.

Newes from the dead (1651) *Newes from the dead, or, A true and exact narrative of the miraculous deliveries of Anne Greene… Written by a scholar in Oxford*. Oxford: T. Robinson.

Pepys, Samuel (1970 [1665]) The Diary of Samuel Pepys, edited by Robert Latham and William Matthews. Berkeley, CA: University of California Press.

'Philo-dicæus' (1647) *The standard of equality in subsidiary taxes and payments, or a just and strong preserver of publique liberty conducing towards the most happy government of kingdomes and states*. London: printed by D. H.

Philosophical Transactions (1665–) *Philosophical Transactions, giving some accompt of the present undertakings, studies and labors of the ingenious in many considerable parts of the world* [afterwards *Philosophical Transactions of the Royal Society*]. London.

Prendergast, John P. (1870) *The Cromwellian settlement in Ireland*, second edition, enlarged. London: Longmans, Green, Reader & Dyer. [The first (1865) edition was reprinted in 1994; the second (1870) edition was reprinted in 1922.]

Ricardo, David (1971 [1817]) *On the principles of political economy and taxation*, edited by Ronald M. Hartwell. London: Penguin Books.

Robinson, Henry (1649) *Briefe considerations concerning the advancement of trade and navigation, tendred unto all ingenious patriots...* London: Matthew Simmons.

Robinson, Henry (1652) *Certain proposalls in order to the peoples freedome and accommodation in some particulars, with the advancement of trade and navigation of this commonwealth in general.* London: Matthew Simmons.

Roscher, Wilhelm G. F. (1857) *Zur Geschichte der englischen Volkswirthschaftslehre im sechzehnten und siebzehnten Jahrhundert.* Leipzig: S. Hirzel [*Abhandlungen der Königlich Sächsische Gesellschaft der Wissenschaften*, Band 3; *philologisch-historischen Classe*, Band 2: 1–146].

Rousseau, Jean-Jacques (1986 [1750]) *The first and second discourses, together with the replies to critics, and Essay on the origin of languages*, edited and translated by Victor Gourevitch. New York: Harper Row.

Smith, Adam (1976 [1776]) *An inquiry into the nature and causes of the wealth of nations*, edited by Roy H. Campbell, Alexander S. Skinner and William B. Todd. Oxford: Oxford University Press.

Some observations (1695) *Some observations upon the Bank of England.* London: John Whitlock.

Southwell, Robert (1757 [1675]) "Discourse concerning water", presented to the Royal Society on 8 April; reproduced in Birch, Thomas, *The history of the Royal Society of London for Improving of Natural Knowledge, from its first rise, in which the most considerable of those papers communicated to the Society which have hitherto not been published are inserted in their proper order...*, volume III. London: printed for A. Millar: 196–216.

Sprat, Thomas (1667) *The history of the Royal Society of London for Improving of Natural Knowledge.* London: J. Martyn.

Steuart, James (1966 [1767]) *An inquiry into the principles of political economy*, edited by Alexander S. Skinner, 2 volumes. Edinburgh: Oliver & Boyd.

Stewart, Dugald [1855] *Collected works*, edited by William Hamilton, volume VIII, part II: *Lectures on political economy*. Edinburgh: Thomas Constable.

Swift, Jonathan (1726) [*Gulliver's travels.*] *Travels into several remote nations of the world. By Lemuel Gulliver. Compendiously methodized, for publick benefit; with observations and explanatory notes throughout.* London: Benjamin Motte.

Swift, Jonathan (1729) *A modest proposal for preventing the children of poor people from becoming a burthen to their parents or country, and for making them beneficial to the publick.* Dublin: S. Harding; London: J. Roberts.

Thurloe Papers (1742) *A collection of the state papers of John Thurloe Esq., Secretary first to the Council of State and afterward to the two Protectors Oliver and Richard Cromwell*, 7 volumes, edited by Thomas Birch. London: Woodward and Davis.

Von Thünen, Johann H. (1826) *Die isolierte Staat*, part I. Hamburg: Friedrich Perthes.

Von Thünen, Johann H. (1875) *Die isolierte Staat*, parts I–III, edited by H. Schumacher [the first complete edition]. Berlin: Wiegandt, Hempel & Parey [reprinted in 1966 by Wissenschaftliche Buchgesellschaft of Darmstadt].

Von Thünen, Johann H. (1966 [1826]) *The isolated state [Die isolierte Staat]*, edited by Peter Hall, translated by Carla M. Wartenberg. Oxford: Pergamon Press.

Ward, John (1740) *The lives of the professors of Gresham College, to which is prefixed the life of the founder, Sir T. Gresham.* London.

Ware, James (1745) *The whole works of Sir J. W. concerning Ireland*, volume II, section II: The writers of Ireland, part II: Such who, though foreigners, enjoyed preferments or offices there, translated from the Latin by Walter Harris, revised and improved. Dublin.

Webb, Alfred (1878) *A compendium of Irish biography: comprising sketches of distinguished Irishmen, and of eminent persons connected with Ireland by office or by their writings.* Dublin: Gill.

Wood, Anthony À (1691–92) *Athenae Oxonienses: an exact history of all the writers and bishops who have had their education in the most ancient and famous University of Oxford, from…1500 to the end of…1690. To which are added the Fasti or Annals of the said university for the same time.* London: Thomas Bennett.

Works published since 1890 (editions of earlier works are included in the previous list)

Anderson, Matthew S. (1998) *War and society in Europe of the old regime, 1618–1789,* revised edition. Guernsey: Sutton Publishing.

Andrews, John H. (1970) "Geography and government in Elizabethan Ireland", in Stephens, Nicholas, and Glasscock, Robin E., eds., *Irish geography studies in honour of E. Estyn Evans.* Belfast: Queen's University of Belfast: 178–191.

Andrews, John H. (1985) *Plantation acres: an historical study of the Irish land surveyor and his maps.* Omagh: Ulster Historical Foundation.

Andrews, John H. (1997) *Shapes of Ireland: maps and their makers, 1564–1839.* Dublin: Geography Publications.

Andrews, John H., and Rankin, K. J. (2012) "William Petty, topographer", in Duffy, Patrick, and Nolan, William, eds., *At the anvil: essays in honour of William J Smyth.* Dublin: Geography Publications: 241–270.

Appleby, Joyce O. (1978) *Economic thought and ideology in seventeenth-century England.* Princeton, NJ: Princeton University Press.

Arena, Richard, Dow, Sheila, and Klaes, Matthias, eds. (2009) *Open economics: economics in relation to other disciplines.* Abingdon, UK: Routledge.

Arndt, Heinz W. (1981) "Economic development: a semantic history". *Economic Development and Cultural Change* 29 (3): 456–466.

Arrow, Kenneth J., ed. (1988) *The balance between industry and agriculture in economic development,* volume I: *Basic issues.* London: Macmillan, for the International Economic Association.

Ashley, Maurice P. (1934) *Financial and commercial policy under the Cromwellian Protectorate.* Oxford: Oxford University Press.

Aspromourgos, Tony (1996) *On the origins of classical economics: distribution and value from William Petty to Adam Smith.* Abingdon, UK: Routledge.

Aspromourgos, Tony (1997 [1988]) "The life of William Petty in relation to his economics: a tercentenary interpretation" [from *History of Political Economy* 20 (3): 337–356], in Hutchison, Terence W., ed., *Sir William Petty: critical responses.* London: Routledge: 35–67.

Aspromourgos, Tony (1998) "William Petty", in Kurz, Heinz D., and Salvadori, Neri, eds., *The Elgar companion to classical economics.* Cheltenham, UK: Edward Elgar: 195–198.

Aspromourgos, Tony (2000) "New light on the economics of William Petty (1623–1687): some findings from previously undisclosed manuscripts". *Contributions to Political Economy* 19 (1): 53–70.

Aspromourgos, Tony (2001) "Political economy, political arithmetic and political medicine in the thought of William Petty", in Groenewegen, Peter D., ed., *Physicians and political economy: six studies of the work of doctor-economists*. Abingdon, UK: Routledge: 10–25.

Aspromourgos, Tony (2005) "The invention of the concept of social surplus: Petty in the Hartlib circle". *European Journal of the History of Economic Thought* 12 (1): 1–24.

Attis, David (2014) *Mathematics and the making of modern Ireland: Trinity College Dublin from Cromwell to the Celtic Tiger*. Boston: Docent Press.

Aubrey, Philip (1990) *Mr Secretary Thurloe: Cromwell's Secretary of State, 1652–1660*. London: Athlone Press.

Backhouse, Roger E. (2002) *The Penguin history of economics*. London: Penguin Books.

Balfour, Robert, ed. (2010) *Culture, capital and representation*. Basingstoke, UK: Palgrave Macmillan.

Barnard, Toby C. (1973a) "Lord Broghill, Vincent Gookin, and the Cork elections of 1659". *English Historical Review* 88: 352–365.

Barnard, Toby C. (1973b) "Planters and policies in Cromwellian Ireland". *Past and Present* 61 (1): 31–69.

Barnard, Toby C. (1974) "The Hartlib circle and the origins of the Dublin Philosophical Society". *Irish Historical Studies* 19: 56–71.

Barnard, Toby C. (1979) "Sir William Petty, his Irish estates and Irish population". *Irish Economic and Social History* 6: 64–69.

Barnard, Toby C. (1981a) "Fishing in seventeenth-century Kerry: the experience of Sir William Petty". *Journal of the Kerry Archaeological and Historical Society* 14: 14–25.

Barnard, Toby C. (1981b) "Sir William Petty, Irish landowner", in Lloyd-Jones, Hugh, Pearl, Valerie, and Worden, Blair, eds., *History and imagination: essays in honour of H. R. Trevor Roper*. London: Duckworth: 201–217.

Barnard, Toby C. (1982) "Sir William Petty as Kerry ironmaster". *Proceedings of the Royal Irish Academy* 82 section C (1): 1–32.

Barnard, Toby C. (1993) "Irish images of Cromwell", in Richardson, Roger C., ed., *Images of Oliver Cromwell: essays for and by Roger Howell Jr*. Manchester: Manchester University Press: 180–206.

Barnard, Toby C. (2000 [1975]) *Cromwellian Ireland: English government and reform in Ireland, 1649–1660*, with a new introduction. Oxford: Clarendon Press.

Barnard, Toby C. (2003) *A new anatomy of Ireland: the Irish Protestants, 1649–1770*. New Haven, CT: Yale University Press.

Barnard, Toby C. (2004) "Petty, Sir William (1623–1687)", in Matthew, H. C. G., and Harrison, B., eds., *Oxford dictionary of national biography*. Oxford: Oxford University Press, www.oxforddnb.com.libproxy.ucl.ac.uk/search?q=Petty.

Barnard, Toby C. (2008) *Improving Ireland? Projectors, prophets and profiteers, 1641–1786*. Dublin: Four Courts Press.

Barnes, Trevor J., and Sheppard, Eric (2000) "Introduction: the art of economic geography", in Sheppard, Eric, and Barnes, Trevor J., eds., *A companion to economic geography*. Oxford: Blackwell: 1–7.

Barro, Robert J., and Sala-i-Martin, Xavier (1995) *Economic growth*. New York: McGraw-Hill.

Barzel, Yoram (2002) *A theory of the state: economic rights, legal rights, and the scope of the state*. Cambridge: Cambridge University Press.

Beckett, J. V. (1985) "Land tax or excise: the levying of taxation in seventeenth- and eighteenth-century England". *English Historical Review* 100: 285–308.

Beckmann, Martin J. (1981) "Land use theory then and now: a tribute to Sir James Steuart". *Papers of the Regional Science Association* 48 (1): 1–6.

Beer, Max (1938) *Early British economics: from the XIIIth to the middle of the XVIIIth century*. London: George Allen & Unwin.

Berg, Maxine (1983) "Political economy and the principles of manufacture, 1700–1800", in Berg, Maxine, Hudson, Pat, and Sonenscher, Michael, eds., *Manufacture in town and country before the factory*. Cambridge: Cambridge University Press: 33–58.

Berg, Maxine, Hudson, Pat, and Sonenscher, Michael, eds. (1983) *Manufacture in town and country before the factory*. Cambridge: Cambridge University Press.

Berry, Brian J. L. (2002) "Review" [of Fujita, Krugman and Venables 1999]. *Annals of the Association of American Geographers* 92 (2): 359–360.

Bevan, Wilson L. (1893) *Sir William Petty: a dissertation presented to the Faculty of Political Science at the University of Munich*. Canterbury: J. A. Jennings.

Bevan, Wilson L. (1894) "Sir William Petty: a study in English economic literature". *Publications of the American Economic Association* 9 (4): 370–472.

Blaug, Mark (1979) "The German hegemony of location theory; a puzzle in the history of economic thought". *History of Political Economy* 11 (1): 21–29.

Blaug, Mark (1985) *Economic theory in retrospect*, fourth edition. Cambridge: Cambridge University Press.

Boddy, Martin (1999) "Geographical economics and urban competitiveness: a critique". *Urban Studies* 36 (5/6): 811–842.

Boehm, Stephan, Gehrke, Christian, Kurz, Heinz D., and Sturn, Richard, eds. (2002) *Is there progress in economics? Knowledge, truth and the history of economic thought*. Cheltenham, UK: Edward Elgar.

Bonney, Margaret, and Ormrod, W. Mark (1999) "Introduction: Crises, revolutions and self-sustained growth: towards a conceptual model of change in fiscal history", in Ormrod, W. Mark, Bonney, Margaret, and Bonney, Richard, eds., *Crises, revolutions and self-sustained growth: essays in European fiscal history, 1130–1830*. Stamford, UK: Shaun Tyas: 1–21.

Bonney, Richard, ed. (1995a) *Economic systems and state finance*. Oxford: Clarendon Press.

Bonney, Richard (1995b) "Early modern theories of state finance", in Bonney, Richard, ed., *Economic systems and state finance*. Oxford: Clarendon Press: 163–229.

Bonney, Richard, ed. (1999) *The rise of the fiscal state in Europe, c. 1200–1815*. Oxford: Oxford University Press.

Bottigheimer, Karl S. (1971) *English money and Irish land: the 'adventurers' in the Cromwellian settlement of Ireland*. Oxford: Clarendon Press.

Bottigheimer, Karl S. (1972) "The Restoration land settlement: a structural view". *Irish Historical Studies* 18: 1–21.

Bowley, Martin (1973) *Studies in the history of economic theory before 1870*. London: Macmillan.

Braddick, Michael J. (1994) *Parliamentary taxation in seventeenth-century England: local administration and response*. London: Royal Historical Society.

Braddick, Michael J. (1996) *The nerves of state: taxation and the financing of the English state, 1558–1714*. Manchester: Manchester University Press.

Braddick, Michael J. (2000) *State formation in early modern England, c. 1550–1700*. Cambridge: Cambridge University Press.

Bradshaw, Brendan (1994 [1989]) "Nationalism and historical scholarship in modern Ireland" [from *Irish Historical Studies* 26: 329–351], in Brady, Ciaran, ed., *Interpreting*

Irish history: the debate on historical revisionism, 1938–1994. Dublin: Irish Academic Press: 191–216.

Bradshaw, Brendan, Hadfield, Andrew, and Maley, Willie, eds. (1993) *Representing Ireland: literature and the origins of conflict, 1534–1660*. Cambridge: Cambridge University Press.

Brady, Ciaran, ed. (1994) *Interpreting Irish history: the debate on historical revisionism, 1938–1994*. Dublin: Irish Academic Press.

Brand, Paul, and Costello, Kevin, eds. (2005) *Adventures in the law: proceedings of the 16th British Legal History Conference*. Dublin: Four Courts Press, for the Irish Legal History Society.

Brenner, Robert (1976) "Agrarian class structure and economic development in pre-industrial Europe". *Past and Present* 70 (1): 30–75.

Brewer, Anthony (1992a) "Petty and Cantillon". *History of Political Economy* 24 (3): 711–728.

Brewer, Anthony (1992b) *Richard Cantillon: pioneer of economic theory*. London: Routledge.

Brewer, Anthony (2003) "Pre-classical economics in Britain", in Samuels, Warren J., Biddle, Jeff E., and Davis, John B., eds., *A companion to the history of economic thought*. Malden, MA: Blackwell: 78–93.

Brewer, Anthony (2011) "The concept of an agricultural surplus, from Petty to Smith". *Journal of the History of Economic Thought* 33 (4): 487–505.

Brewer, John (1989) *The sinews of power: war, money and the English state, 1688–1783*. London: Unwin Hyman.

Briggs, Peter M. (2005) "John Graunt, Sir William Petty, and Swift's *Modest Proposal*". *Eighteenth-Century Life* 29 (2): 3–24.

Buchwald, Jed Z., and Cohen, I. Bernard, eds. (2001) *Isaac Newton's natural philosophy*. Cambridge, MA: MIT Press.

Buck, Peter (1977) "Seventeenth-century political arithmetic: civil strife and vital statistics". *Isis* 68 (1): 67–84.

Butler, William F. T. (1917) *Confiscation in Irish history*. Dublin: Talbot Press.

Butterfield, Herbert (1931) The Whig interpretation of history. London: G. Bell and Sons.

Canny, Nicholas (1987) *From Reformation to Restoration*. Dublin: Helicon.

Canny, Nicholas, ed. (1998) *The Oxford history of the British Empire*, volume I: *The origins of empire*. Oxford: Oxford University Press.

Cantillon, Richard (2015) *Essay on the nature of trade in general: a variorum edition*, edited by Richard Van den Berg. Abingdon, UK: Routledge.

Cantlie, Neil (1974) *History of the army medical department*, 2 volumes. Edinburgh: Churchill Livingstone.

Carlin, Norah (1993) "Extreme or mainstream? The English Independents and the Cromwellian reconquest of Ireland, 1649–1651", in Bradshaw, Brendan, Hadfield, Andrew, and Maley, Willie, eds., *Representing Ireland: literature and the origins of conflict, 1534–1660*. Cambridge: Cambridge University Press: 209–226.

Carroll, Patrick (2006) *Science, culture, and modern state formation*. Berkeley, CA: University of California Press.

Chalk, Alfred F. (1951) "Natural law and the rise of economic individualism in England". *Journal of Political Economy* 59 (4): 332–347.

Chandaman, C. D. (1975) *The English public revenue, 1669–1688*. Oxford: Clarendon Press.

Chaplin, Joyce E. (2001) *Subject matter: technology, the body and science on the Anglo-American frontier, 1500–1676*. Cambridge, MA: Harvard University Press.

Chenery, Hollis, and Srinavasan, Thirukodikaval N., eds. (1988–89) *Handbook of development economics*, 2 volumes. Amsterdam: Elsevier Science.

Christensen, Paul P. (1989) "Hobbes and the physiological origins of economic science". *History of Political Economy* 21 (4): 689–709.

Clark, Audrey N. (2003) *The Penguin dictionary of geography*, third edition. London: Penguin Books.

Clark, Colin G. (1940) *The conditions of economic progress*. London: Macmillan.

Clark, Colin G. (1957) *The conditions of economic progress*, third edition [rewritten]. London: Macmillan.

Clark, Colin G. (1984) "Development economics: the early years", in Meier, Gerald M., and Seers, Dudley, eds., *Pioneers in development*. New York: Oxford University Press [for the World Bank]: 59–83.

Clark, Gordon L. (1998) "Stylised facts and close dialogue: methodology in economic geography". *Annals of the Association of American Geographers* 88 (1): 73–87.

Clark, Gordon L., Feldmann, Maryann P., and Gertler, Meric S., eds. (2000) *The Oxford handbook of economic geography*. Oxford: Oxford University Press.

Clarke, Aidan (1999) *Prelude to Restoration in Ireland: the end of the Commonwealth, 1659–1660*. Cambridge: Cambridge University Press.

Clément, Alain (2003) The influence of medicine on political economy in the seventeenth century. *History of Economics Review* 38 (1): 1–22.

Coleman, William O. (1995) *Rationalism and anti-rationalism in the origins of economics: the philosophical roots of 18th century economic thought*. Aldershot, UK: Edward Elgar.

Corish, Patrick J. (1976) "The Cromwellian regime, 1650–60", in Moody, Theodore W., Martin, Francis X., and Byrne, Francis J., eds., *A new history of Ireland*, volume III: *Early modern Ireland, 1534–1691*. Oxford: Clarendon Press: 353–386.

Corsten, Severin, Füssel, Stephan, Pflug, Günther, and Schmidt-Künsemüller, Friedrich A., eds. (1990) *Lexicon des gesamten Buchwesens*, 8 volumes, second edition. Stuttgart: Anton Hiersemann.

Costello, Kevin (2005) "Sir William Petty and the Court of Admiralty in Restoration Ireland", in Brand, Paul, Costello, Kevin, and Osborough, W. N., eds., *Adventures in the law: proceedings of the 16th British Legal History Conference, Dublin, 2003*. Dublin: Four Courts Press, for the Irish Legal History Society: 106–138.

Costello, Kevin (2011) *The Court of Admiralty of Ireland, 1575–1893*. Dublin: Four Courts Press, for the Irish Legal History Society.

Coughlan, Patricia (1990) "'Cheap and common animals': the English anatomy of Ireland in the seventeenth century", in Healy, Thomas, and Sawday, Jonathan, eds., *Literature and the English Civil War*. Cambridge: Cambridge University Press: 205–223.

Coulomb, Fanny (1998) "Adam Smith: a defence economist". *Defence and Peace Economics* 9 (3): 299–301.

Coward, Barry (2002) *The Cromwellian Protectorate*. Manchester: Manchester University Press.

Cowen, Michael P., and Shenton, Robert W. (1995) "The invention of development", in Crush, Jonathan, ed., *Power of development*. Abingdon, UK: Routledge: 27–43.

Cronin, Nessa (2014) "Writing the 'new geography': cartographic discourse and colonial governmentality in William Petty's *The Political Anatomy of Ireland* (1672)". *Historical Geography* 42: 58–71.

Crush, Jonathan, ed. (1995) *Power of development*. Abingdon, UK: Routledge.

Cunningham, John (2011) *Conquest and land in Ireland: the transplantation to Connacht, 1649–1680.* Woodbridge, UK: Boydell & Brewer.

Dainville, François de (1940) *La géographie des humanistes: les Jésuites et l'éducation de la société française.* Paris: Beauchesne et ses fils.

Dale, Peter G. (1987) *Sir W. P. of Romsey.* Romsey, UK: LTVAS Group.

Dale, Sue (2011) Sir William Petty's 'Ten Tooles': a programme for the transformation of England and Ireland during the reign of James II. PhD thesis, Birkbeck College, University of London.

Daunton, Martin J. (1995) *Progress and poverty: an economic and social history of Britain, 1700–1850.* Oxford: Oxford University Press.

Daunton, Martin J. (2002) "Trusting Leviathan: the politics of taxation, 1815–1914", in Winch, Donald, and O'Brien, Patrick K., eds., *The political economy of British historical experience, 1688–1914.* Oxford: Oxford University Press, for the British Academy: 318–350.

Deane, Phyllis (1968) "William Petty", in Sills, David L., ed., *International encyclopedia of the social sciences*, volume XII. New York: Macmillan: 66–68.

Debus, Allen G. (1968) "Mathematics and nature in the chemical texts of the Renaissance". *Ambix* 15 (1): 1–28.

Dennehy, Coleman, ed. (2008) *Restoration Ireland: always settling and never settled.* Aldershot, UK: Ashgate.

Desai, S. S. M. (1967) *History of economic thought: being an account of Western economic thought from mercantilism to Alfred Marshall*, second revised edition. Poona: Continental.

Désert, Gabriel, ed. (1981) *Histoire de Caen.* Toulouse: Privat.

Desmedt, Ludovic (2005) "Money in the 'Body Politick': the analysis of trade and circulation in the writings of seventeenth-century political arithmeticians". *History of Political Economy* 37 (1): 79–101.

Dicken, Peter, and Lloyd, Peter E. (1990) *Location in space: theoretical perspectives in economic geography*, third edition. New York: HarperCollins.

Dickson, Peter G. M. (1993) *The financial revolution in England: a study in the development of public credit, 1688–1756*, reprint. Aldershot, UK: Gregg.

Dictionary of National Biography (1885–1900) *The Dictionary of National Biography*, edited by Leslie Stephen and Sidney Lee. London: Smith, Elder.

Dimock, Wai Chee, and Gilmore, Michael T., eds. (1994) *Rethinking class: literary studies and social formations.* New York: Columbia University Press.

Dimou, M., and Pecqueur, B. (2012) "L'éspace urbain dans l'œuvre de William Petty". *Canadian Journal of Regional Science* 35 (1): 1–9.

Dixit, Avinash K., and Stiglitz, Joseph E. (1977) "Monopolistic competition and optimum product diversity". *American Economic Review* 67 (3): 297–308.

Dockès, Pierre (1969) *L'espace dans la pensée économique du XVIe au XVIIIe siècle.* Paris: Flammarion.

Dockès, Pierre (2013) "L'économie politique de William Petty et les colonies". Paper delivered at Journées d'étude de l'Association Charles Gide, Martinique, 28–29 November, "Les économistes et les colonies".

Downing, Brian M. (1992) *The military revolution and political change: origins of democracy and autocracy in early modern Europe.* Princeton, NJ: Princeton University Press.

Downs, Michael (1977) *John Harrington.* Boston: Twayne Publishers.

Duffy, Patrick, and Nolan, William, eds. (2012) *At the anvil: essays in honour of William J Smyth*. Dublin: Geography Publications.

Dunlop, Robert, ed. (1913) *Ireland under the Commonwealth: being a selection of documents relating to the government of Ireland from 1651 to 1659*, 2 volumes. Manchester: Manchester University Press.

Dymski, Gary A. (1996) "On Krugman's model of economic geography". *Geoforum* 27 (4): 439–452.

Eatwell, John, Milgate, Murray, and Newman, Peter, eds. (1987) *The new Palgrave: a dictionary of economics*. London: Macmillan.

Edinburgh Review (1895) "Review" [of Fitzmaurice (1895)]. *Edinburgh Review* 373: 45–77.

Ekelund, Robert B., and Tollison, Robert D. (1981) *Mercantilism as a rent-seeking society: economic regulation in historical perspective*. College Station, TX: Texas A&M University Press.

Ekelund, Robert B., and Tollison, Robert D. (1997) *Politicised economies: monarchy, monopoly, and mercantilism*. College Station, TX: Texas A&M University Press.

Ellis, Peter Berresford (1988) *Hell or Connaught: the Cromwellian colonisation of Ireland, 1652–1660*, new edition. Belfast: Blackstaff.

Endres, Anthony M. (1985) "The functions of numerical data in the writings of Graunt, Petty, and Davenant". *History of Political Economy* 17 (2): 245–264.

Epstein, Stephan R. (2000) *Freedom and growth: the rise of states and markets in Europe, 1300–1750*. London: Routledge.

Erba, Alighiero (1998) "William Petty's model and the analysis of socio-economic phenomena". *International Review of Sociology* 8 (1): 5–37.

Ertman, Thomas (1997) *Birth of the Leviathan: building states and regimes in medieval and early modern Europe*. Cambridge: Cambridge University Press.

Evans, Peter B., Rueschemeyer, Dietrich, and Skocpol, Theda, eds. (1985) *Bringing the state back in*. Cambridge: Cambridge University Press.

Everitt, Alan (1967) "The marketing of agricultural produce", in Thirsk, Joan, ed., *The agrarian history of England and Wales*, volume IV: *1500–1640*. Cambridge: Cambridge University Press: 466–592.

Feingold, Mordechai (2001) "Mathematicians and naturalists: Sir Isaac Newton and the Royal Society", in Buchwald, Jed Z., and Cohen, I. Bernard, eds., *Isaac Newton's natural philosophy*. Cambridge, MA: MIT Press: 77–102.

Feld, Maury (1977) *The structure of violence: armed forces as social systems*. Beverly Hills: Sage Publications.

Fernández López, Manuel (2002) "Location theory and mathematical programming: progress or rediscovery?", in Boehm, Stephan, Gehrke, Christian, Kurz, Heinz D., and Sturn, Richard, eds., *Is there progress in economics? Knowledge, truth and the history of economic thought*. Cheltenham, UK: Edward Elgar: 273–292.

Fine, Ben (1982) *Theories of the capitalist economy*. London: Edward Arnold.

Fine, Ben (2001) "Economics imperialism as Kuhnian revolution". *International Papers in Political Economy* 8 (3): 1–58.

Fine, Ben (2002) "Economics imperialism and the new development economics as Kuhnian paradigm shift". *World Development* 30 (12): 2057–2070.

Fine, Ben, and Leopold, Ellen (1993) *The world of consumption*. London: Routledge.

Fine, Ben, and Milonakis, Dimitris (2003) "From principle of pricing to pricing of principle: rationality and irrationality in the economic history of Douglass North". *Comparative Studies in Society and History* 45 (3): 120–144.

Fine, Ben, and Saad-Filho, Alfredo, eds. (2012) *Elgar companion to Marxist economics*. Cheltenham, UK: Edward Elgar.

Finkelstein, Andrea (2000) *Harmony and the balance: an intellectual history of seventeenth-century English economic thought*. Ann Arbor, MI: University of Michigan Press.

Finkelstein, Joseph, and Thimm, Alfred (1973) *Economists and society: the development of economic thought from Aquinas to Keynes*. New York: Harper & Row.

Firth, Charles H. (1909) *The last years of the Protectorate, 1656–1658*, 2 volumes. London: Longman.

Firth, Charles H. (1962 [1902]) *Cromwell's army: a history of the English soldier during the Civil Wars, the Commonwealth and the Protectorate*, fourth edition. London: Longman.

Firth, Charles H., and Rait, Robert S., eds. (1911) *Acts and ordinances of the Interregnum, 1642–1660*, 3 volumes. London: HMSO.

Fitzmaurice, Edmond (1895) *The life of Sir William Petty, 1623–1687*. London: John Murray.

Fitzmaurice, Edmond (1896) "Sir William Petty, 1623–1687", in DNB: 113a–119a.

Fitzmaurice, Edmond (1899) "Sir William Petty, 1623–1687", in Palgrave, Robert H. I., ed., *Dictionary of political economy*, volume III. London: Macmillan: 99–102.

Foley, Vernard (1984 [1974]) "The division of labor in Plato and Smith" [from *History of Political Economy* 6: 220–242], in Wood, John Cunningham, ed., *Adam Smith: critical assessments*, volume III. London: Routledge: 330–347.

Fox, Adam (2009) "Sir William Petty, Ireland, and the making of a political economist, 1653–87". *Economic History Review*, new series 62 (2): 388–404.

Fujita, Masahisa, Krugman, Paul R., and Venables, Anthony J. (1999) *The spatial economy: cities, regions, and international trade*. Cambridge, MA: MIT Press.

Furniss, Edgar S. (1920) *The position of the laborer in a system of nationalism: a study in the labor theories of the later English mercantilists*. Boston: Houghton Mifflin.

Gardiner, Samuel R. (1899) "The transplantation to Connaught". *English Historical Review* 14: 700–734.

Gentles, Ian (1992) *The New Model Army in England, Ireland and Scotland, 1645–1653*. Oxford: Blackwell.

Ghosh, B. N. (2001) *The living ideas of dead economists: a short history of economic thought*. Leeds: Wisdom House.

Goblet, Yann Morvran (1930) *La transformation de la géographie politique de l'Irlande au XVIIe siècle, dans les cartes et essais anthropogéographiques de Sir William Petty*, 2 volumes. Paris: Berger-Levrault.

Goblet, Yann Morvran (1955) *Political geography and the world map*. London: George Philip & Son.

Gooch, George P. (1914) *Political thought in England from Bacon to Halifax*. London: Williams & Norgate.

Goodacre, Hugh J. (2005a) "Development and geography: current debates in historical perspective", in Jomo, Kwame Sundaram, and Fine, Ben, eds., *The new development economics*. Delhi: Oxford University Press: 249–268.

Goodacre, Hugh J. (2005b) "William Petty and early colonial roots of development economics", in Jomo, Kwame Sundaram, ed., *The pioneers of development economics: great economists on development*. London: Zed Books: 10–30.

Goodacre, Hugh J. (2008) "From Petty to Ricardo up to Sraffa" [review article on Roncaglia (2005)]. *Economic Issues* 13 (1): 106–108.

Goodacre, Hugh J. (2009) "Economics, geography and colonialism in the writings of William Petty", in Arena, Richard, Dow, Sheila, and Klaes, Matthias, eds., *Open economics: economics in relation to other disciplines*. Abingdon, UK: Routledge: 233–246.

Goodacre, Hugh J. (2010a) "Colonialism, displacement and cannibalism in early modern economic thought", in Balfour, Robert, ed., *Culture, capital and representation*. Basingstoke, UK: Palgrave Macmillan: 16–34.

Goodacre, Hugh J. (2010b) "Limited liability and the wealth of 'uncivilised nations': Adam Smith and the limits to the European Enlightenment". *Cambridge Journal of Economics* 34 (5): 857–867.

Goodacre, Hugh J. (2010c) "Technological progress and economic analysis from Petty to Smith". *European Journal for the History of Economic Thought* 17 (5): 1149–1168 [special issue on technology and economics with keynote article by Robert Solow].

Goodacre, Hugh J. (2012) "Classical political economy", in Fine, Ben, and Saad-Filho, Alfredo, eds., *The Elgar companion to Marxist economics*. Cheltenham, UK: Edward Elgar: 53–59.

Goodacre, Hugh J. (2014) "The William Petty problem and the Whig history of economics". *Cambridge Journal of Economics* 38 (3): 563–583.

Goodacre, John D. (1994) *The transformation of a peasant economy: townspeople and villagers in the Lutterworth area, 1500–1700*. Aldershot, UK: Scolar Press.

Goodchild, Philip (2017) "On the origins of modern debt and value: revisiting Friedrich Nietzsche and William Petty". *Continental Thought and Theory* 1 (2): 306–332.

Goodwin, Craufurd D., ed. (1991) *Economics and national security: a history of their interaction*. Durham, NC: Duke University Press [annual supplement to *History of Political Economy*, volume 23].

Greenleaf, William H. (1964) *Order, empiricism and politics: two traditions of English political thought, 1500–1700*. Oxford: Oxford University Press.

Greenwood, Major (1928) "Graunt and Petty". *Journal of the Royal Statistical Society* 91 (1): 79–85.

Groenewegen, Peter D. (1973) "A note on the origin of the phrase 'supply and demand'". *Economic Journal* 83: 505–509.

Groenewegen, Peter D. (1997 [1967]) "Authorship of the natural and political observations upon the Bills of Mortality" [from *Journal of the History of Ideas* 28 (4): 601–602], in Hutchison, Terence W., ed., *Sir William Petty: critical responses*. London: Routledge: 69–71.

Groenewegen, Peter D., ed. (2001) *Physicians and political economy: six studies of the work of doctor-economists*. London: Routledge.

Gyorgy, Andrew (1944) *Geopolitics: the new German science*. Berkeley, CA: University of California Press.

Hadfield, Andrew, and Maley, Willie (1993) "Irish representations and English alternatives", in Bradshaw, Brendan, Hadfield, Andrew, and Maley, Willie, eds., *Representing Ireland: literature and the origins of conflict, 1534–1660*. Cambridge: Cambridge University Press: 1–23.

Hall, A. Rupert (1970) *From Galileo to Newton, 1630–1720*, second edition. New York: Constable.

Hanson, Gordon H. (1998) "North American economic integration and industry location". *Oxford Review of Economic Policy* 14 (2): 30–45.

Harris, Frances (1998) "Ireland as a laboratory: the archive of Sir William Petty", in Hunter, Michael, ed., *Archives of the scientific revolution: the formation and exchange of ideas in seventeenth-century Europe.* Woodbridge, UK: Boydell and Brewer: 73–90.

Harris, Frances (2000) *The Petty papers: the British Library catalogue of additions to the manuscripts: additional manuscripts 72,850–72,908, additional charters 76,966–76,990.* London: British Library.

Hartley, Harold B., ed. (1960) *The Royal Society: its origins and founders.* London: Royal Society.

Harvey, David (1990) *The conditions of postmodernity.* Oxford: Blackwell.

Harvey, David (2000) *Spaces of hope.* Edinburgh: Edinburgh University Press.

Healy, Thomas, and Sawday, Jonathan, eds. (1990) *Literature and the English Civil War.* Cambridge: Cambridge University Press.

Hébert, Robert F. (1981) "Richard Cantillon's early contributions to spatial economics". *Economica* 48: 71–77.

Henderson, James P., ed. (1997) *The state of the history of political economy.* London: Routledge, for the History of Economics Society.

Henry, Aaron James (2014) "William Petty, the Down Survey, population and territory in the seventeenth century". *Territory, Politics, Governance* 2 (2): 218–237.

Herrnstein, Richard J., and Murray, Charles (1994) *The bell curve: intelligence and class structure in American life.* New York: Free Press.

Hoare, Anthony G. (1992) "Review" [of Krugman 1991]. *Regional Studies* 26 (7): 679.

Hodgen, Margaret T. (1964) *Early anthropology in the sixteenth and seventeenth centuries.* Philadelphia: University of Pennsylvania Press.

Hoffman, Philip T., and Norberg, Kathryn, eds. (1994) *Fiscal crises, liberty, and representative government, 1450–1789.* Stanford, CA: Stanford University Press.

Holmes, Geoffrey (1993) *The making of a great power: late Stuart and early Georgian Britain, 1660–1722.* London: Longman.

Hooper, Mary (2008) *Newes from the dead: being a true story of Anne Greene.* London: Bodley Head.

Hoppen, K. Theodore (1965) "Sir William Petty: polymath, 1623–1687". *History Today* 15 (2): 126–134.

Hoppen, K. Theodore (1970) *The common scientist in the seventeenth century: a study of the Dublin Philosophical Society, 1683–1708.* London: Routledge & Kegan Paul.

Houghton, Walter E. (1941) "The history of trades: its relation to seventeenth-century thought". *Journal of the History of Ideas* 2 (1): 33–60.

Hueckel, Glenn (1986) "Sir William Petty on value: a reconsideration". *Research in the History of Economic Thought and Methodology* 4: 37–66.

Hughes, J. T. (1982) "Miraculous deliverance of Anne Green: an Oxford case of resuscitation in the seventeenth century". *British Medical Journal* 285: 1792–1793.

Hughes, J. T. (1999) "William Petty, Oxford anatomist and physician". *Journal of Medical Biography* 7 (1): 11–16.

Hull, Charles H. (1899) Introduction to EW: xiii–xci.

Hull, Charles H. (1997 [1900]) "Petty's place in the history of economic theory" [from *Quarterly Journal of Economics* 14: 307–340], in Hutchison, Terence W., ed., *Sir William Petty: critical responses.* London: Routledge: 73–108.

Hunter, Michael C. W. (1975) *John Aubrey and the realm of learning.* New York: Science History Publications.

Hunter, Michael C. W. (1989) *Establishing the new science: the experience of the early Royal Society*. Woodbridge, UK: Boydell & Brewer.

Hunter, Michael C. W. (2010) "Review" [of McCormick 2009]. *American Historical Review* 115 (5): 1524–1525.

Hunter, Michael C. W., ed. (1998) *Archives of the scientific revolution: the formation and exchange of ideas in seventeenth-century Europe*. Woodbridge, UK: Boydell & Brewer.

Hutchison, Terence W., ed. (1997) *Sir William Petty: critical responses*. London: Routledge.

Hutchison, Terence W. (1997] [1988]) "Petty on policy, theory and method" [from *Before Adam Smith: the emergence of political economy, 1662–1776*. Oxford: Blackwell], in Hutchison, Terence W., ed., *Sir William Petty: critical responses*. London: Routledge: 1–26.

Isard, Walter (1956) *Location and space-economy: a general theory relating to industrial areas, land use, trade, and urban structure*. Cambridge, MA: MIT Press.

Isard, Walter (1990 [1949]) "The general theory of location and space-economy", in Smith, Christine, ed., *Locational analysis and general theory, economic, political, regional and dynamic: selected papers of Walter Isard*. London: Macmillan: 27–55.

Isserman, Andrew M. (1996) "It's obvious, it's wrong, and anyway they said it years ago? Paul Krugman on large cities". *International Regional Science Review* 19 (1/2): 37–48.

Jacob, Margaret C., ed. (1992) *The politics of Western science, 1640–1990*. Amherst, NY: Humanity Books.

Johnson, Edgar A. J. (1937) *Predecessors of Adam Smith: the growth of British economic thought*. New York: Augustus Kelley.

Johnston, R. J. (1992) "Review" [of Krugman 1991]. *Environment and Planning A* 24 (7): 1066.

Jomo, Kwame Sundaram, ed. (2005) *Pioneers of economic development*. London: Zed Books. [Also published in Vietnamese as *Kinh tê hoc phât triên câc nha kinh têe vi dai vê phat triên*, 2007, translated by Trân Doàn Lâm. Hanoi: Nhà Xuât Bản Thế Giới.]

Jomo, Kwame Sundaram, and Fine, Ben, eds. (2005) *The new development economics*. Delhi: Oxford University Press.

Jones, J. R. (1994) "Fiscal policies, liberties, and representative government during the reigns of the last Stuarts", in Hoffman, Philip T., and Norberg, Kathryn, eds., *Fiscal crises, liberty, and representative government, 1450–1789*. Stanford, CA: Stanford University Press: 67–95.

Jordan, Thomas E. (2007a) *A copper farthing: Sir William Petty and his times, 1623–1687*. Houghton-le-Spring, UK: University of Sunderland Press.

Jordan, Thomas E. (2007b) *Sir William Petty, 1623–1687: the genius entrepreneur of seventeenth-century Ireland*. Lewiston, NY: Edwin Mellen Press.

Jordan, Thomas E. (2010) *Sir William Petty, 1674: letters to John Aubrey*. Lewiston, NY: Edwin Mellen Press.

Kaldor, Nicholas (1954) "The relation of economic growth and cyclical fluctuations". *Economic Journal* 64: 53–71.

Kargon, Robert (1965) "William Petty's mechanical philosophy". *Isis* 56 (1): 63–66.

Kearns, Gerry (2013) "Colonial contexts and postcolonial legacies". *Historical Geography* 41: 22–34.

Keller, Alex (1993) "Technological aspirations and the motivation of natural philosophy in seventeenth-century England". *History of Technology* 15: 76–92.

Kelly, James (1987) "The origins of the Act of Union: an examination of unionist opinion in Britain and Ireland, 1650–1800". *Irish Historical Studies* 25: 236–263.

Kendrick, John W. (1970) "The historical development of national-income accounts". *History of Political Economy* 2 (2): 284–315.

Kennedy, Paul M. (1976) *The rise and fall of British naval mastery*. London: Allen Lane.

Kennedy, Paul M. (1988) *The rise and fall of the great powers: economic change and military conflict from 1500 to 2000*. London: Unwin Hyman.

Kennedy, William (1913) *English taxation, 1640–1799: an essay on policy and opinion*. London: London School of Economics and Political Science.

Kern, Stephen (1983) *The culture of time and space, 1880–1918*. London: Weidenfeld & Nicolson.

Keynes, Geoffrey, ed. (1971) *A bibliography of Sir William Petty FRS and of Observations on the bills of mortality by John Graunt FRS*. Oxford: Clarendon Press.

Keynes, John M. (1936) *The general theory of employment, interest and money*. London: Macmillan.

Kiker, B. F. (1967) "The concept of human capital in the history of economic thought". *Indian Economic Journal* 14 (4): 467–486.

Kitson, Frank (1994) *Prince Rupert: portrait of a soldier*. London: Constable.

Klein, Judy L. (1997) *Statistical visions in time: a history of time series analysis, 1662–1938*. Cambridge: Cambridge University Press.

Krugman, Paul R. (1991) *Geography and trade*. Leuven: Leuven University Press.

Krugman, Paul R. (1995) *Development, geography, and economic theory*. Cambridge, MA: MIT Press.

Krugman, Paul R. (1996) *The self organizing economy*. Malden, MA: Blackwell.

Krugman, Paul R. (1998) "What's new about the new economic geography?" *Oxford Review of Economic Policy* 14 (2): 7–17.

Krugman, Paul R. (1999) "The role of geography in development". *International Regional Science Review* 22 (2): 142–161 [paper for annual World Bank Conference on Development Economics 1998].

Krugman, Paul R. (2000) "Where in the world is the 'new economic geography'?", in Clark, Gordon L., Feldmann, Maryann P., and Gertler, Meric S., eds., *The Oxford handbook of economic geography*. Oxford: Oxford University Press: 49–60.

Krugman, Paul R., and Obstfeld, Maurice (2003) *International economics: theory and policy*, sixth edition. New York: HarperCollins.

Krugman, Paul R., and Venables, Anthony J. (1995) "Globalisation and the inequality of nations". *Quarterly Journal of Economics* 110 (4): 857–880.

Kuhn, William E. (1963) *The evolution of economic thought*. Cincinnati: South-Western Publishing.

Kurz, Heinz D., and Salvadori, Neri, eds. (1998) *The Elgar companion to classical economics*. Cheltenham, UK: Edward Elgar.

Kurz, Heinz D., and Salvadori, Neri (2003 [2000]) "'Classical' roots of input–output analysis: a short account of its long prehistory" [from *Economic Systems Research* 12 (2): 153–179], in Kurz, Heinz D., and Salvadori, Neri, *Classical economics and modern theory: studies in long-period analysis*. London: Routledge: 38–67.

Kurz, Heinz D., and Salvadori, Neri (2003) *Classical economics and modern theory: studies in long-period analysis*. London: Routledge.

Kurz, Heinz D., and Salvadori, Neri (2005) "Representing the production and circulation of commodities in material terms: on Sraffa's objectivism". *Review of Political Economy* 17 (3): 413–441.

Lanaspa, Luis F., Pueyo, Fernando, and Sanz, Fernando (2001) "The public sector and core–periphery models". *Urban Studies* 38 (10): 1639–1649.

Landreth, Harry, and Colander, David C. (2001) *History of economic thought*, fourth edition. Boston: Houghton Mifflin.

Lansdowne, Marquis of [Henry W. E. Petty Fitzmaurice] (1937) *Glanerought and the Petty-Fitzmaurices*. Oxford: Oxford University Press.

Laslett, Peter (1992) "Natural and political observations on the population of late seventeenth-century England: reflections on the work of Gregory King and John Graunt", in Schurer, Kevin, and Arkell, Tom, eds., *Surveying the people: the interpretation and use of document sources for the study of population in the later seventeenth century*. Oxford: Leopard's Head: 6–30.

Lepenies, Philipp (2013) *The power of a single number: a political history of GDP*. Cambridge: Cambridge University Press.

Letwin, William L. (1963) *The origins of scientific economics: English economic thought, 1660–1776*. London: Methuen.

Lewis, Rhodri (2006) "An unpublished letter from Andrew Marvell to William Petty". *Notes and Queries* 53 (2): 181–183.

Lewis, Rhodri (2011) "William Petty's anthropology: religion, colonialism, and the problem of human diversity". *Huntington Library Quarterly* 74 (2): 261–288.

Lewis, Rhodri (2012a) *William Petty on the order of nature: an unpublished manuscript treatise*. Tempe, AZ: Arizona Center for Medieval and Renaissance Studies.

Lewis, Rhodri (2012b) "William Petty", in Stewart, Alan, and Sullivan, Garrett, eds., *Encyclopedia of English Renaissance literature*. Oxford: Blackwell): 780–782.

Lewis, William Arthur (1954) "Economic development with unlimited supplies of labour". *The Manchester School* 22 (2): 139–191.

Lewis, William Arthur (1988) "The roots of development theory, in Chenery, Hollis, and Srinavasan, Thirukodikaval N., eds., *Handbook of development economics*, volume I. Amsterdam: Elsevier Science: 27–37.

Leyshon, Andrew (2000) "Money and finance", in Sheppard, Eric, and Barnes, Trevor J., eds., *A companion to economic geography*. Oxford: Blackwell: 432–449.

Linklater, Andro (2013) *Owning the earth: the transforming history of land ownership*. New York: Bloomsbury USA.

Little, Patrick (2000) "The first unionists? Irish Protestant attitudes to union with England, 1653–9". *Irish Historical Studies* 32: 44–58.

Lloyd-Jones, Hugh, Pearl, Valerie, and Worden, Blair, eds. (1981) *History and imagination: essays in honour of H. R. Trevor Roper*. London: Duckworth.

Lösch, August (1954 [1940]) *The economics of location [Die raümliche Ordnung der Wirtschaft]*, translated by William H. Woglom. New Haven, CT: Yale University Press.

Love, Harold (2007) "Sir William Petty, the London coffee houses, and the Restoration 'leonine'". *The Seventeenth Century* 22 (2): 381–394.

Lowry, S. Todd, ed. (1987) *Pre-classical economic thought from the Greeks to the Scottish Enlightenment*. Boston: Kluwer Academic.

Lowry, S. Todd (1991) "Preclassical perceptions of economy and security", in Goodwin, Craufurd D., ed., *Economics and national security: a history of their interaction*. Durham, NC: Duke University Press: 5–21.

Lynam, Edward W. O'F. (1932) "Irish political geography" [review of Goblet (1930)]. *Geographical Journal* 79 (5): 415–418.

Lynch, William T. (2001) *Solomon's child: method in the early Royal Society of London*. Stanford, CA: Stanford University Press.

McCormick, Ted (2006) "Alchemy in the political arithmetic of Sir William Petty (1623–1687)". *Studies in History and Philosophy of Science* part A 37 (2): 290–307.

McCormick, Ted (2007) "Transmutation, inclusion, and exclusion: political arithmetic from Charles II to William III". *Journal of Historical Sociology* 20 (3): 259–278.

McCormick, Ted (2008) "'A proportionable mixture': William Petty, political arithmetic, and the transmutation of the Irish", in Dennehy, Coleman, ed., *Restoration Ireland: always settling and never settled.* Aldershot, UK: Ashgate: 123–140.

McCormick, Ted (2009) *William Petty and the ambitions of political arithmetic.* Oxford: Oxford University Press.

McCormick, Ted (2013a) "Governing model populations: queries, quantification, and William Petty's 'Scale of salubrity'". *History of Science* 51 (2): 179–198.

McCormick, Ted (2013b) "Political arithmetic and sacred history: population thought in the English Enlightenment, 1660–1750". *Journal of British Studies* 52 (4): 829–857.

McCormick, Ted (2014) "Political arithmetic's 18th century histories: quantification in politics, religion, and the public sphere". *History Compass* 12 (3): 239–251.

McCormick, Ted (2016) "Alchemy into economy: material transmutation and the conceptualisation of utility in Gabriel Plattes (c. 1600–1644) and William Petty (1623–1687)", in Richter, Sandra, and Garner, Guillaume, eds., *'Eigennutz' und 'gute Ordnung': Ökonomisierungen der Welt im 17. Jahrhundert.* Wiesbaden: Harrassowitz: 339–352.

MacFarlane, Alan (1997) *The savage wars of peace: England, Japan and the Malthusian trap.* Oxford: Blackwell.

McKenny, Kevin (1995) "The seventeenth-century land settlement in Ireland: towards a statistical interpretation", in Ohlmeyer, Jane H., ed., *Ireland from independence to occupation, 1641–60.* Cambridge: Cambridge University Press: 181–200.

McNally, David (1988) *Political economy and the rise of capitalism: a reinterpretation.* Berkeley, CA: University of California Press.

Mahaffy, Robert P., ed. (1903) *Calendar of the State Papers relating to Ireland preserved in the Public Records Office: adventurers for land, 1642–1659.* London: Mackie, for HMSO.

Mandelbrote, Scott (2017) "William Petty and Anne Greene: medical and political reform in Commonwealth Oxford", in Mandelbrote, Scott, and Pelling, Margaret, eds., *The practice of reform in health, medicine, and science, 1500–2000: essays for Charles Webster.* Abingdon, UK: Routledge: 125–149.

Marshall, Alfred (1920) *Principles of economics*, eighth edition. London: Macmillan.

Marshall, Peter J., ed. (1998) *The Oxford History of the British Empire*, volume II: *The eighteenth century.* Oxford: Oxford University Press.

Martin, Ron (1999) "The new 'geographical turn' in economics: some critical reflections". *Cambridge Journal of Economics* 23 (1): 65–91.

Martin, Ron (2000) "Local labour markets: their nature, performance, and regulation", in Clark, Gordon L., Feldmann, Maryann P., and Gertler, Meric S., eds., *The Oxford handbook of economic geography.* Oxford: Oxford University Press: 455–476.

Martin, Ron, and Sunley, Peter (1996) "Paul Krugman's geographical economics and its implications for regional development theory: a critical assessment". *Economic Geography* 72 (3): 259–292.

Masson, Irvine, and Youngson, Alexander J. (1960) "Sir William Petty FRS", in Hartley, Harold B., ed., *The Royal Society: its origins and founders.* London: Royal Society: 79–90.

Matsukawa, Shichiro (1977) "Sir William Petty: an unpublished manuscript". *Hitotsubashi Journal of Economics* 17 (2): 33–50

Meardon, Stephen J. (2002) "On the new economic geography and the progress of geographical economics", in Boehm, Stephan, Gehrke, Christian, Kurz, Heinz D., and Sturn, Richard, eds., *Is there progress in economics? Knowledge, truth and the history of economic thought*. Cheltenham: Edward Elgar: 217–239.

Meek, Ronald L. (1984 [1954]) "Adam Smith and the classical concept of profit" [from *Scottish Journal of Political Economy* 1: 138–153], in Wood, John Cunningham, ed., *Adam Smith: critical assessments*, volume III. London: Routledge: 58–70.

Meek, Ronald L. (1973a) *Studies in the labour theory of value*, second edition. London: Lawrence & Wishart.

Meek, Ronald L., ed. (1973b) *Precursors of Adam Smith 1750–1775*. London: Dent.

Meier, Gerald M. (1984) "The formative period", in Meier, Gerald M., and Seers, Dudley, eds., *Pioneers in development*. New York: Oxford University Press, for the World Bank: 3–22.

Meier, Gerald M. (1994a) "Introduction", in Meier, Gerald M., ed., *From classical economics to development economics*. London: Macmillan: 1–4.

Meier, Gerald M. (1994b) "The 'progressive state' in classical economics", in Meier, Gerald M., ed., *From classical economics to development economics*. London: Macmillan: 5–27.

Meier, Gerald M. (1994c) "From colonial economics to development economics", in Meier, Gerald M., ed., *From classical economics to development economics*. London: Macmillan: 173–196.

Meier, Gerald M., and Rauch, James E. (2000) *Leading issues in economic development*, seventh edition. New York: Oxford University Press.

Meier, Gerald M., and Seers, Dudley, eds. (1984) *Pioneers in development*. New York: Oxford University Press, for the World Bank.

Mellinger, Andrew, Sachs, Jeffrey D., and Gallup, John (2000) "Geography and economic development", in Clark, Gordon L., Feldmann, Maryann P., and Gertler, Meric S., eds., *The Oxford handbook of economic geography*. Oxford: Oxford University Press: 169–194.

Mendoza Herrejon, M. B. E. (2017) "William Petty y el mercantilismo Anglo-Holandés: su impacto en el surgimiento del derecho mercantil". *Revista Internacional de Ciencias Jurídicas* 5 (9).

Mirowski, Philip (1989) *More heat than light: economics as social physics: physics as nature's economics*. Cambridge: Cambridge University Press.

Mirowski, Philip (2002) *Machine dreams: economics becomes a cyborg science*. Cambridge: Cambridge University Press.

Mitchell, Wesley C. (1967) *Types of economic theory: from mercantilism to institutionalism*, 2 volumes. New York: Augustus Kelley.

Montes, Leonidas (2003) "Smith and Newton: some methodological issues concerning general economic equilibrium theory". *Cambridge Journal of Economics* 27 (5): 723–747.

Monthly Review (2002) "A prizefighter for capitalism: Paul Krugman versus the Quebec protesters". *Monthly Review* 53 (2): 1–5.

Moody, Theodore W., Martin, Francis X., and Byrne, Francis J., eds. (1976) *A new history of Ireland*, volume III: *Early modern Ireland, 1534–1691*. Oxford: Clarendon Press.

Morgan, Hiram (1985) "The colonial venture of Sir Thomas Smith in Ulster, 1571–1575". *Historical Journal* 28 (2): 261–278.

Morgan, Hiram (1999) "Beyond Spenser? A historiographical introduction to the study of political ideas in early modern Ireland", in Morgan, Hiram, ed., *Political ideology in Ireland, 1541–1641*. Dublin: Four Courts Press: 9–21.

Morgan, Hiram, ed. (1999) *Political ideology in Ireland, 1541–1641*. Dublin: Four Courts Press.

Morgan, Kenneth (2002) "Mercantilism and the British Empire, 1688–1815", in Winch, Donald, and O'Brien, Patrick K., eds., *The political economy of British historical experience, 1688–1914*. Oxford: Oxford University Press, for the British Academy: 165–191.

Morrissey, John (2012) "Foucault and the colonial subject: emergent forms of colonial governmentality in early modern Ireland", in Duffy, Patrick, and Nolan, William, eds., *At the anvil: essays in honour of William J Smyth*. Dublin: Geography Publications: 135–150.

Mountfield, David (1976) *The coaching age*. London: Robert Hale.

Murata, Yasusada (2008) "Engel's law, Petty's law, and agglomeration". *Journal of Development Economics* 87 (1): 161–177.

Murphy, Antoin (2009) *The genesis of macroeconomics: new ideas from Sir William Petty to Henry Thornton*. Oxford: Oxford University Press.

Mykkänen, Juri (1994) "'To methodise and regulate them': William Petty's governmental science of statistics". *History of the Human Sciences* 7 (3): 65–88.

Neveux, Hugues (1981) "Une croissance ambigüe, XVIe–XVIIIe siècles", in Désert, Gabriel, ed., *Histoire de Caen*. Toulouse: Privat: 115–148.

North, Douglass C. (1981) *Structure and change in economic history*. New York: Norton.

North, Douglass C., Anderson, Terry L., and Hill, Peter J. (1983) *Growth and welfare in the American past: a new economic history*, third edition. Englewood Cliffs, NJ: Prentice Hall.

Ó Siochrú, Micheál (2008) *God's executioner: Oliver Cromwell and the conquest of Ireland*. London: Faber & Faber.

Ó Tuathail, Gearóid, Dalby, Simon, and Routledge, Paul, eds. (1998) *The geopolitics reader*. London: Routledge.

Oberhauser, Ann M. (2000) "Feminism and economic geography: gendering work and working gender", in Sheppard, Eric, and Barnes, Trevor J., eds., *A companion to economic geography*. Oxford: Blackwell: 60–76.

O'Brien, Denis P. (1997 [1992]) "Petty's political arithmetick" [from "Sir William Petty" (in German), in Schefold, Bertram, ed., Sir William Petty und seine Political Arithmetic. Dusseldorf: Verlag Wirtschaft und Finanzen: 55–75], in Hutchison, Terence W., ed., *Sir William Petty: critical responses*. London: Routledge: 145–158.

O'Brien, Denis P. (2003) "Classical economics", in Samuels, Warren J., Biddle, Jeff E., and Davis, John B., eds., *A companion to the history of economic thought*. Malden, MA: Blackwell: 112–129.

O'Brien, Patrick K. (1988) "The political economy of British taxation, 1660–1815". *Economic History Review* 41 (1): 1–32.

O'Brien, Patrick K. (1998) "Inseparable connections: trade, economy, fiscal state, and the expansion of empire, 1688–1815", in Marshall, Peter J., ed., *The Oxford History of the British Empire*, volume II: *The eighteenth century*. Oxford: Oxford University Press: 53–77.

O'Brien, Patrick K. (2002) "Fiscal exceptionalism: Great Britain and its European rivals from civil war to triumph at Trafalgar and Waterloo", in Winch, Donald, and O'Brien, Patrick K., eds., *The political economy of British historical experience, 1688–1914*. Oxford: Oxford University Press, for the British Academy: 245–265.

O'Brien, Patrick K., and Hunt, Philip A. (1999a) "England, 1485–1815", in Bonney, Richard, ed., *The rise of the fiscal state in Europe, c. 1200–1815*. Oxford: Oxford University Press: 53–100.

O'Brien, Patrick K., and Hunt, Philip A. (1999b) "Excises and the rise of a fiscal state in England, 1586–1688", in Ormrod, W. Mark, Bonney, Margaret, and Bonney, Richard, eds., *Crises, revolutions and self-sustained growth: essays in European fiscal history, 1130–1830.* Stamford, UK: Shaun Tyas: 198–223.

Ochs, Kathleen H. (1985) "The Royal Society of London's history of trades programme: an early episode in applied science". *Notes and Records of the Royal Society of London* 39 (2): 129–158.

Ohlin, Bertil (1933) *Interregional and international trade.* Cambridge, MA: Harvard University Press.

Ohlmeyer, Jane H., ed. (1995) *Ireland from independence to occupation, 1641–60.* Cambridge: Cambridge University Press.

Ohta, Hiroshi, and Thisse, Jacques-François, eds. (1993) *Does economic space matter? Essays in honour of Melvin L. Greenhut.* Basingstoke, UK: Macmillan.

Olson, Richard (1993) *The emergence of the social sciences, 1642–1792.* New York: Twayne Publishers.

Ormrod, W. Mark, Bonney, Margaret and Bonney, Richard, eds. (1999) *Crises, revolutions and self-sustained growth: essays in European fiscal history, 1130–1830.* Stamford, UK: Shaun Tyas.

Ottaviano, Gianmarco I. P., and Puga, Diego (1997) *Agglomeration in the global economy: a survey of the 'new economic geography'*, Discussion Paper no. 356. London: London School of Economics and Political Science, Centre for Economic Performance.

Oxford English Dictionary (1989) *The Oxford English Dictionary*, second edition, prepared by John A. Simpson and Edmund S. C. Weiner. Oxford: Clarendon Press.

Palgrave, Robert H. I., ed. (1894–99) *Dictionary of political economy*, 3 volumes. London: Macmillan.

Parel, Véronique (1997) "Lois naturelles de production, prix et normativité chez William Petty". *Économies et Sociétés: Œconomia, Histoire de la pensée économique*, série PE 25 (1): 109–123.

Parker, Geoffrey (1996) *The military revolution: military innovation and the rise of the West, 1500–1800*, second edition. Cambridge: Cambridge University Press.

Pasquier, Maurice (1903) *Sir William Petty: ses idées économiques.* Paris: V. Giard et E. Brière.

Patnaik, Prabhat (2005) "Karl Marx as a development economist", in Jomo, Kwame Sundaram, ed., *The pioneers of development economics: great economists on development.* London: Zed Books: 62–73.

Peet, Richard (2002) "Book review" [Clark et al. 2000]. *Economic Geography* 78 (3): 387–392.

Perelman, Michael (2000) *The invention of capitalism: classical political economy and the secret history of primitive accumulation.* Durham, NC: Duke University Press.

Perrotta, Cosimo (1997) "The pre-classical theory of development: increased consumption raises productivity". *History of Political Economy* 29 (2): 295–326.

Perrotta, Cosimo (2003) "The legacy of the past: ancient economic thought on wealth and development". *European Journal of the History of Economic Thought* 10 (2): 177–229.

Pinto, James V. (1997) *English economists' descriptive accounts of location theory*, Working Paper no. 97–2. Flagstaff, AZ: Northern Arizona University, College of Business Administration.

Pomeranz, Kenneth (2000) *The great divergence: China, Europe, and the making of the modern world economy.* Princeton, NJ: Princeton University Press.

Poovey, Mary (1994) "The social constitution of class: towards a history of classificatory thinking", in Dimock, Wai Chee, and Gilmore, Michael T., eds., *Rethinking class: literary studies and social formations*. New York: Columbia University Press: 15–56.

Poovey, Mary (1998) *A history of the modern fact: problems of knowledge in the sciences of wealth and society*. Chicago: University of Chicago Press.

Pressman, Steven (1999) *Fifty major economists*. Abingdon, UK: Routledge.

Purver, Margery (1967) *The Royal Society: concept and creation*. London: Routledge & Kegan Paul.

Pyatt, Graham (1984) "Comment" [on Clark (1984)], in Meier, Gerald M., and Seers, Dudley, eds., *Pioneers in development*. New York: Oxford University Press, for the World Bank: 78–83.

Ramsey, Robert W. (1933) *Henry Cromwell*. London: Longmans, Green.

Reilly, Tom (1999) *Cromwell: an honourable enemy*. London: Phoenix Press.

Reungoat, Sabine (2004) *William Petty, observateur de la population des îles britanniques*. Paris: INED.

Reungoat, Sabine (2015) "Les reformateurs anglais et l'Irlande dans la seconde moitié du XVIIème siècle: les traités économiques de Williiam Petty, Richard Lawrence et William Temple". *Quaderna 3*.

Reungoat, Sabine (2017) *William Petty: genèse de l'arithmétique politique* [translations of TTC, VS and PA, with an introduction]. Geneva: Slatkine Erudition.

Richardson, Roger C., ed. (1993) *Images of Oliver Cromwell: essays for and by Roger Howell Jr*. Manchester: Manchester University Press.

Richter, Sandra, and Garner, Guillaume, eds. (2016) *'Eigennutz' und 'gute Ordnung': Ökonomisierungen der Welt im 17. Jahrhundert*. Wiesbaden: Harrassowitz.

Riley, James C. (1985) *Population thought in the age of the demographic revolution*. Durham, NC: Carolina Academic Press.

Robbins, Lionel (1998) *A history of economic thought: the LSE lectures*, edited by Steven G. Medema and Warren J. Samuels. Princeton, NJ: Princeton University Press.

Roberts, Michael (1956) *The military revolution, 1560–1660: an inaugural lecture delivered before the Queen's University Belfast*. Belfast: M. Boyd.

Rodriguez Braun, Carlos (1987) "Capital's last chapter". *History of Political Economy* 19 (2): 299–310.

Rohrbasser, Jean-Marc (2008) "Süssmilch lecteur de Petty: arithmetique politique et théologie naturelle". *Journal electronique d'histoire de la probabilité et des statistiques* 4 (1).

Roll, Eric (1973) *A history of economic thought*, fourth edition, revised. London: Faber & Faber.

Romano, Antonella (1999) *La contre-réforme mathématique: construction et diffusion d'une culture mathématique jésuite à la Renaissance, 1540–1640*. Rome: École Française de Rome.

Roncaglia, Alessandro (1985 [1977]) *Petty: the origins of political economy* [*Petty: la nascita dell'economia politica*], translated by Isabella Cherubini. Cardiff: University College Cardiff Press.

Roncaglia, Alessandro (1987) "William Petty", in Eatwell, John, Milgate, Murray, and Newman, Peter, eds., *The new Palgrave: a dictionary of economics*. London: Macmillan: 853–855.

Roncaglia, Alessandro (1988) "William Petty and the conceptual framework for the analysis of economic development", in Arrow, Kenneth J., ed., *The balance between industry and agriculture in economic development*, volume I: *Basic issues*. London: Macmillan, for the International Economic Association: 157–174.

Roncaglia, Alessandro (2005 [2001]) *The wealth of ideas: a history of economic thought* [*La ricchezza delle idee: storia del pensiero economico*]. Cambridge: Cambridge University Press.

Roncaglia, Alessandro (2017) *A brief history of economic thought*. Cambridge: Cambridge University Press.

Roseveare, Henry (1991) *The financial revolution 1660–1760*. London: Longman.

Roseveare, Henry (2001) "Review" [of Ormrod, Bonney and Bonney (1999)]. *Economic History Review* 54 (2): 391–392.

Rothbard, Murray N. (1995) *Economic thought before Adam Smith: an Austrian perspective on the history of economic thought*, volume I. Aldershot, UK: Edward Elgar.

Routh, Guy (1975) *The origin of economic ideas*. London: Macmillan.

Rubin, Isaac I. (1979 [1929]) *A history of economic thought* [*Istoriya ekonomicheskoi mysli*], translated by Don Filtzer. London: Pluto Press.

Sadler, David (2000) "Concepts of class in contemporary economic geography", in Sheppard, Eric, and Barnes, Trevor J., eds., *A companion to economic geography*. Oxford: Blackwell: 325–340.

Samuels, Warren J., Biddle, Jeff E., and Davis, John B., eds. (2003) *A companion to the history of economic thought*. Malden, MA: Blackwell.

Schmutzler, Armin (1999) "The new economic geography". *Journal of Economic Surveys* 13 (4): 355–379.

Schoenberger, Erica (2000) "Creating the corporate world: strategy and culture, time and space", in Sheppard, Eric, and Barnes, Trevor J., eds., *A companion to economic geography*. Oxford: Blackwell: 377–391.

Schoenberger, Erica (2004 [1998]) "Discourse and practice in human geography" [from *Progress in Human Geography* 22 (1): 1–14), in Barnes, Trevor J., Peck, Jamie, Sheppard, Eric, and Tickell, Adam, eds., *Reading economic geography*. Oxford: Blackwell: 389–402.

Schumpeter, Joseph A. (1955) History of economic analysis, second printing. London: George Allen & Unwin.

Schurer, Kevin, and Arkell, Tom, eds. (1992) *Surveying the people: the interpretation and use of document sources for the study of population in the later seventeenth century*. Oxford: Leopard's Head.

Seligman, Edwin R. A. (1910) *The shifting and incidence of taxation*, third edition, revised and enlarged. New York: Columbia University Press.

Sen, Amartya K. (1988) "The concept of development", in Chenery, Hollis, and Srinavasan, Thirukodikaval N., eds., *Handbook of development economics*, volume I. Amsterdam: Elsevier Science: 9–26.

Sewall, Hannah R. (1901) *The theory of value before Adam Smith*. New York: Macmillan.

Shapin, Steven (1996) *The scientific revolution*. Chicago: University of Chicago Press.

Sharp, Lindsay G. (1975) "The Royal College of Physicians and interregnum politics". *Medical History* 19 (1): 107–128.

Sharp, Lindsay G. (1977) "Sir William Petty and some aspects of seventeenth century natural philosophy". D.Phil. thesis D19432/77, University of Oxford [unpublished].

Sheppard, Eric (2000a) "Geography or economics? Conceptions of space, time, interdependence, and agency", in Clark, Gordon L., Feldmann, Maryann P., and Gertler, Meric S., eds., *The Oxford handbook of economic geography*. Oxford: Oxford University Press: 99–119.

Sheppard, Eric (2000b) "Competition in space and between places", in Sheppard, Eric, and Barnes, Trevor J., eds., *A companion to economic geography*. Oxford: Blackwell: 169–186.

Sheppard, Eric, and Barnes Trevor J., eds. (2000) *A companion to economic geography*. Oxford: Blackwell.

Sills, David L., ed. (1968) *International encyclopedia of the social sciences*, 17 volumes. New York: Macmillan.

Simington, Robert C., ed. (1931–61) *The Civil Survey, A.D. 1654–1656*, 10 volumes. Dublin: Stationery Office, for the Irish Manuscripts Commission.

Simington, Robert C., ed. (1970) *The transplantation to Connacht, 1654–58*. Shannon: Irish University Press, for the Irish Manuscripts Commission.

Sivado, Akos (2017) "Resurrecting the body politic: physiology's influence on Sir William Petty's political arithmetick". *Early Science and Medicine* 22 (2/3): 157–182.

Skinner, Alexander S., and Wilson, Thomas, eds. (1975) *Essays on Adam Smith*. Oxford: Clarendon Press.

Slack, Paul (2004) "Measuring the national wealth in seventeenth-century England". *Economic History Review* 57 (4): 607–635.

Smith, Christine, ed. (1990) *Locational analysis and general theory, economic, political, regional and dynamic: selected papers of Walter Isard*. London: Macmillan.

Smyth, William J. (2006) *Map-making, landscapes and memory: a geography of colonial and early modern Ireland, c. 1530–1750*. Cork: Cork University Press.

Sorokin, Pitirim A. (1956) *Fads and foibles in modern sociology and related sciences*. Chicago: Henry Regnery.

Spiegel, Henry W. (1983) *The growth of economic thought*, revised and expanded edition. Durham, NC: Duke University Press.

Spurr, John (2000) *England in the 1670s: 'this masquerading age'*. Oxford: Blackwell.

Sraffa, Piero (1960) *Production of commodities by means of commodities: prelude to a critique of economic theory*. Cambridge: Cambridge University Press.

Stephens, Nicholas, and Glasscock, Robin E., eds. (1970) *Irish geography studies in honour of E. Estyn Evans*. Belfast: Queen's University of Belfast.

Stevens, David (1975) "Adam Smith and the colonial disturbances", in Skinner, Alexander S., and Wilson, Thomas, eds., *Essays on Adam Smith*. Oxford: Clarendon Press: 202–217.

Stewart, Alan, and Sullivan, Garrett, eds. (2012) *Encyclopedia of English Renaissance literature*. Oxford: Blackwell.

Stiglitz, Joseph E. (2002) *Globalisation and its discontents*. London: Penguin Books.

Stone, Richard (1988) "When will the war end?" *Cambridge Journal of Economics* 12 (2): 193–201.

Stone, Richard (1997) *British empiricists in the social sciences, 1650–1900*. Cambridge: Cambridge University Press.

Strauss, Erich (1954) *Sir William Petty: portrait of a genius*. London: Bodley Head.

Studenski, Paul (1958) *The income of nations*, part I: *History*. New York: New York University Press.

Stull, William J. (1994 [1986]) "The urban economics of Adam Smith" [from *Journal of Urban Economics* 20 (3): 291–311], in Wood, John Cunningham, ed., *Adam Smith: critical assessments*, volume VI. London: Routledge: 80–100.

Sturdy, David J. (2002) *Fractured Europe, 1600–1721*. Oxford: Blackwell.

Sunley, Peter (2000) "Urban and regional growth", in Sheppard, Eric, and Barnes, Trevor J., eds., *A companion to economic geography*. Oxford: Blackwell: 187–201.

Sussman, Charlotte (2004) "The colonial afterlife of political arithmetic". *Cultural Critique* 56: 86–126.

Sy, Aida, and Tinker, Tony (2014) "Early European accounting theory: Sir William Petty's contributions to accounting". *International Journal of Critical Accounting* 6 (3): 211–232.

Tallett, Frank (1992) *War and society in early modern Europe, 1495–1715*. Abingdon, UK: Routledge.

Tarr, László (1969 [1968]) *History of the carriage*, translated by Elizabeth Hoch. London: Vision.

Terrier, Max (1981) "The researches of the Royal Society of London on carriage springs". *Carriage Journal* 19 (1): 11–17.

Thirsk, Joan, ed. (1967) *The agrarian history of England and Wales*, volume IV: *1500–1640*. Cambridge: Cambridge University Press.

Thomson, Herbert F. (1984 [1965]) "Adam Smith's philosophy of science" [from *Quarterly Journal of Economics* 79 (2): 212–233], in Wood, John Cunningham, ed., *Adam Smith: critical assessments*, volume I. London: Routledge: 323–341.

Thomson, Herbert F. (1987) "The Scottish Enlightenment and political economy", in Lowry, S. Todd, *Pre-classical economic thought: from the Greeks to the Scottish Enlightenment*. Boston: Kluwer Academic: 221–255.

Thomson, Mark A. (1938) *A constitutional history of England*, volume IV: *1642 to 1801*. London: Methuen.

Tilly, Charles (1985) "War making and state making as organised crime", in Evans, Peter B., Rueschemeyer, Dietrich, and Skocpol, Theda, eds., *Bringing the state back in*. Cambridge: Cambridge University Press: 169–191.

Tilly, Charles (1990) *Coercion, capital and the European states, A.D. 990–1990*. Oxford: Blackwell.

Tribe, Keith (1978) *Land, labour and economic discourse*. London: Routledge & Kegan Paul.

Ullmer, James H. (2004) "The macroeconomic thought of Sir William Petty". *Journal of the History of Economic Thought* 26 (3): 401–413.

Ullmer, James H. (2011) "The scientific method of William Petty". *Erasmus Journal for Philosophy and Economics* 4 (2): 1–19.

Vaggi, Gianni, and Groenewegen, Peter D. (2003) *A concise history of economic thought from mercantilism to monetarism*. Basingstoke, UK: Palgrave Macmillan.

Valeri, Mark (2010) "William Petty in Boston: political economy, religion and money in provincial New England". Early American Studies 8 (3): 549–580.

Van Creveld, Martin L. (1991) *Technology and war from 2000 BC to the present*. Oxford: Brassey's.

Veenendaal, A. J. (1994) "Fiscal crises and constitutional freedom in the Netherlands, 1450–1795", in Hoffman, Philip T., and Norberg, Kathryn, eds., *Fiscal crises, liberty, and representative government, 1450–1789*. Stanford, CA: Stanford University Press: 96–137.

Vélez Tamayo, Julián Mauricio (2017) *Sir William Petty y la conformación de la ley Petty–Clark* [*Sir William Petty and the conformation of the Petty–Clark law*]. Munich Personal RePEc Archive Paper no. 76345.

Venables, Anthony J. (1998) "The assessment: trade and location". *Oxford Review of Economic Policy* 14 (2): 1–6.

Walsh, Vivian, and Gram, Harvey (1980) *Classical and neoclassical theories of general equilibrium*. New York: Oxford University Press.

Weatherill, Lorna (1996) *Consumer behaviour and material culture in Britain, 1660–1760*, second edition. London: Routledge.

Webster, Charles (1975) *The great instauration: science, medicine and reform, 1626–1660*. London: Duckworth.

Webster, Charles (1979) *Utopian planning and the Puritan revolution: Gabriel Platte, Samuel Hartlib, and 'Macaria'*, Research Publication no. 2 [with a facsimile reprint of

A description of the famous kingdome of Macaria]. Oxford: Wellcome Unit for the History of Medicine.

Welch, Patrick J. (1997) "Cromwell's occupation of Ireland as judged from Petty's observations and Marx's theory of colonialism", in Henderson, James P., ed., *The state of the history of political economy*. London: Routledge, for the History of Economics Society: 157–172.

Welch, Patrick (2013) "Jonathan Swift on the lives of the poor native Irish as seen through 'A Modest Proposal' and other of his writings". *Journal of the History of Economic Thought* 35 (4): 471–489.

Wendt, Holger (2014) William Petty und der Fortschritt der Wissenschaften: Eine Untersuchung geistesgeschichtlicher Quellen Pettys ökonomischer Theorie. Duisburg: Universitätsverlag Rhein-Ruhr.

Wheeler, James S. (1999) *Cromwell in Ireland*. New York: St. Martin's Press.

Whittaker, Edmund (1960) *Schools and streams of economic thought*. Chicago: Rand McNally.

Wightman, William P. D. (1975) "Adam Smith and the history of ideas", in Skinner, Alexander S., and Wilson, Thomas, eds., *Essays on Adam Smith*. Oxford: Clarendon Press: 44–67.

Willan, Thomas S. (1936) *River navigation in England, 1600–1750*. Oxford: Oxford University Press.

Winch, Donald (2002) "Introduction", in Winch, Donald, and O'Brien, Patrick K., eds., *The political economy of British historical experience, 1688–1914*. Oxford: Oxford University Press, for the British Academy: 1–28.

Winch, Donald, and O'Brien, Patrick K., eds. (2002) *The political economy of British historical experience, 1688–1914*. Oxford: Oxford University Press, for the British Academy.

Wood, Ellen Meiksins (2002) *The origin of capitalism: a longer view*. London: Verso [originally published by Monthly Review Press, 1999].

Wood, Herbert (1934) "Sir William Petty and his Kerry estate". *Journal of the Royal Society of Antiquaries of Ireland* 4 (1): 22–40.

Wood, John Cunningham, ed. (1984–94) *Adam Smith: critical assessments*, 8 volumes. London: Routledge.

Wrightson, Keith (2000) *Earthly necessities: economic lives in early modern Britain*. New Haven, CT: Yale University Press.

Yang, Xiaokai (2003) *Economic development and the division of labor*. Malden, MA: Blackwell.

Zöllner, Frank (2003) *Leonardo da Vinci, 1452–1519: the complete paintings and drawings*. Cologne: Taschen.

Author citation index

For discussion and quotation of the works of the authors listed here, see the General Index.

Where more than one reference is found on the same page of endnotes, the individual notes are indicated in brackets, e.g. a number of endnote references to the same author on page 19 is shown as: 19(nn59, 60, 65, 67, 69).

Page numbers in *italic* refer to figures or tables.

General index

This index includes entries for subjects, and also for authors when their works are quoted and discussed. For full lists of citations of their works, see the Author Citation Index.

As in the Author Citation Index, where more than one reference is found on the same page of endnotes, the individual notes are indicated in brackets, e.g. a number of endnote references to the same author on page 19 is shown as: 19(nn59, 60, 65, 67, 69).

Page numbers in *italic* refer to figures or tables.

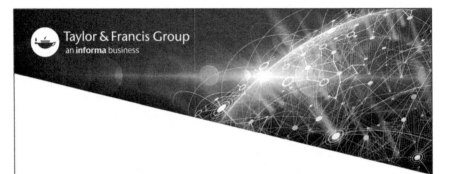

Printed in the United States
by Baker & Taylor Publisher Services